DRUGS
and Contemporary Warfare

RELATED TITLES FROM POTOMAC BOOKS

After the Taliban: Nation-Building in Afghanistan
by James F. Dobbins

DRUGS
and Contemporary Warfare

PAUL REXTON KAN

Foreword by Moisés Naím

Potomac Books, Inc.
Washington, D.C.

Published in the United States by Potomac Books, Inc. All rights reserved. No part of this book may be reproduced in any manner whatsoever without written permission from the publisher, except in the case of brief quotations embodied in critical articles and reviews.

Library of Congress Cataloging-in-Publication Data
Kan, Paul Rexton.
  Drugs and contemporary warfare / Paul Rexton Kan ; foreword by Moisés Naím. — 1st ed.
    p. cm.
  Includes bibliographical references and index.
  ISBN 978-1-59797-256-7 (hardcover : alk. paper) — ISBN 978-1-59797-257-4 (pbk. : alk. paper)
  1. Drug traffic—Economic aspects—Developing countries. 2. Drug traffic—Social aspects—Developing countries. 3. Paramilitary forces—Drug use. 4. Guerrillas—Drug use. I. Title.
  HV5840.D44K36 2009
  363.4509172'4—dc22

                                                                        2008049462

Printed in the United States of America on acid-free paper that meets the American National Standards Institute Z39-48 Standard.

Potomac Books, Inc.
22841 Quicksilver Drive
Dulles, Virginia 20166

First Edition

10 9 8 7 6 5 4 3 2 1

CONTENTS

TABLES

FOREWORD

by Moisés Naím

THE FACT THAT DRUGS FUEL THE WAR IN AFGHANISTAN is an interesting paradox that says much about our times. The paradox is that while the situation in Afghanistan should be a drug warrior's dream, the drug trade creates a nightmare for the world's mightiest military machine. In the pages ahead, Dr. Paul Kan expertly dissects this paradox and in the process unveils a situation that needs urgent attention and innovative thinking.

He starts from the obvious notion that to successfully tackle drug production it is indispensable to have a detailed knowledge of the geography and other characteristics of the producing region as well as a deep understanding of the trade logistics that link the producing area with consumer markets often located continents away. That is the case of Afghanistan, a country that produces over 90 percent of the poppies that feed the world's heroin market. We know how difficult it is to do business in a rugged, landlocked, war-torn, and very poor country with paltry infrastructure like Afghanistan. This is especially true of any business whose success rests on complex transportation and distribution logistics. Yet, Afghanistan is home to some of the world's most imaginative, audacious, ruthless, and profitable export business organizations: drug traders. Hence another paradox: Developing any kind of profitable, export-oriented business in Afghanistan is close to impossible. Unless it is the drug business.

In Afghanistan, the source country is not only well known, but has a large external military presence that could arguably do something about the poppy crop. Indeed, it has been mandated to do so. Furthermore, it is an international military presence composed by the armies of countries that adhere to the global anti-narcotics regime. However, there isn't a nation in NATO with forces in Afghanistan that seeks to overturn the international ban on illicit drug trafficking. These forces have been there for *years* and they will likely be an abiding feature of the Afghan institutional landscape for the foreseeable future. This confluence of circumstances could not be more conducive to eradicating a major supplier of the global drug trade—a sustained international military presence, backed by nations opposed to drug trafficking, that operates freely inside the borders of a country that grows the overwhelming majority of crops used to produce a dangerous narcotic. Yet—and here is the paradox—the trade thrives, and may very well contribute to the defeat of one history's largest and most successful military alliances.

Figuring out how we got to this point—of how a drug warrior's dream has turned into a military strategist's nightmare—not just in Afghanistan, but in other countries such as Colombia, Myanmar, Peru, and Turkey, is the essential contribution that Dr. Kan makes in this book. He describes how these "drug-fueled conflicts" point to a growing intimacy between war and drug trafficking that is unlikely to lessen and that urgently needs to be better understood. He brings to bear in his analysis interesting insights drawn from political science, history, economics, military strategy, law enforcement, and even pharmacology and epidemiology. As a result, we now have a better analytical foundation to understand these conflicts and their effects on national, regional, and international security. Such an interdisciplinary approach is not only welcomed, but required in a world where diverse actors like terror groups, insurgent movements, paramilitary organizations, professional militaries, multinational peacekeepers, military contractors, the justice system, the medical establishment, and, of course, politicians shape the contours of the global drug trade.

Kan explains how today's wars are not just being fought with and over drug money, but they are fought by belligerents who are often "high." The drugs consumed by fighters are as varied as the weapons they employ against each other and they are equally as destructive of human life and civil society. Warring groups see another advantage in participating in the drug trade than just earning money for their activities. Drug use among combatants and gruesome scenes of human suffering go hand-in-hand.

Those who work so diligently to ease human suffering in conflict zones know the frustration of failed efforts of a peaceful settlement. This book also goes a long way in explaining why some conflicts have proven to be so intractable. Drug profits are not easily relinquished and drug intoxicated recruits are not easily controlled.

The law of supply and demand tells only part of the story. To paraphrase one of the detectives in the HBO television drama *The Wire*, if you follow the drugs, they will lead you to the dealer and the user; but if you follow the money, you never know where that will take you. Understanding drug-fueled conflicts means a new perspective as well as having appropriate strategies to deal with them. Once again, this book, with its examination of past approaches to these conflicts and its outlining of possible paths to overcome heir shortcomings, will be an indispensable reference for anyone—policy maker, military strategists, or concerned citizen—who wants to understand a threat that is only growing larger and more ominous.

PREFACE

THROUGHOUT MY CHILDHOOD, there were many reminders of the Opium Wars. I was born in Hong Kong to a Chinese father and an Australian mother. Over the course of their many discussions, I can recall that they could not agree on the cause of the Opium Wars— was it because the British Empire was built on the opium trade and could not afford to lose a market or because so many Chinese were addicted to smoking opium? It was the classic supply versus demand argument that still permeates the drug debate.

In 2006 I returned to Hong Kong for my father's funeral. While there, I noticed many warnings about thieves and pickpockets. I asked my uncle why there were so many warnings; hadn't the Chinese government been able to take a tougher line on crime than the British? He said that crime was on the rise because of drugs like heroin and methamphetamine coming from Myanmar, North Korea, and Afghanistan. It appeared that the latest drug scourge had not overlooked an old market.

The scourge of drugs is not only rediscovering old markets, it is nurturing new markets while contributing to ongoing violent conflicts. Since the Opium Wars and the outlawing of narcotics for non-medical use, new violent actors have entered the illicit global drug market, forcing us to reconsider the causes and complications of war. As such, this book is not about America's War on Drugs or about proposing solutions to the global drug trade per se. Its focus is narrowed to an examination of the various roles drugs now play in modern warfare and the ways to address these roles on the battlefield and in post-conflict nation-building situations. Although the focus is narrow, the book is written with varying audiences in mind.

Those in political science and international relations should find this book useful for debates in the evolving school of the political economy of armed conflicts. It will also be valuable to historians and sociologists who are interested in the social and political history of the drug trade. There is a new and powerful dialectic now at work—drug trafficking currently contributes to higher levels of organized political violence that challenges the international community's ability to bring about stability, thereby providing greater incentive for violent groups to participate in drug trafficking opportunities.

Policy makers and military professionals should likewise find this book helpful in understanding the new parameters of the post-Cold War international security environment. The Army War College describes this environment as violent, unstable, complex, and ambiguous (VUCA)—the intersection of drugs and warfare stands as a strong example of this description. Those who are involved in studying and enforcing drug control policies may find this book useful to their efforts. While the book discusses the dynamics of drug-fueled conflicts, members of the drug control and law enforcement community may see the process as one that is more recognizable as the militarization of drug trafficking.

Finally, a general reader may enjoy a book on the less savory side of globalization. While the world may be "flat" according to authors such as Tom Friedman, it is no less dangerous as it gets "tilted" toward drug dealers, violent political actors, and corrupt politicians. The hijacking of globalization by these actors will have consequences for everyone.

ACKNOWLEDGMENTS

All books begin with a good idea but are carried through to completion by the contributions of a number of kindhearted and generous people.

Much of this book was written under the auspices of the General George C. Marshall Research Grant from the U.S. Army War College, and special thanks are owed to Tony Echevarria, director of research at the Strategic Studies Institute, and my department chair, Col. Jim Helis, for helping me earn the grant. My faculty colleagues Joe Nunez, Craig Nation, Tami Davis-Biddle, and Phil Williams were excellent mentors for me as I took on this writing project.

For their professional expertise, I am indebted to Jorrit Kamminga at the Senlis Council, the agents at the DEA New York Field Division, Moisés Naím, editor of *Foreign Policy,* and Carolyn Bryan, the USAID country director for Tajikistan.

Bill Dean, Alex Lassner, and Chris Luck at Air University were instrumental in helping sharpen my ideas and my prose, as was Bruce Bechtol at the Marine Corps Command and Staff College. Even with all the benefits of a research grant, I simply could not have completed this book without them.

For their research assistance, I am indebted to the librarians at USAWC, Virginia Shope and Nancy Sneed, my department's administrative assistants, BJ Saylor, Jill Wolfert, and Donna Moyer, members of Seminar Ten's teaching team, George Woods, Dave Armitage, and Louis Hicks as well as to the many students in my classes over the years who challenged me to define my thoughts and concepts (They know who they are!). Special thanks are also owed to Chrisi Arrighi, Pat and Kathy Cox, Shawn Morris, Troy Gagliano, Chris Meskow, Michael Powers, and Daniel Owins.

I would also like to recognize the important contributions of my mother, Elwyn, my sister, Monique, and nieces Janae and Kiani. Throughout my writing, they were my good luck charms. In addition to my family members, I would also like to thank the Morris family in Austin, Texas, and the Gagliano family in New Orleans, Louisiana, for their continued support of my professional efforts.

1

HAZY SHADES OF WAR

WARFARE AND DRUGS SHARE many characteristics—they prolong human suffering, bedevil political leaders, and enrich a select few. Further, they have been intertwined at various times throughout history. However, the pernicious role of drugs in organized political violence is often overlooked. Drugs have caused wars, funded military operations, been used by combatants, and have been part of the postwar political landscape by financing some legitimate political actors and parties. Drugs have corrupted militaries, toppled governments, prompted interventions, and taken thousands of lives. The insidious nature of drugs is especially visible in today's wars.

Contemporary wars generally involve sharp asymmetries where one party wields a superior conventional military against the irregular forces of a militarily weaker party; they are by their very nature fertile environments for a variety of drug-related activities. Today's wars are structured differently from traditional, large-scale interstate wars of the past. The military dimension of current conflicts is generally overshadowed by political, social, economic, and psychological concerns.[1] These concerns are where the influence of drugs is most acutely felt by societies in conflict. It is no coincidence that some of the most persistent wars, from the Balkans to the Hindu Kush and from the Andes to the Golden Triangle, occur in areas of widespread drug production and well-traveled distribution routes. In fact, the rate at which civil wars occur is much higher among drug producing countries than non-drug producing countries.[2] Astonishingly, 95 percent of the world's production of hard drugs takes place in contexts of armed conflict.[3]

In many of the wars in the post-Cold War world, such as the Colombian government's ongoing struggle against the Revolutionary Armed Forces of Colombia (FARC) guerrillas, drugs are so deeply embedded in the politics, society, economy, and daily life of a country that it is often difficult to separate counternarcotics operations from counterinsurgency campaigns. As the director of the Colombian national police declared, "One does not know

1

if the drug trafficker is a guerrilla or if the guerrilla is a drug trafficker. The line is now blurred; it is a brotherhood community."[4] Other brotherhood communities threaten the conventional military successes of recent U.S. interventions. The 2007 poppy season in Afghanistan produced 92 percent of the world's heroin and lined the pockets of Taliban loyalists and other warlords who opposed the American presence in the country.[5]

Meanwhile in Iraq drug trafficking sharply increased and Iraqi drug abuse rose by 75 percent between February 2003 and July 2003. Both activities subvert efforts to build a stable nation.[6] In some conflict situations, along with troops and bullets, drugs have the potential to alter the course of conflicts.

Following the Cold War, numerous civil wars erupted, creating new demands for funds. Without the ideological competition of the Cold War, newly armed groups and many former clients of the superpowers have become more entrepreneurial in their quests to keep their political movements or governments viable. A variety of warring groups, such as insurgents, guerrillas, paramilitaries, militias, terrorists, and professional armies, have found wider opportunities to generate support from illicit activities to meet varying goals, including carving out a new ethnic homeland, overthrowing an established authority, changing the course of state's domestic or foreign policy, and defeating an urban or rural insurgency.

Drugs are especially attractive to those engaged in violent conflicts for many reasons. First, drug trafficking is a highly profitable business. Estimates of the illicit global trade in narcotics are between $150 billion and $500 billion in annual sales.[7] By the year 2000, drug trafficking already accounted for 2 percent of the world's economy.[8] Drug profits can be used to pay for arms, equipment, and training, bribe governmental officials, and recruit sympathizers. Because of its participation in the cocaine trade, the FARC is the world's richest insurgent group with assets believed to be approximately $600 million.[9] Second, unlike the illicit trade in diamonds, copper, and oil, commodities with a sometimes irregular availability, drug crops are a reliable means of generating income for they can be regularly harvested in the proper conditions. Third, illegal narcotics are appealing during violent conflicts because they are easy to manufacture, transport, and conceal, which allows for greater distribution and larger profits. Trade in oil, alluvial gems, and timber requires the use of skilled labor and sophisticated technology whereas drug trafficking requires unskilled labor and limited technology. Most drugs are lightweight, high value commodities, making profitable quantities relatively easy to move. Fourth, drugs have an additional benefit that other commodities do not—combatants consume them for battle. Individual fighters can use drugs to alter their behavior in ways that may seem beneficial to them in combat. Finally, drugs can be a means to attack an adversary's military and society in the belief that this will lead to battlefield or ideological victory. Encouraging drug use within the enemy's military or the enemy's society provides a warring group with one more weapon against its enemy. As a result of these qualities, drugs are the most fungible commodity in some of the most persistent conflicts.

The presence of drugs in today's conflicts has contributed to the volatile nature of international and regional security in the post-Cold War era. Drug trafficking contributes to prolonged intrastate conflicts and high levels of arms trafficking and cross border migrations. Intoxicated combatants have committed gross violations of human rights, adding to humanitarian catastrophes that the international community has felt compelled to limit through military intervention. Additionally, when irregular forces use the drug economy, it can contribute to higher casualty figures for professional militaries—in September 2006, with the resurgent Taliban funded by drug profits, it became statistically as dangerous for American service members to serve in Afghanistan as in Iraq.[10]

To understand more thoroughly the role of drugs in contemporary warfare, this interdisciplinary work examines warring groups that are involved in the drug trade, the ways they are involved, the types of drugs they traffic and use, and how these components affect the nature and character of today's warfare. This book examines and analyzes lessons learned from previous and ongoing attempts to counter the influence of drugs in violent conflicts and offers possible strategies to counter the influence of drugs in such conflicts.

THE SIGNIFICANCE OF DRUG TRAFFICKING TO
THE STUDY OF WARFARE

The complicated and convoluted relationship between drugs and today's wars affect international relations, national security, and military operations in powerful ways.

> In fact, the drug trade affects both so-called hard or military security issues as well as soft security issues (such as economic and societal security). In doing so, it practically penetrates the academic security debate: whether security is understood in a traditionalist, state-centered sense focusing on military threats, or in a wider, broader sense encompassing non-state actors and non-military threats, organized crime in general and drug trafficking in particular is an increasingly obvious element of concern in international security.[11]

Although the influence of drug trafficking has been examined in the disciplines of international relations, political science, and military and diplomatic history, there is disagreement over the degree of importance the drug-security linkage should have in world politics discussions. Is drug trafficking merely a criminal matter or a significant transnational threat to the preeminent role of the state?[11] This book focuses on a narrow slice of the security debate—war—and how drugs intersect with it, making the parameters of the discussion more manageable while demonstrating the trade's distorting effects on contemporary conflicts.

Coming to grips with the influence of drugs in contemporary warfare is long overdue. Unique to the post-Cold War era is the proportion of wars occurring within states to wars occurring between states—from 1990–2004, only four out of fifty-seven conflicts were traditional interstate conflicts.[12] In the mid-1990s an important debate centered on why some long-standing civil wars that began during the Cold War in Latin America, Central Asia, and Africa continued long after its end, while other conflicts in these areas were sparked and seemed to be both protracted and bloody. One explanation is that economic agendas linked to the accessibility of natural resources, "greed," have supplanted ideological and political sources, "grievance," as causes for the outbreak and protraction of intrastate war. Greed is a particularly persuasive argument—even though war brings depravation to significant segments of a society in conflict, warring parties often commit acts of predation to extract licit and illicit resources that are then funneled into legitimate and illegitimate global commerce. Armed conflicts present many participants opportunities to exploit commercial resources to pay for military operations and gain private profit.[13] This linkage suggests one cause of prolonged conflicts—there is little economic incentive for a group to relinquish the profits they receive from illegal trade. Although numerous civil wars begin with a political agenda, many transform into profit-motivated violence. Paul Collier notes that "to get started, a rebellion needs a grievance, whereas to be sustained, it needs greed."[14]

The greed argument is even more compelling when looking at the influence of drug trafficking on warfare because drugs have not been a *cause* of war since the Opium Wars during the nineteenth century. Drugs have not provided the basis for any grievance that has led to widespread social, political, or economic movements that were grounds for organized violence. Because of their profitability and ease of distribution, drugs have also supported other greed-related struggles. In some cases, drugs are bartered for other illegally traded commodities, such as diamonds and timber, that are part of other resource-driven conflicts. Nonetheless, by providing funding and intoxication, drugs also support conflicts where grievance issues, such as land distribution, resource allocation, and political rights, are at the center of the disputes. For example, drug funding and use were components of conflicts in Angola, Liberia, and Sri Lanka, but were not the central issue of the fighting.

While some conflicts can be explained by either greed or grievance arguments, both groups illicit commodities together without pointing out the unique qualities of each. Although there are similarities among cases of illicit trafficking, there are important differences that require greater explanation to more fully comprehend how drugs affect contemporary warfare. Even grouping illicit narcotics together into a single analysis overlooks the differences in trafficking drugs, such as heroin, cocaine, marijuana, and amphetamine-type stimulants (ATS). Each drug is uniquely produced, processed, and distributed, meaning that the number of types of violent actors who participate and the ways they participate in trafficking a given narcotic are distinct. The differences among narcotics production and distribution influence profit and labor, which can determine the depth and breadth of a warring group's participation and whether a group is involved in the drug trade out of greed or to support a cause related to a political, economic, or social grievance.

Battlefield intoxication is also an important element when discussing the role of drugs in warfare. With civil wars now comprising the vast majority of violent clashes, very few wars are between professional militaries. Civilians account for the majority of fighting forces. As a result of diminished professionalism, narcotic usage allows for "combat narcosis," which alters a person's fear, stress, and inhibition. Drug abuse by combatants not only presents professional militaries with operational and tactical challenges, but it has a range of effects as well—from public health issues to human rights abuses as well as post-conflict settlement and nation-building.

Terms like "narcoterrorist" and "narcoguerrilla" reveal the degree to which antagonists involved in contemporary wars combine narcotraffickers' activities with techniques of political violence. These new actors have led many to argue that the nature and character of modern warfare is changing.

Martin Van Creveld argues that war has become "transformed" as we enter a "new era, not of peaceful competition between trading blocks, but of warfare between ethnic and religious groups" waged "not by armies but by groups whom we today call terrorists, guerrillas, bandits and robbers." Barbara Ehrenriech, too, points to a "new kind of war," one "less disciplined and more spontaneous than the old," and "one often fought by ill-clad bands more resembling gangs than armies." In a similar vein, Mary Kaldor writes about "new wars" ones centrally about "identity politics," fought in a context of globalization by "a disparate range of different types of groups such as paramilitary units, local warlords, criminal gangs, police forces, mercenary groups and also regular armies including breakaway units of regular armies."[15]

In response to such changes, some argue that the West should place greater focus on ongoing conflicts that "involve limited engagements and attrition, guerrilla warfare, terrorism and other types of low intensity conflicts."[15] In many cases, the widespread violence created by the actors involved in these types of conflicts is fueled by their active links to the drug trade.

Operating in such environments means greater involvement by international organizations and multinational troops to generate conflict settlements and to attempt nation-building activities. Yet, drugs complicate conflict resolution and nation-building efforts. For example, the deputy commander of American forces in Afghanistan recognized the complicating role of drugs in nation-building efforts when he expressed, "We would prefer not to be in the [drug crop] eradication business. We have spent a lot of capital in trying to build relationships with the people and now this has the potential for us to do things that wouldn't be popular."[16]

Drugs range from being one complicating factor among many to the central problem in post-conflict settlement by stymieing efforts to generate sustainable and legitimate paths to stability and prosperity. From false starts at reaching cease-fire agreements to rampant criminality in post-conflict settings, the presence of drugs in contemporary warfare lingers after the violence has stopped.

While engaging in armed conflict does not naturally generate money, many individuals involved in drug-fueled conflicts "do well out of war."[17] These conflicts are not necessarily the result of a breakdown in a particular system; some drug-fueled conflicts are better understood as the continuation of economics by other means.[18] "Some economic aims [of rebel groups] can be furthered by controlling the state. Others are more immediate, and do not depend upon holding the reins of power; they usually involve breaking the law, rather than changing or preserving a system of laws."[19] To support this notion, there are far fewer coups and revolutions in the post-Cold War era. The drug trade allows warring groups to foster their own links to the international economy without controlling the apparatus of the state.

THE HISTORY OF THE DRUG TRADE'S INFLUENCE ON WARFARE

One reason that the intersection between drugs and warfare has not been thoroughly explored is because of the slow evolution of their link. Yet, history reveals that an intimate link between narcotics and organized political violence has grown and now affects international security in new and dangerous ways. In many historical instances, the dimensions of wars were shaped by the major powers' views of psychoactive drugs and by the drug habits of Western societies.

Though psychoactive narcotics were discovered in regions beyond the shores of Europe and America between the sixteenth and twentieth centuries, "the history of drugs is essentially a history of expansion, with technological change and capitalist enterprise providing most of the driving power."[20] The expansion of commercial capitalism in Europe and America, in combination with technological innovation, allowed drug crops to be stored and transported over greater distances. During this time period, coca plants, opium poppies, and cannabis became part of ordinary international trade in agricultural products and were part of the way of life in many European and American societies. These drugs were not only valued because of their mood altering qualities, but also for their usefulness in the production of other goods, such as beverages, medicines, and clothing. Very few, if any, restrictions were placed on their sale and purchase, and overseas territories were actively encouraged to grow drug crops.

Because psychoactive narcotics were treated like any other commodity during the commercial expansion of the West, they became part of a significant trade dispute, which was the *casus belli* for a major power to initiate a war against a weaker trading power. The First Opium War between England and China reflected the political motivations of the wars during that era, for the conflict was more about gaining open trade concessions for British merchants within the Chinese kingdom than opium. These political motivations were also evident during the Second Opium War, which expanded trade rights for the British, extended trade rights to the French and Americans, and ceded Chinese territory to the British. In short, many countries, such as France, Britain, the United States, and the Netherlands, made huge profits from drug commodities.

As the twentieth century progressed, Western countries that had made huge profits from drugs began limiting them to medical and scientific purposes through international treaties. Drugs encountered heavy prohibition, and by extension, profits and management by illegal entities increased. Drugs such as cocaine, heroin, and marijuana that were once legal were no longer freely traded commodities; they were prohibited items that fell into the realm of law enforcement rather than that of legitimate commerce. Western industrialized countries saw illegal narcotics as disruptive to the social, political, and moral order of their societies. Western states, whose governments actively encouraged and engaged in the drug trade in past centuries, now sought to rid their societies of what was seen as a growing curse of addiction, public health crises, and criminality. The culmination was the signing of the 1912 International Opium Convention and the passing of the Harrison Narcotics Tax Act in 1914 by the United States.

Drug policies during this phase alternated between controlling the licit trade and rolling back illicit trade. Both, however, ultimately sought to return the geographic limitations on drugs that existed before commercial capitalism expanded. Though many developed countries sought to ban drug distribution and use in their societies, many communities in the Third World saw drug production as a profitable business. Decolonization also shifted the drug trade into the hands of warring groups. As colonial powers divested themselves of drug producing territories, drug production became unchecked and more difficult to control from far away capitals. Criminal groups stepped in to take over drug control policies from the colonial authorities. Insurgent groups and governments of newly independent states sought kickbacks and payoffs from drug lords in exchange for the use of territory or for overlooking anti-drug laws. For example, ineffective efforts by the British colonial government to limit the opium trade in Burma meant that by the time Burma became independent, the drug industry was no longer controlled by local feudal lords and colonial bureaucrats but by organized crime and numerous insurgent and counterinsurgent groups.

Because it was prohibited, drug trafficking was a lucrative business; few other businesses provided such a large profit margin. In fact, tighter international controls during the

Cold War increased its profitability, leading many warring groups to further their participation in the illicit trade. [21] This was apparent during the 1980s in conflicts between the Sandinista government and the Contra guerrilla group in Nicaragua[22] and the Colombian government and the FARC guerrilla group in Colombia.[23]

While prohibition of the drug trade did not prevent the funding of warring groups, it also did not end the use of narcotics by combatants. In fact, drug use expanded especially among Western troops. For example, draftees fighting in Vietnam turned to marijuana and heroin to relieve combat stress and alleviate homesickness associated with fighting a protracted war.[24] The widespread use of heroin by American troops threatened to undermine military discipline and, owing to the suppression of the drug trade, placed many soldiers in legal jeopardy because drug possession was an offense under military law.[25]

Drugs became more noticeable in wars that occurred in the shadow of the Cold War. Scott MacDonald and Bruce Zagaris identified eight developments during the 1980s and 1990s that influenced changes in the drug trade, which resulted in the higher degree of participation by warring groups.[26]

- The dramatic increase in cocaine demand in the United States provided more profits that were used to undermine Colombian law enforcement and military operations.
- The 1979 Soviet invasion of Afghanistan facilitated an increase in opium production and allowed profits to be put toward the anti-Soviet effort while exploiting transit routes in Iran and Pakistan.
- The 1979 Iranian Islamic Revolution increased support to Islamic militants in the Bekaa Valley at the expense of narcotics countermeasures in Lebanon.
- The 1988 collapse of the Ne Win government in Burma created increased national instability, led to fewer counternarcotics operations, and increased drug production by rebel groups who opposed the new government.
- The 1989 U.S. invasion of Panama led to the sharp restriction of Panama's ability to be used as a transit country, thereby forcing traffickers to shift routes through countries where rebel groups actively challenged governments.
- The saturation of the U.S. cocaine market in the early 1990s forced product and market diversification. New drugs were produced, and markets in Asia, the Middle East, Africa, and Europe expanded, thereby adding opportunities for more violent actors to participate in the drug trade than before.
- The development of synthetic psychotropic drugs, which could be produced anywhere, permitted violent groups to participate in the drug trade even though they were not located in drug crop regions or along familiar transit routes.

These changes in the drug trade directly impact the nature of contemporary war. From the 1990s to the present, some insurgent groups and governments have not merely turned a blind eye to drug cartels, but produce and distribute narcotics as the largest source of funding rather than as an ancillary one. Frequently, humanitarian catastrophes in which the West intervenes to stem are exacerbated by the pernicious influence of narcotics. For example, several warring groups in Yugoslavia were heavily involved in the drug trade to purchase arms and to pay combatants used in paramilitary operations against civilians.[27] The expansion of the drug trade permitted use by combatants in new regions. For example, new markets in Africa made cocaine accessible to fighters in Liberia for the first time.

Illegal narcotics have also been part of the wars linked to the U.S. Global War on Terrorism. In addition to poppy production in Afghanistan, American and coalition forces have contended with the drug trade in Iraq. U.S. Marines who participated in the November 2004 assault on the Iraqi town of Falluja claim that many of their adversaries were on drugs. Amphetamines, crack, and stockpiles of needles and pipes were found in homes used by insurgents.[28] Moreover, as countries begin to seize the financial assets of terror groups and rein in sympathetic charities, transnational terror organizations like al Qaeda and violent groups linked to them have very few avenues left to fund their activities. Reportedly, Hezbollah imports raw materials for heroin and cocaine production into Lebanon and sells the finished products on the streets of the U.S. and Western Europe as a way to continue its campaign against Israel and the West.[29]

The presence of the drug trade in some conflicts has increased the frustration of efforts aimed at ending violence. Drugs have special features and connections to the prolongation of war. "They are 'lootable,' that is, they are easily 'extracted and transported by individuals and small teams of unskilled workers.'"[30] The lootability and the high profits associated with drugs have created many wars *over* drugs—or military campaigns to gain access to drug crops or to preserve drug routes. Although many violent actors state their commitment to ideological, political, or ethnic goals, they routinely place these goals behind their desires to protect and nurture the drug trade. This means that some forces are less predictable than the conventional militaries that were involved in previous conflicts. Many rebel forces that rely on drugs do not attack military installations or strategic choke points, such as airports and harbors, but target places that are related to drug trafficking.[31] Such a break from traditional notions of warfare requires a greater understanding of the levels of drug-trafficking influence and varying degrees of combatant drug use.

LEVELS OF INTENSITY OF DRUG TRADE AND DRUG USE IN CONTEMPORARY WARS

Since the signing of the 1912 International Opium Convention, drug control has shifted from empires and corporations to near monopolization by irregular combatants and

TABLE 1.1: DRUG TRADE PRESENCE IN CONFLICTS

COLD WAR	POST-COLD WAR	
Afghanistan	Afghanistan	Northern Ireland
Angola	Algeria	Pakistan
Cambodia	*al Qaeda	Palestinian Authority
Colombia	Angola	Peru
Myanmar (Burma)	Bosnia	Philippines
Nepal	Cambodia	Russia (Chechnya)
Nicaragua	Colombia	Rwanda
Peru	Congo	Sierra Leone
South Africa	Indonesia	Senegal
Sri Lanka	Iraq	Somalia
Turkey	Kosovo	Sudan
	Lebanon	Sri Lanka
	Liberia	Turkey
	Morocco	Uganda
	Myanmar	Uzbekistan
	Nepal	

besieged governments who are tightly linked to the globalized world economy. In the post-Cold War era, the number of conflicts where the drug trade plays a part, for funding or consumption by combatants, has grown. (Table 1.1)

The increase in the number of conflicts does not mean the countries listed have been affected by the drug trade or drug use to the same extent; there is a spectrum of intensity in today's conflicts. The following section details the various intensity levels of ongoing conflicts where combatant groups are financially linked to the drug trade. The incipient level represents conflicts weakly linked to the drug trade, while the advanced level represents conflicts with the strongest ties to the drug trade.[32]

Some conflicts have moved through various levels. Colombia, for example, continues to move among high levels, while Afghanistan has rapidly moved from the low to the high intensity level. At the serious level, the role of drugs crosses a threshold from being a peripheral issue for the continuation of violence to being a central issue where clashes occur over resources related to the drug trade. The serious level represents a dangerous crossroads where drugs move from being the sinews of war to becoming its stakes.[33] High intensity levels mean that traditional conceptions of war, based on notions of familiar patterns of violence used to pursue political objectives, are diluted. Political programs and ideology become covers for participation in the drug trade, while violence is used to maintain or increase a group's involvement in drug trafficking or its access to drugs for its

INTENSITY LEVELS OF DRUG TRAFFICKING'S INFLUENCE ON CONFLICTS

Incipient: Congo, Iraq, Nepal, Northern Ireland (Provisional Irish Republican Army), Spain (Euskadi Ta Askatasuna), Palestinian Authority (Hamas), Russia (Chechnya)
- Combatant leadership does not restrict or impede drug trafficking in exchange for payment from drug traffickers.
- Alternatively, combatant leadership may also attempt to control the level of drug-related crime in their territories to demonstrate their authority.

Developing: Algeria, Indonesia, Morocco, Philippines, Senegal, Somalia, Sudan
- Combatants protect crops and/or key nodes of trafficking network from counternarcotics operations or assist in drug transit through their territory in exchange for payment.
- Leaders and troops who are corrupted by drug money permeate government forces.
- Cross border links with other groups associated with the drug trade increase.

Serious: Bosnia, Cambodia, Kosovo, Lebanon (Hezbollah), Liberia, Sierra Leone, Sri Lanka, Turkey
- Combatants collaborate with drug cartels to help produce and transport drugs.
- Combatants actively side with drug cartels in violent confrontations with counternarcotics officials.
- Cross border ties among combatant groups and criminal organizations and other combatant groups expand through personnel and expertise exchange.

Critical: Pakistan, Peru, Uzbekistan
- Combatant leadership is intimately involved in directing and controlling key nodes of drug trafficking, such as transportation, processing labs, and crop harvesting.
- The local population, whether involved in drug trade or not, becomes more economically linked to combatants.
- Combatants fight to protect segments of the drug trade in addition to their stated ideological and political goals.
- Combatants actively fight across borders to support their dependence on drug trafficking.

Advanced: Afghanistan, Colombia, Myanmar
- Combatant leadership uses the drug economy to enmesh its troops and supporters into the legitimate political and economic life of a community.
- The local population not involved in drug trafficking actively supports the violence for economic reasons.
- Drug trade becomes the objective of violence, and there is greater resistance to end the violence.
- Cross border actors actively assist negotiation resistance.

fighters. For example, the Islamic Movement of Uzbekistan (IMU), which states its commitment to a pan-Islamic caliphate in Central Asia, routinely conducts small-scale incursions in the months after the opium harvests in Afghanistan as diversionary tactics designed to confuse and divert law enforcement and military operations, thereby permitting the transit of heroin through several mountain passes.[34]

Intensity levels, however, are not immovable. Depending on variables such as the vagaries of the drug market, involvement by major regional powers, and shifts in international politics, intensity levels can diminish or rise. For example, the Angolan civil war, which lasted beyond the Cold War, exhibited elements of a developing intensity level in the early nineties, but was brought to conclusion with heavy international and regional involvement. The drug trade in Angola has returned to the incipient level.

Intensity levels have increased in the post-Cold War era. Fewer Cold War conflicts were not only drug related, but also did not reach the critical level. For example, the conflicts in Angola, Nicaragua, and Turkey during the 1980s did not move beyond the incipient level, and other conflicts during the Cold War rose only to the serious level. However, the conflicts in Afghanistan, Colombia, Myanmar, and Peru, which have persisted beyond the Cold War's end, have surpassed the serious level.

Moreover, given today's international environment, there is potential for other groups

---

DEGREES OF DRUG USE BY COMBATANTS

Minimal: Haiti, Iraq (Sunni Insurgents, al Qaeda in Iraq, U.S. forces, UK forces)
- Leadership of an irregular group ignores drug use by individual fighters.
- Alternatively, leadership of an irregular group recruits fighters via intoxication or addiction.
- Members of professional militaries deployed abroad in protracted conflicts consume drugs.

Acute: Bosnia, Colombia, Congo, Peru, Philippines, Russia (Chechen rebels), Rwanda
- Leadership of an irregular group uses drugs as a reward.
- Leadership of an irregular group encourages drug use as a motivation for atrocities against civilians.
- Command and control problems begin to occur among the ranks.

Unrestrained: Liberia, Sierra Leone, Somalia, Uganda
- Increasing intoxication or addiction among irregular troops who may conduct violent operations to support their habits.
- Command and control over irregular troops is nearly non-existent because of widespread drug use among fighters.

in more recent conflicts to become involved in drug trafficking. The conflict in Iraq shows signs of reaching the incipient level of intensity with militias and organized crime using areas as transshipment points for heroin.[35] Increasing civil unrest in Haiti and Zimbabwe, combined with their current place in the network of regional drug trafficking, could play a part in future conflicts. The same may be said about the young "insurgency with no name" in southern Thailand, which lies at a geographic crossroads for methamphetamine and heroin from Myanmar bound for Bangkok.[36]

Like the differing drug-trafficking intensity levels in conflicts, drug use by combatants in conflicts also occurs in degrees and has affected several post-Cold War conflicts. Fights that exhibit acute and unrestrained levels of drug use among irregular combatants begin at the minimal level by forcing recruited fighters to consume drugs. For example, drug use blossomed in Bosnia and Rwanda when groups of irregular combatants looted pharmacies, clinics, and hospitals, while conflicts in Liberia and Sierra Leone were unrestrained, primarily because of the use of drugs to recruit child soldiers. At the acute and unrestrained levels, there is an increasing potential for committing human rights abuses against civilians by intoxicated combatants because the mind-altering qualities of drugs permit atrocities to be more widespread.

Professional troops consume drugs in conflict settings as well. Drug use among members of professional militaries has only reached the acute level and has not risen to the unrestrained level. Drug use among members of professional militaries is, however, largely associated with long deployments in protracted conflicts. Drug use by soldiers affects public opinion about the war, which was apparent in America during the Vietnam War and in the Soviet Union during its war in Afghanistan.

As mentioned in the previous section, globalization and the change in drug-trafficking patterns have also contributed to expanding the variety of drugs available to fighters. At times, combatants' drug usage followed drug-smuggling routes. As mentioned previously, this is the case in Liberia where cocaine became available to the Liberians United for Reconciliation and Democracy (LURD) movement fighters on its way to Europe.[37]

Today, the higher the degree of drug involvement by warring groups and drug use by combatants, the greater the effects on dimensions of contemporary warfare. The following are some effects of drug presence in today's wars: protraction of intrastate conflict, undermining of governmental authority in weak states, proliferation of small arms and dual-use technology, corruption of the licit economy, creation of regional instability, undermining legitimate agriculture, enabling human rights abuses and atrocities, deterioration of public health, corruption of professional militaries and police services, challenging accepted military doctrines, encouragement of child soldiery, and combatant unpredictability. The wide-ranging effects of drugs in conflict settings mean murkier operational environments for future political and military leaders. To limit the number of drug-fueled conflicts, lessen their intensity, and reduce the attendant effects of drugs on warfare, the roles that drugs play in conflicts and the lessons learned must be seriously examined so that more effective strategies can be formulated.

THE PLAN OF THIS BOOK

It is not merely the presence of drugs in contemporary conflicts that requires further study; their scope and growing centrality to warfare merits deeper analysis as well. This evolution has created difficult questions for government and military leaders. When do the effects of drugs on conflicts require forceful intervention by outside powers? What level of attention is required when drugs are present in violent conflicts—should they be the major focus, ignored entirely, or something in between? How should conventional military operations take into account combatant drug use? What drug policies would contribute to successful post-conflict rebuilding? The following chapters offer insight into answering these questions.

Chapter 2 examines the flexible and adaptive nature of the drug market and its intersection with the changing face of war from colonial conflicts to the modern battlefield. The chapter also explores how the prohibition of the drug trade created a more lucrative business, initially making it an attractive reservoir of funds for Western militaries.

Chapter 2 then turns its attention to the reasons drugs have become more ubiquitous during wars after the Cold War. Without the competition between the Soviet Union and the United States for the title of global superpower, the calculations of many violent groups assumed a more market-oriented approach. A thorough understanding of the intersection between drugs and warfare requires an examination of the drug-trafficking business, its dynamics, and its effects. Therefore, chapter 2 includes an analysis of the drug production and distribution stages, focusing on the unique qualities of heroin, cocaine, marijuana, and ATS and why these drugs are appealing funding choices for certain violent actors.

Today, drug trafficking involves violent actors at more stages of drug trading than ever before. Chapter 2 also identifies the drugs and the combatants who are involved in their trafficking. The chapter concludes by discussing how armed groups that are financed by drug trafficking affect the dimensions of warfare.

Chapter 3 discusses the various ways intoxicated combatants have affected battlefield conflicts and the difficulties they have presented to various militaries. The chapter discusses how the reasons for combat narcosis add to the strategic problems for many political and military leaders. Troops under the influence of narcotics act in ways that are counterintuitive to many military and political leaders. In conflicts where the drug use intensity level is acute or unrestrained, some insurgent groups have encouraged addiction among children to make them fight for the movement.[38] Such acts create moral complications for troops from developed countries.

Chapter 3 continues with an examination of the four categories of drug usage among belligerents: traditional, transshipped, looted, and synthetically produced. In some conflicts, notably in Africa, fighters have combined drugs from the four categories for added battlefield potency. Because widespread drug use among fighters is now a common feature of post-Cold War conflicts, this chapter argues for the need to develop new ways of fighting. In fact, no Western military has developed a doctrine to outline the ways to cope with intoxicated combatants. Chapter 3 also discusses the separate and distinct ways drugs are used to encourage addiction among the enemy. Rather than combatants themselves ingesting drugs for advantages on the battlefield, some combatant groups have encouraged drug use among their adversaries to undercut their war efforts.

In the aftermath of many wars, several former members of insurgent groups allowed drug traffickers to use their territory. The fourth chapter details the ways the drug trade has made it difficult for insurgent groups to sign and enforce peace accords to end wars. Seeking ways to provide employment for their constituents, and thereby maintaining power in a post-conflict political landscape, former members of militias have actively cultivated ties with drug barons who use areas as drug transit points.[39] As such, the war economy based on illicit drug cultivation, production, or trafficking either precludes or survives a peace deal.

Access to legal commodities such as oil, timber, diamonds, and gas can be more easily impeded through traditional military, diplomatic, and economic actions that can pressure the parties involved. The illegality and profitability of the drug trade makes it difficult to employ such actions and coerce actors to reach a post-conflict settlement among those who participated in both the political violence and the drug trade. Giving up a profitable resource is a powerful disincentive to sign a peace accord.[40] In some cases, "cheating" by an insurgent group or warlord to protect ties to drug money has led to the resurgence of violence. As such, wars are longer and punctuated by numerous "false starts" at resolving the conflict. The chapter continues by discussing how the mutually reinforcing dynamics of violent internal conflict and the drug market make generating a peacetime economy exceptionally difficult. In a world where many warring groups find possessing a hectare of a drug crop more valuable than a seat in Parliament, an analysis of the drug trade's relationship to post-conflict settlement is needed.

Chapter 5 examines the lessons learned from previous and ongoing counternarcotics operations in conflict zones, as well as battlefield dynamics that have indicated avenues for success and paths to failure. Many policymakers find it difficult to understand the characteristics of the drug they are dealing with, which has led to strategic failure. For example, misunderstanding how drug crops are harvested has thwarted crop substitution programs that sap the strength of violent political groups and create favorable conditions for the development of peacetime economies in the aftermath of conflicts.

Chapter 5 argues that troops who are charged with enforcing the parameters of a post-conflict agreement must assess how counternarcotics operations affect the local populace who reside in a country of conflict. Political, military, economic, and social strategies aimed at both curtailing the drug trade and defeating insurgent movements have been crippled from the inception when the local population has not been taken into account. This chapter looks at the variety of factors that military leaders and policymakers must take into account to develop successful strategies.

The final chapter looks at the shaky path ahead to limit the effects of the drug trade on contemporary conflicts. Given the link between drugs and contemporary conflicts, "drug control policies must be adjusted to complement and reinforce the goals of conflict resolution."[41] This chapter argues that there are several underlying assumptions generated from the lessons learned in chapter 5 that produce certain core principles that any strategy must take into account in an era when drugs are enmeshed with violent political conflicts. Several broad strategies are offered that refine assessments, policies, and operations to promote social, economic, and political conditions that lead to the building of a sustainable society and robust government in countries where conflicts are taking place in the shadow of the drug trade. Developing strategies and programs to combat the drug trade increase the likelihood of success in meeting the nation-building goals of building a peacetime economy, empowering the locals, isolating the warlords, and ensuring political promises.

The chapter concludes by arguing that no single strategy addresses all of the dynamics of the drug trade's growing intimacy with warfare. Rather, a multilayered effort from international organizations, major powers, and non-state actors is required to fully address the effects of the drug trade on warfare in today's world. The final chapter also pays special attention to the vital role of intelligence to monitor new drug trends and how these trends may intersect with warfare in the future. The broad conclusions of the outlined strategies suggest that international relations, development studies, and military theory can help generate new understanding, but must first be adapted to match the drug trade's influence within the conflict.

Currently, few forces exist to limit the widespread presence of drugs in warfare. It is likely that the number and intensity of conflicts that are affected by the drug trade will increase. The national security of states in the developed world are also affected by the link between drugs and ongoing conflicts. As an economic resource, drugs have spread violence far from the actual battlefields as strategic theaters for some warring groups have seemingly expanded. Conflicts have spilled into societies of the developed world and led to violent confrontations over urban distribution networks and markets. Lebanese, Kosovar, and Turkish rings violently struggled for control over areas in Frankfurt, Berlin, Zurich, and Budapest. Rather than mere criminal conflicts among ethnic gangs, these were "paramilitary operations conducted by veteran troops who [came] to the rescue from their native countries."[42]

Meanwhile, there is little evidence that the strategic and doctrinal implications of the intersection between drugs and contemporary warfare are being adequately addressed in the halls of power—or in the halls of academia. Because of the ways the drug trade affects contemporary warfare, reliance on traditional strategies and military operations will not be enough. In an international environment that appears violent, uncertain, and complex, creative solutions and deeper intellectual efforts must be crafted to cope more thoroughly with the effects of the intersection between drugs and violent conflicts. This book is a small attempt to find ways to link the battle against illegal narcotics trafficking to the struggle for peace.

2

DRUGGING THE BATTLEFIELD
Drugs as War Funding

CONFLICTS FUNDED BY SALES OF ILLEGAL NARCOTICS SHARE components of other re-source-driven wars funded by diamonds, oil, and timber. Conflicts financed by illicit commodities demonstrate the licit and illicit taxation on resource extraction by various actors of uncertain legitimacy, the ability to keep revenues "off the books," the enrichment of corrupt elites, and the use of extreme violence against civilians to establish and enforce control over the resources.[1] Income from the narcotics trade, more than any other illicit trade, however, has become especially seductive to those involved in violent armed conflicts, while the effects of drug-financed warfare have created far-reaching effects on international security. The dynamics and pressures of the modern drug-trafficking business also allow warring groups to draw profit more directly and more actively than before. As mentioned in chapter 1, today's war financing from drug trade profits stems from the lack of the overarching global superpower competition, the change in the drug trade during the 1980s and 1990s, and the increasing pace of globalization. This chapter explores the warring groups involved in the trafficking of particular drugs, how they are involved, and the effects of their involvement on warfare.

Financing war with drug profits is not unique to the present international environment. This pattern originated in overseas production and distribution by major powers that used the profits in their competition with one another to expand their power—often violently. From the sixteenth to the twentieth century, the drug trade was "a crucial element in the course of European expansion."[2] Opium was especially influential, for it was not only valued for its intoxicating and medicinal qualities, but also because it spawned other commodities. Land, labor, finance, and government were all commercialized by opium. The British, French, and Dutch were actively involved in the global trade of opium as part of their routine imperial commerce. In the Dutch Indies, opium contributed to 30 percent of net revenues,[3] while in French Indochina, opium was the largest single revenue generating operation.[4]

The British Empire especially relied on the Chinese opium market, for "although it is difficult to prove beyond question, it seems likely that without opium, there would have been no empire."[5]

Profits from opium not only offset the deficit of the British East India Company's tea investment, but by the time of the Opium Wars, Britain's broader Far East trade was largely financed by Chinese silver earned from the opium trade.[6]

During World War II, the Japanese used opium trafficking to extend their influence in Asia. Imperial Japan and its elites "latched onto opium as a poor empire's fiscal panacea."[7] In fact, opium became one of the financial underpinnings of Japan's occupation of China. The last Chinese Emperor, Pu Yi, who was installed as a figurehead for the Japanese puppet regime of Manchukuo, reported one sixth of the budget came from opium.[8] The Japanese also used opium profits to fund covert operations against Chinese territory outside of Japan's control.[9]

Even liberal democracies succumbed to the temptation of the drug trade as a way to finance covert operations. The worldwide ban on opium trafficking coincided with the development of more transparent and accountable democratic practices in Europe and the United States. Governments, like the French, that ignored the international ban on trading opium, turned to it to hide *covert* activities beyond the view of domestic constituencies. "Operation X" was designed by the French intelligence services and members of the French Expeditionary Corps to sell opium grown in Laos and Vietnam to Vietnamese and Corsican criminal syndicates and use the profits to fund the counterinsurgency campaign against the Viet Minh.[10] All of this occurred while the French civil administration and home government promoted anti-opium measures at home and abroad.

Colonial powers were not the only political actors participating in the drug trade. As civil wars and wars over decolonization began, so did the Cold War's influence on drug-financed conflicts. Chinese belligerents during the Chinese Revolution of 1949 used the opium trade to support their causes. Both Mao Zedong and Chiang Kai-shek gained funding for their campaigns from growing and selling opium. As one Chinese Nationalist Army general, who was continuing the struggle against the People's Republic of China from the mountains of Burma in 1967, commented, "to fight you must have an army, and an army must have guns, and to buy guns you must have money. [Here] the only money is opium."[11]

Many groups and governments with grievances in the developing world consistently turned to the drug trade as an economic bulwark against foreign encroachment.[12] Cuban members of the Bay of Pigs operation organized Brigade 2506 to fight their own private war to liberate Cuba from Soviet influence. Using their clandestine skills, they formed "La Compania," an underground drug syndicate dedicated to raising money to put toward the undermining of the Castro regime. In Bolivia, military officers in collusion with drug traffickers organized a "cocaine coup" in 1980 to protect the drug proceeds of high-ranking governmental officials while justifying the seizure of power as a means to "eliminate the Marxist cancer." As a precursor to events in the post-Cold War era, several groups engaged in armed clashes over drug resources that were needed to prevail against ideological rivals. In 1967, a local opium war was fought in Burma with Khun Sa's rebel forces on one side and the Chinese Kuomintang Party (KMT) and Royal Lao Army on the other.

Warring groups continue to use drug money to fund conflicts occurring in the post-Cold War era. From the 1990s to the present, many insurgent groups and governments participate in various stages of drug production and distribution rather than relying on state support for their operations. Using drugs to finance military operations has given groups greater autonomy and has weakened the ability of outside powers to influence warring groups. While organized criminal syndicates still provide middlemen, they are increasingly sharing their status with combatants themselves. This ability to "self-finance" armed conflict via drug profits reflects the advantages that globalization gives to contemporary armed groups and points to an increasingly complex international security environment.

GLOBALIZATION AND ILLICIT TRADE

With the number of intrastate conflicts outstripping interstate conflicts, the international landscape of contemporary warfare is distinct from the landscape of war in the past. The end of the Cold War created the motivation, changes in the pattern of drug trafficking provided the opportunity, and elements of a globalizing economy provided the means for warring groups to take a more active role in the drug trade. However, the most important factor was, and continues to be, the power of the globalizing economy.

As a largely economic phenomenon, globalization is expanding the capitalist marketplace around the world. The embrace of free market capitalism by former communist countries and by those formerly aligned with the Soviet Union has meant that previously insulated societies are now increasingly integrated into the larger global economy. Agreements within the European Union (and with those seeking EU membership) and the signing of NAFTA have further removed barriers to the flow of goods and capital. Advances in technology, instant access to information, and lower transportation costs permit greater access to resources in developing countries. These political and economic reforms and technological advances in the wake of the Cold War's end all point in one direction—

toward what economists call an "open economy." In this view, barriers to trade or investment should be as few and as low as possible; rules are known in advance, transparent, coherent, and uniformly enforced; and government interventions are bounded, meaning that few or no prices are set by the government and the economic weight of the state is reduced thanks to balanced budgets and the shedding of state-owned enterprises.[13]

Looser border controls and government authority over international trade is advantageous for illicit goods traffickers. Just as the liberalization of trade and free flow of capital no longer restrict legitimate and illegitimate investor opportunities, combatants more easily find new partners and funding sources around the globe.

Additionally, the structural adjustment policies promoted by developed countries to put Third World countries in line with the international economy created the conditions for social-economic disparities while "increasing exclusion, unemployment, and consequently, illicit activity."[14] The belt-tightening requirements insisted on by Western donors and international development institutions not only disenfranchised and alienated many citizens of developing states, it also meant that many developing states could no longer maintain large military forces. Underpaid and unpaid soldiers sought other sources of funding. Some disenfranchised military commanders became de facto warlords over sprawling criminal fiefdoms.

With the rise in the number of civil conflicts taking place in a world devoid of superpower sponsorship and with traditional enforcement barriers against illegal trade diminished, warring groups have firmly stepped into this burgeoning illicit global marketplace. Because many warring groups seek to change the nature, shape, or policy of a state's government, their members and their financial sources are routinely targeted by governments. Such actions push their members and activities underground where they come into greater contact with the black market and its links to the illicit global economy. In fact, many leaders of warring groups were active criminals before joining a political cause. The head of the Islamic Movement of Uzbekistan (IMU) as well as various leaders of warring groups in the Balkans such as Arkan's Tigers, a Serb paramilitary group, and members of the Kosovo Liberation Army (KLA), were well-known ethnic mafia figures.

Pressure to remain a viable fighting force is considerably eased by turning to a primary commodity like drugs as a source of funding, which thrives in a globalized economy. "Like car making, pharmaceuticals, or even banking, the drug trade has become a truly global industry: it knows no frontiers and has no particular national identity."[15] The worldwide expansion of the drug trade was also aided by the global diffusion of technical expertise and internationalization of manufacturing, making possible the cultivation and refinement of drugs in remote places but within reach of distant markets.[16] The result is that the illegal narcotics business is estimated to be the second largest industry in the world, meeting the demand of nearly 5 percent of the world's population and making up nearly 2 percent of the world's economy.[17] With looser customs inspections, greater facilitation of currency movements, and increased access to transportation facilities, drugs and their profits can move more freely to their destinations. Market pressures favor the involvement of warring groups in the drug trade, and profits have increased for traffickers and smugglers while budgets have declined for governmental agencies that are responsible for countering them.

The drug-trafficking business and its dynamics demonstrate why the drug trade and contemporary warfare empower each other.

THE STRUCTURE OF THE DRUG-TRAFFICKING BUSINESS AND OPPORTUNITIES FOR WARRING GROUPS

The structure and dynamics of modern drug trafficking lie at the foundation for understanding how drug profits are being used to wage war in a globalized world. For those willing to participate in drug trafficking, there are many stages of production and distribution, creating many points of entry. Drug crops that are used to make heroin, cocaine, and marijuana must be grown, harvested, transported to labs for processing, moved to distribution points, sold to wholesale markets, and purchased at retail. Profits are made at each stage of the enterprise, creating multiple funding opportunities. For combatants, each stage represents the potential for the "accumulation of power, or military force."[18]

> Unless a successful rebel organization is bankrolled by another country or an extensive and willing diaspora, it must generate income by operating some business activity alongside its military operations. The question then becomes the type of business activity in which a rebel group is likely to be competitive. Unfortunately, the obvious answer is that the rebel groups' only competitive advantage is their large capacity for organized violence and mayhem. Since, for military reasons, rebel groups tend to be based in rural areas, they turn to business activities such as various forms of extortion and the exploitation and trade of primary commodities.[19]

The multiple stages of drug trafficking work to the advantage of irregular combatant groups, such as insurgents, guerrillas, militias, terrorists, and governments who wish to covertly fund operations. The average cost of organizing and carrying out a violent operation by one of these groups is approximately $100,000.[20] Therefore, a warring group does not require much money to remain lethal and can participate in a very limited number of drug-trafficking stages to earn the needed funding. A warring group does not require a monopoly over all aspects of a particular narcotic; it merely needs to participate in one of the nodes or a linkage between nodes that make up a drug-trafficking network.

As law enforcement succeeded in breaking down drug cartels and organized criminal syndicates, drug trafficking evolved from hierarchical organizations based on kinship, ethnicity, common experience, and tradition to networked enterprises with a flattened lateral structure based on ad hoc arrangements with other groups. While members of the inner core of a drug network may be more closely bonded along the lines of a hierarchical organization, the peripheries of networks allow them to interact more extensively and with greater impact.[21] Today's drug trafficking is akin to a flexible exchange network that expands and contracts according to market opportunities and barriers.[22] As a result, there is little desire, or ability, for a drug cartel to own a monopoly over an entire drug-trafficking process.

> The Colombian cocaine trade of the 1980s and early 1990s was very much a directed network—at least at the core—which came into existence to transport cocaine to the United States. The heroin trade from Southeast Asia, in contrast, is far more of a transaction network, in which brokers play a critical role at almost every stage of the process. Producers supply heroin to independent distributors, and it is then passed along a chain of brokers until it reaches the retail market.[23]

Warring groups are now the brokers, leading to a hybrid quality of drug trafficking where, in practice, a directed network can be part of a larger transaction network.[24] Criminal contacts with warring groups, much like contacts among various criminal groups, can take a number of forms: joint ventures, strategic alliances, "subcontracting" or franchising for particular functions.[25]

Owing to the global scope of the drug trade, the variety of stages of its trafficking, the limited amount of money needed for a warring group to be lethal, and the network organizational nature of drug traffickers, many rebel groups and besieged governments are involved in virtually every stage of the global drug trade. For violent groups, the drug trade offers consistent profits that can be used to solve key problems for combatant leaders—recruiting, training, and retaining loyal fighters. By generating funding, violent groups can demonstrate their power by organizing successful operations and gain followers through payments. Insurgent movements are involved, from the FARC's cocaine cultivation to Iraqi insurgents' sale of methamphetamine and heroin on the streets. Government militaries that are engaged in conflicts are involved, from Turkey ignoring the use of drug profits of anti-Kurdish militias to Colombian military forces overlooking the drug dealing of right-wing paramilitaries. Violent groups have accepted the axiom: drugs equal money and money equals power.

In many instances, warring groups have been welcomed by drug traffickers because they can provide security and expertise. The most common services provided by violent groups are protection for drug farmers and the transporting of the product. Unlike legitimate agribusiness, the drug trade is surrounded by the possibility of detection, arrest, and death. These dangers can be mitigated by the superior firepower of belligerents. Additionally, against the backdrop of illegality, drug traffickers must balance the need for concealment and stealth with the need for coordination. Armed groups are able to provide an additional layer of security by protecting the product from interdiction, key personnel from arrest, and profits from seizure. This protection provides a degree of certainty for profiting at all stages of drug trafficking. Warring groups do not need to control a node to earn income from drug traffickers. Like many entrepreneurs, drug barons are willing to make market speculations and give warring groups advance payments to secure future prospects that may prove lucrative to the trade.[26] Drug cartels also offer violent groups expertise in money laundering and additional networks for smuggling weapons. In some cases, a symbiosis between drug traffickers and warring groups has developed as with Hezbollah and the criminal gangs in Ciudad del Este or the Taliban and organized crime in Pakistan.

Warring groups are least active in retail distribution at the street level. This is largely because of the lack of a violent group's physical presence in the main marketplaces within developed countries. At the retail distribution stage, arrangements with organized crime groups are almost always needed, for criminal groups possess the networks to sell the product for retail distribution in developed countries. However, lack of a physical presence in a market has not completely obstructed retail sales. Ethnic ties between violent political groups and organized crime in developed countries, as with the Tamil Tigers of Sri Lanka, can also aid the retail distribution process. The increase in global migration and the growth of ethnic networks that transcend numerous national boundaries have permitted profits from retail sales to return to the coffers of groups who are committed to an armed struggle in a diaspora community's home country. Ideological affinity can also assist in profits from retail sales being used in a similar manner. For example, in 1993 French authorities believed that drug sales in suburban Muslim slums were under the control of Afghan war veterans with ties to Algerian terror groups and had penetrated a significant portion of the Moroccan hashish trade.[27]

To make up for the inability to conduct retail sales, rather than cash payment, violent groups barter for other illicit goods, such as weapons, or exchange services. For example, members of the United Self-Defense Forces of Colombia (AUC), Colombia's right wing paramilitary group, were caught attempting to trade drugs for weapons.[28] While organized crime furnishes weapons for a warring group, warring groups who participate in organized crime, like the Irish Republican Army, offer personnel training in exchange for drugs.

Yet there are significant differences that separate a warring group from an organized criminal syndicate. Although these differences are often subtle, they can still lead to a warring group taking on functions of criminality to gain autonomy and financial strength. Some warring groups compete for governmental legitimacy, while organized criminal syndicates generally do not and merely favor weakened governmental control. Collusion with an antigovernment group can expose the criminal syndicate to greater violence from professional military forces. Warring groups generally have more ideologically inspired goals than criminal groups; the main goals for a criminal organization are the generation and accumulation of profit. High levels of violence associated with warfare can often hamper the achievement of these goals for criminals.

Moreover, the accumulation of profit over time is not a wartime goal nor immediately useful to a combatant group. As previously mentioned, because the costs of funding a violent operation are relatively cheap, warring groups are more interested in money disbursement than profit accumulation. Warring groups need their drug earnings to purchase arms, equipment, and training whereas criminal groups invest proceeds in legitimate sectors of an economy and dedicate profits to improving their business.

In some instances, when warring groups and organized criminal syndicates have colluded in drug trafficking they have parted company because of competing interests and priorities. Some warring groups have developed "in-house" capabilities for conducting segments of the drug-trafficking business. In Afghanistan, Colombia, and Myanmar, irregular forces pursue drug activities that were traditionally associated with organized crime. Some warring groups in these nations have established processing labs to refine the product, which allows them to be involved in the intermediate stages of production rather than outsourcing the activity to organized crime syndicates in other territories. Often, the proximity of a profitable drug crop to an active insurgency has led a warring group to become nearly indistinguishable from organized crime. Warring groups who were active in transit countries often demobilize after conflict settlements and degenerate into organized criminal groups that are linked to political movements and parties.

The high-risk nature of the drug trade, its global distribution, and the number of stages the product must pass through create the conditions for a very profitable industry. The most trafficked drugs continue to be heroin, cocaine, and marijuana. There is also a substantial rise in the trafficking of synthetic drugs, including ecstasy and meth. Traditional drugs like *khat* and *datura* are not widely sold outside of conflict zones. While the trafficking of any illegal narcotic shares similar stages of production and distribution, each drug is unique in how and where it is grown, harvested, processed, and transported. Each drug is also distinctive because of the actors who are involved in the specific stages of its trafficking.

VIOLENT POLITICAL ACTORS AND THE STAGES OF DRUG TRAFFICKING

Drug trafficking supports a variety of warring groups around the globe. The economic forces of supply and demand, when applied to the drug trade, reveal that it is a consistent and reliable trade for those who participate. Worldwide demand for drugs has remained relatively steady since the 1990s; in 2006 the customer base was roughly 200 million users.[29] Although interdiction efforts have improved, the economics of the drug trade can make up for any shortfall by passing down the costs to users who are more than willing to pay higher prices. If street prices fall, street sellers will accept lower profits, while the profit margin for the traffickers remains relatively stable. With an addictive product, demand can be manipulated by intentionally lowering the price of drugs to attract new users or opening new markets.

The consistent and high rate of profit also creates a "hydra-effect" in the labor and management force of drug trafficking.[30] Named after the mythical animal that could lose a head, only to have two grow back in its place, this dynamic refers to the drug trade's ability to absorb losses of personnel at any place in the trafficking chain. Owing to the drug trade's profitability, there is a large reservoir of people, including combatants, who are willing to replace the loss of any person. Changes in the drug trade in the '80s and '90s stand as a testament to the hydra-effect's influence on warfare. For example, the FARC and the National Liberation Army (ELN) became more active in the cocaine trade partially because law enforcement significantly reduced the power of the Cali and Medellin drug-trafficking cartels through arrests and extraditions.

Unlike oil, timber, and diamonds, drugs are highly mobile, and because of their relatively low weight-to-value ratio, new production areas can be found easily if a source or production stage is eradicated. Even successful eradication and interdiction efforts run aground because the drug trade can absorb the loss of resources and product. The "balloon effect" of drug enforcement is also unique to the drug trade. Just as pressing on a particular area of a balloon creates an expansion in another area, pressure in one area of a drug-trafficking network means that traffickers simply move their operations where there is less pressure or make up for losses in another node of the distribution chain. From the standpoint of a combatant who is growing drug crops or providing protection for crops, a ton of finished heroin, morphine, or cocaine that is seized is no different from a ton consumed since it is the demand at the next stage of distribution that sets the price and the profits. The street price of the drug does little to affect their bottom line, meaning that the price at the retail end can be manipulated either higher or lower to compensate for any disruptions in the network.

Unlike other commodities that warring groups use for funding that are traded in the global marketplace, the drug trade possesses an additional advantage because it is illegal. It is highly compartmentalized by region and drug. For example, prices for poppy are high in the Golden Crescent but low in the Golden Triangle, while the price of coca is the same everywhere because its production is geographically limited to the Andes.[31] The differences among drugs permits the prices of drugs at different production stages to be more easily manipulated than prices of legal commodities, which are tied to the world market. Legal commodities that are illegally traded can be mixed and remixed with those that are legally acquired and legally traded, sold, and resold on the world market. Prime examples are diamonds and timber taken illegally from conflict zones in Africa and intermingled with diamonds and timber that have been legitimately acquired. Illegal narcotics, while they cannot be mixed in a legal market, are not subject to price shocks and market collapses of legal commodities.

Opium, Morphine, and Heroin

The opium poppy continues to be highly valued for its narcotic quality. As the primary ingredient in the manufacturing of morphine and heroin, it is also a more weight-efficient producer of profit than cocaine or marijuana. A single smuggler on foot or as a passenger can carry between $50,000 to $200,000 worth of high-grade heroin.[32] At the farm gate in Afghanistan, production is worth an estimated $600 million.[33] The cultivation of poppies for heroin requires proper climate, appropriate soil acidity, access to ample water, generous fertilization, and semi-skilled labor. Because of these requirements, poppy growing is limited to certain geographic areas. Many of these areas lie in countries of conflict, such as Myanmar, Colombia, Afghanistan, and Pakistan, or border these countries such as Laos, Thailand, and Tajikistan.

Heroin is processed from morphine, which is a naturally occurring substance extracted from seedpods of poppy plants. Because poppy fields contain thousands of poppy capsules, harvesting is labor intensive.[34] At this stage of production, rurally based violent groups who operate near these plantations have "taxed" the farmers for protection. Combatants have also made up for any shortages in labor necessary to extract the gum. Also known as opium, this gum or paste does not rot, allowing for longer storage compared to other plant-based narcotics. In Afghanistan, it is believed that there is a four to eight year inventory stashed away in order to survive any counterdrug actions by coalition forces.[35]

Opium's long shelf life means that it can gain value over time, allowing violent groups to manipulate the price it receives at the processing stage. In addition, few legitimate crops in countries where opium is cultivated can be transported great distances without spoiling or being damaged because of insecurity and poor roads. By comparison, because poppy resin, the main ingredient in heroin, is robust and can keep for years, it is an attractive option for peasants and a prime target for exploitation by violent groups.

Heroin production and distribution allow for numerous stages in which violent groups can become involved. In 2000–2001, the Taliban government was able to manipulate the heroin market by focusing on the first node of production: it banned the growing of opium while recommending its criminal allies store enough opium gum until the sale price rose. This allowed the Taliban to generate more funding to prosecute its campaign against the Northern Alliance shortly before the American-led intervention in October 2001. Afghan drug kingpin Bashir Noorzai was not only paying the Taliban for protection but also supplied al Qaeda with $28 million worth of heroin annually.[36] Remnants of al Qaeda continue to feed off the heroin trade as does the Islamic Movement of Uzbekistan, which is dedicated

TABLE 2.1: WARRING GROUPS INVOLVED IN THE OPIUM/MORPHINE/HEROIN TRADE

COUNTRY	GROUP(S)	STAGE(S) OF TRAFFICKING
Afghanistan	Taliban	Protection for farmers, transportation to labs, transportation to wholesalers
	Northern Alliance	Protection for farmers, transportation to labs, transportation to wholesalers
Colombia	FARC, ELN	Protection for farmers, transportation to labs, transportation to wholesalers
Indonesia	GAM	Transportation to wholesalers
Iraq	Mahdi Militia	Transportation to wholesalers
Kosovo	KLA	Transportation to wholesalers, wholesale distribution, and retail sales
Liberia	LURD	Transportation to wholesalers
Myanmar	UWSA	Protection for farmers, transportation to labs, transportation to wholesalers
Northern Ireland	IRA	Retail sale
	UVF, UDA	Retail sale
North Korea	Central Committee Bureau 39	Production, wholesale, and retail distribution
Pakistan	Jaish al Mohammad	Transportation to wholesalers, wholesale distribution, and retail sales
Philippines	Abu Sayyaf	Protection and transportation to wholesale market
Spain	ETA	Retail sale
Sri Lanka	Tamil Tigers	Transportation to wholesalers and retail sale
Turkey	PKK	Transportation to wholesalers, wholesale distribution, and retail sales
	Grey Wolves	Transportation to wholesalers, wholesale distribution, and retail sales
Uzbekistan	IMU	Transportation to wholesalers

to establishing a radial "pan-Arab caliphate" across Central Asia.[37]

Refining raw opium gum into heroin is a slow, multi-step process. Once the opium gum is transported to a laboratory, it is converted into morphine, an intermediate product. When dried, the morphine is pressed into bricks. The Taliban and members of the Northern Alliance have established their own labs in Afghanistan for this process.[38] The processing reduces the bulk of the product by 90 percent, aiding in smuggling it outside the country. From the labs, heroin passes through many hands. Again, security for storage can be taxed, and transportation provided by a violent group that, in collusion with smugglers, ensures the product's delivery to wholesalers and then retailers in or near markets in Europe, the United States, Australia, and Southeast Asia.

The distance between the remote regions where poppies are grown and heroin is introduced to the market requires numerous participants who are often involved in ongoing armed conflicts. Opium is not only grown in or near countries of conflict, but depending on the organization, the processed drug may be transshipped via restless countries, such as Indonesia, the Philippines, Uzbekistan, Kyrgyzstan, Syria, Egypt, Turkey, Russia, Israel, and Nigeria. Iraq has also recently entered the heroin trafficking business as a transit point, thereby complicating ongoing efforts to build a stable society.[39] Table 2.1 outlines the violent actors and where they participate in the stages of production and distribution.

Cocaine

Unlike the trafficking of opium, heroin, and morphine, the cocaine exporting business is relatively young. Although coca and cocaine were commercially available in Western societies before its prohibition, its illicit trafficking skyrocketed in the 1970s and fully matured in the 1980s. With the help of figures such as Pablo Escobar and Carlos Lehder, cocaine was brought into the United States in quantities that generated a burgeoning demand for the drug, a demand that continues today. The relative youth of the cocaine trafficking business, however, has not prevented it from playing a role in contemporary conflicts.

The unique qualities of cocaine set it apart from other illicit narcotics and the ways it intersects violent conflicts. Coca plants require a tropical climate with high amounts of rainfall and elevations between 1,600 and 5,000 meters. Because of the geographic idiosyncrasies of growing the coca plant, crops are limited to the Andes region of South America, specifically in the countries of Bolivia, Peru, and Colombia and along the border areas of Ecuador and Venezuela. These countries either contain or border active insurgencies. Unlike opium-based narcotics, cocaine is geographically much closer to its main market of the United States, sharply limiting the number of distribution nodes and therefore constricting the number of violent actors who participate in its trafficking (Table 2.2). However, similar to opium, finished cocaine can produce generous profits. Five hundred kilograms of coca leaves is worth about $750 to the farmer but yields eight to ten kilos of cocaine worth about $200,000.[40]

Coca farming is well suited for clandestine production and participation by violent political actors. Coca fields are grown in isolated and difficult to access areas; in fact, the higher the altitude, the richer the concentration of cocaine in the leaves. The remote areas of coca fields are also in areas where guerrillas and paramilitaries seek sanctuary and draw support from the local population. Most coca fields are less than one hectare in size. This is to the advantage of traffickers since small plots make locating the coca and eradicating it very difficult. Because coca takes a long time to grow, farmers sometimes plant corn or yucca to make money while the coca plants are growing. The interspersing of other crops adds to the difficulty in detecting coca fields, providing another benefit to the trafficker.

The presence of an insurgent group in coca-producing regions has provided beneficial opportunities for guerrillas and traffickers. Since picking coca leaves is labor intensive, requiring three hundred people per day per hectare, and can be harvested four times a year, irregular combatants have added to the labor force and have increased the efficiency of coca harvesting. Leaves are picked from the coca plant, dried, and bundled for carriers who transport them to processing labs. At this stage, guerrillas have taxed farmers and plantation owners for protection. In certain areas of Colombia, a *gramaje* (payment in grams) has been charged to the plantation owners for protection in exchange for a percentage of the grams of coca paste produced in the area.[41] In fact, the FARC and ELN have colluded in standardizing the gramaje to reduce conflict between the groups and generate

TABLE 2.2: WARRING GROUPS INVOLVED IN THE COCAINE TRADE

COUNTRY	GROUP(S)	STAGE(S) OF TRAFFICKING
Angola	UNITA	Wholesale distribution
Colombia	FARC, ELN, AUC	Protection for farmers, transportation to labs, processing, transportation to wholesalers
Lebanon	Hezbollah	Manufacture, wholesale distribution, retail sale
Liberia	LURD	Wholesale distribution, retail sale
Peru	Sendero Luminoso	Protection for farmers, transportation to labs, transportation to wholesalers

a consistent flow of money for their respective groups. Unlike opium-based narcotics, coca leaves cannot be stored for long periods of time. This means that violent groups cannot easily manipulate the price for the product at the coca stage.

Guerrillas have also aided in transporting coca leaves to processing labs where they are made into "base" cocaine. The base is screened, impurities are removed, and chemicals are added to convert the base into finished cocaine. These labs often exist in remote areas where there is no access to roads, making overland transportation of the finished product difficult. This means that much of the security and transportation through these limited routes must be provided by guerrillas as the product makes it way to the next stage of the distribution process—arrival at warehouses, ports, and airstrips. From these sites to wholesalers, street sales, and profit collection, members of the FARC, ELN, and right-wing paramilitary groups each play a role in the stages of contemporary cocaine trafficking.[42] The FARC is so intimately involved in cocaine manufacturing and distribution that the U.S. Department of Justice indicted fifty of its members on drug-trafficking charges in March 2006.[43]

Similar to heroin, small amounts of cocaine can generate hefty profits. Thus, smugglers do not need to transport large amounts of cocaine to the wholesale market. Smuggling smaller amounts makes interdiction more troublesome. Smuggling routes have varied, but cocaine continues to transit through a number of countries that have emerged from years of internal conflict to reach the U.S. main market. Unlike opium and its derivatives, which transit through many countries with active conflicts, cocaine traffickers take advantage of countries where law enforcement and customs inspection are attempting to rebound after violent conflicts. Cocaine trafficking threatens to undermine the newly established stability in countries such as El Salvador, Nicaragua, Guatemala, and Haiti.

The flexibility and adaptability of the cocaine trade is demonstrated by the balloon effect. According to the UN *2007 World Drug Report*, seizures of cocaine are up and hectares used to grow coca are down.[44] According to the same report, demand for cocaine has stabilized. While a seeming victory for anti-drug operations that may lead to lower profits for several warring groups involved in production and transportation of cocaine, street prices for cocaine in its main market in the United States have fallen.[45] In an effort to keep profits unaffected at their end of production and distribution, costs have been pushed down the chain. As a result, for profits to be made at the wholesale level drug bosses in the United States have lowered the wages they pay street pushers or moved the product themselves from one node to another to remove the middle men.

Additionally, in combination with the balloon effect, the hydra-effect is at work in the cocaine trade as well. Although the United States has the largest market for cocaine, Europe's demand for cocaine is rising. As a result, the trafficking routes have expanded to countries in West Africa, including Cape Verde, Ghana, Togo, Nigeria, and Liberia, that have shaky governance structures. They are being used as transshipment points, for there is a ready reservoir of people willing to earn money from the drug trade. Reflecting the increased use of Africa as a transit zone, cocaine use in Africa is rising.[46] A strong market exists in South Africa with transshipment points existing in nearby Zimbabwe and Mozambique.

Marijuana and Hashish

Marijuana is the most widely consumed drug in the world for many reasons. Cannabis is grown in almost every country in the world. Unlike poppies and coca, marijuana can be grown in a wide variety of climates, in poor soil, and indoors with the proper equipment.[47] Additionally, its growth and consumption are not penalized as harshly as other narcotics. Lower penalties mean lower risk, while the ease in which marijuana is grown means that supply is readily available. As a result, marijuana is the least weight efficient producer of profit. The street price for marijuana varies from $400 to $2,000 per pound. Hashish, made by drying and compressing the plant to make a resin, sells for $2,000 to $4,000 per pound. The formula for the cultivation and trafficking appears to be small investment, little risk, but low returns.

Because of smaller profits, marijuana's growth and sale have not led to high levels of influence in a violent conflict. Many warring groups that used marijuana or hashish as financing have entered peace processes, including Angola, Liberia, and Senegal. Few

TABLE 2.3: MARIJUANA AND HASHISH AND WARRING GROUPS

COUNTRY	GROUP(S)	STAGE(S) OF TRAFFICKING
Algeria	GSPC (now, al Qaeda in Maghreb)	Protection for farmers, wholesale distribution, and retail sales
Morocco	GICM	Protection for farmers and production, distribution to retail market
Philippines	New People's Army	Protection for farmers and production, distribution to wholesale market
	Abu Sayyaf	Protection for farmers and production, distribution to wholesale market
Uganda	LRA	Distribution to wholesale market

ongoing conflicts continue to be financed by marijuana profits (see Table 2.3). The primary exporters of marijuana are Colombia, Thailand, Jamaica, and Mexico. While Colombia contains an active internal conflict, the primary drug used to produce revenue is cocaine. Although Thailand borders the troubled state of Myanmar, Thailand's insurgency is embryonic and Myanmar's warring groups rely primarily on the heroin and ATS trade. Marijuana played a limited role in the conflicts in Nepal and Ethiopia and continues to play a minor role in the fighting in Uganda. The Communist Party of the Philippines/New People's Army (CPP/NPA), a U.S.-designated foreign terrorist organization, receives money for providing safe haven and security for many of the marijuana growers in the northern Philippine and collects "revolutionary taxes" on the sale of drugs; yet such funding complements other funding schemes like kidnapping and human trafficking.

The marijuana weed is a hardier plant than poppy or coca. Since harvesting marijuana is not as dependent on large numbers of laborers, manpower shortages are rare, thereby removing an opportunity for a warring group to participate. Unlike heroin and cocaine, marijuana requires virtually no processing to generate a stronger finished product. As a result, marijuana moves quickly from farm to wholesaler and leaves little need for transportation security. Combatants can grow small amounts of marijuana themselves without relying on farmers. Yet, similar to heroin and cocaine, the production and distribution of marijuana permits the participation of violent actors. Insurgent groups in Algeria, Morocco, and the Philippines have taxed farmers and provided transportation for the crops. Growing larger amounts of marijuana, however, makes it more difficult to smuggle to wholesale markets, leaving it particularly susceptible to interdiction by law enforcement. In fact, Nepalese guerrillas found that Indian customs became so adept at confiscating their marijuana loads that they have compensated for diminishing funds by selling stolen gasoline.[48]

Marijuana's role in financing conflicts is different from that of heroin and cocaine. The lower margin of profit constrains a warring group's ability or willingness to continue the struggle. Lower profits may also explain why groups in Angola, Liberia, and Mozambique relied on trafficking in more profitable resources like oil, diamonds, and timber. However, these commodities were more susceptible to obstruction and interdiction efforts created additional pressures to settle the conflicts. As a result, marijuana trafficking is not as useful in sustaining conflicts by itself or playing a large role in the overall financial viability of a warring group. It is more useful as a way for a group to diversify its funding.

In addition, the market for marijuana, though large, shows signs of decreased profitability in the United States, one of its main consumer markets. According to the U.S. Office of National Drug Control Policy, "more marijuana was consumed in 2000, [but] the price decreased from 1990 to 2000, resulting in a decrease in the total amount spent on the drug."[49] This trend has continued. The low profits and the seeming decline in market value may signal the further lessening of marijuana's role in funding violent conflicts.

Amphetamine-Type Stimulants (ATS): Methamphetamine and Ecstasy

The trends in the drug market that are working against the profitability of marijuana are creating new funding streams for violent conflicts. Synthetically produced amphetamine-type stimulants (ATS), like ecstasy and meth, are in increasing demand and are beginning to overshadow the more traditional plant-based narcotics, such as marijuana, cocaine, and heroin, in consumption.[50] Much like marijuana, ATS can be produced in numerous countries. However, like cocaine and heroin, ATS requires precursor chemicals that are not always readily available and must be acquired through various means. As a result, the ease of manufacturing and distributing ATS is comparable to marijuana, but the unreliability of accessing precursors makes them more expensive.

These so-called designer drugs are not agricultural and can be manufactured in almost any environment.[51] Their production is not tied to a specific location and allows them to be easily transported. Designer drugs can be manufactured in small laboratories no larger than an automobile, making them difficult to destroy at the source. Because drug production must almost always be out of the sight of law enforcement and the military, the home-manufacturing of ATS offers a better hedge against detection than large fields of poppy, coca, or cannabis. In addition, instead of one waiting for a harvest to be ready and then transporting the crops to a lab for processing, ATS drugs can be produced and ready for distribution in two to twenty-four hours.

The qualities of ATS manufacturing and distribution allow them to be produced more easily, more quickly, and more clandestinely than plant-based drugs that require crop space, hospitable climate, and a large workforce. Additionally, because meth is home-manufactured, for example, there are few choke points that can be targeted by counternarcotics operations. As a result of few middlemen, unlike the trafficking in plant-based narcotics, the manufacturer receives nearly 100 percent of the profits of ATS drugs.[52] Because of these characteristics, designer drugs are gaining appeal to transnational violent groups who are loosely structured and clandestine. Al Qaeda and sympathizers to its cause have already taken advantage of the ATS trade. Likewise, Spanish authorities believe that those responsible for the March 2004 train bombings financed their operations in part through the sale of ecstasy.[53] ATS is well suited to al Qaeda associated groups which have become more entrepreneurial in their operations in the wake of 9/11 as governments launched greater anti-terrorist campaigns. Rather than depending on outside funding from Bin Laden's al Qaeda or sympathetic organizations to organize an attack, smaller local *jihadist* groups and cells have participated in the ATS trade along with petty crime like credit card fraud.

The heavy reliance on the availability of certain chemical compounds like pseudoephedrine or ephedrine for producing ATS had largely limited the production of designer drugs to developed countries like the United States, Canada, and the Netherlands. However, with the rapid pace of globalization facilitating the transfer of technology and products, acquiring

TABLE 2.4: ATS AND WARRING GROUPS

COUNTRY	GROUP(S)	STAGE(S) OF TRAFFICKING
———	al Qaeda	Wholesale distribution, retail sales
Lebanon	Hezbollah	Production, wholesale distribution, retail sale
Myanmar	United Wa State Army	Production, transportation, wholesale distribution
	Mongko Defense Army	Production, transportation, wholesale distribution
	Kachin Democratic Army	Production, transportation, wholesale distribution
	Myanmar Democratic Alliance Army	Production, transportation, wholesale distribution
North Korea	Central Committee Bureau 39	Production, wholesale and retail distribution
Palestinian Territories	Hamas	Production, transportation, wholesale distribution
Philippines	Abu Sayyaf	Production, transportation, wholesale distribution, retail distribution

precursors is no longer a large obstacle. There are numerous recipes on the Internet that instruct an individual how to make ephedrine in a five-gallon bucket if none is readily available.[54] Today, no region or country is immune from synthetic drug production.[55] Some violent groups produce ATS drugs for markets in rapidly urbanizing areas of the developing world. The influence of Western nightclub culture has been imported into these societies, including the desire of the youth to take part in the latest drug fad.[56] With youth as an increasing percentage of the population in developing countries combined with rapid urbanization, the market for ATS has exploded. Violent actors near these markets are already profiting. In fact, several warring parties in Myanmar have well-developed trafficking networks; the United Wa State Army, the Mongko Defense Army, the Kachin Democratic Army, and the Myanmar National Democratic Alliance Army are active producers and wholesale distributors of meth in Southeast Asia.[57]

Although not as profitable as heroin and cocaine, with demand increasing and the relative ease and mobility of production, ATS drugs are poised to be a large source of funding for many violent groups in the future.

Locally Traded Drugs: Khat and Datura

Other conflicts have been sustained by trading in narrow drug markets. Drug crops of *khat* and *datura* have financed east African conflicts in Somalia and Sudan. These drugs are not widely traded internationally and are more geographically circumscribed. Their narrow trade is mostly owing to the inability of these crops to be stored for long periods of time without losing their narcotic qualities, making transportation over long distances difficult. In fact, these drugs are mainly sold to local supporters or almost always immediately ingested by fighters in these conflicts. Even though khat's potency diminishes shortly after it is picked, overnight worldwide delivery services have mitigated this problem.[58] Khat is also legal in Great Britain and many countries in Europe, making its trade less profitable. It is illegal in the United States where it has a market among African expatriate communities, but it has not expanded significantly. Methcathinone, a drug derived from the khat plant, was gaining popularity in the United States during the early 1990s but was rapidly outpaced by the growing popularity of meth.

EFFECTS ON CONTEMPORARY WARFARE

The variety of drugs and the number of warring groups participating in their trafficking reveal differences in how they affect specific conflicts. Some argue that rebel groups in particular can perpetuate conditions of warlordism whereby *de facto* sovereignty is imposed over areas of drug production and distribution.[59] This only applies in cases where opium and coca are grown and harvested, for the existence of crops far from the center of power "can provide an economically viable fall-back position" in case warring groups fail to achieve their ideological objectives.[60] Although the profits are not high at the growth stage of the heroin or opium trade, they are consistent and reliable and have a higher weight to ratio profit than marijuana. With such a steady profit, warring groups with access to opium and coca crops can dedicate more resources to securing more portions of trafficking nodes from production to protecting routes to wholesalers, thereby more fully funding military operations.

Nonetheless, the botanical peculiarities of coca and opium mean that they are geographically limited; coca and opium crops cannot fund groups outside the regions where these crops can be harvested. For example, coca and opium cannot be grown in Africa and therefore do not feature in the cases of warlordism that occur in conflicts on the continent. Because marijuana is a weed it can be produced in a variety of conditions, which, in combination with lower penalties for its use in certain markets, means that its profits are lower and it has only been useful as supplemental revenue for warring groups.[61]

Conflicts in opium- and coca-producing countries tend to not only be more intense than conflicts where marijuana is produced, but also increase the intensity of conflicts nearby. The cases of the IMU and Jaish al-Mohammad demonstrate how important drug-smuggling routes out of a source country can be in ongoing and high levels of violence. The cases of the KLA, ETA, and paramilitary groups in Northern Ireland demonstrate that the closer cocaine and heroin move to consumer markets, the lower the level of intensity of the drug trade's influence on conflict.

Trafficking in ATS drugs demonstrates the ease with which a number of different types of violent actors can participate. With the backing of the government, North Korea's Central Committee Bureau 39 is able to control all nodes of one trafficking network. Several warring groups in Myanmar are also able to control all the nodes of separate trafficking networks. This is largely because of the long history and well-established networks that have been used to smuggle heroin. Terrorist groups like al Qaeda and the individuals who participated in the Madrid train bombings in 2004 have participated in wholesale distribution and street sales more than activities further up the trafficking chain.[62] However, Hezbollah has been active in manufacturing, wholesale, and retail sales.[63]

However, for all the differences among the variety of drugs in terms of growth, production, and distribution, the broad effects on warfare are similar. Rather than drugs being merely a generator of profit for organized crime, drugs have emerged as a strategic resource in politically motivated violence. This has meant that the duration of conflicts has lengthened and the battlegrounds have expanded beyond the frontlines, providing conflicts with additional layers of complexity and asymmetry. These conflicts now include larger aspects of civil society such as crop space, travel routes, transportation hubs, smuggling routes, financial institutions, and institutions of governance. The drug trade influences contemporary warfare in wide-ranging and interdependent ways that policymakers and military leaders have been coping with for decades but have only now begun to recognize more clearly.

Protraction of Intrastate Conflict
Because warfare can now be more easily sustained with drug funding and other illicit trade, the expected length of conflicts is more than double that of conflicts that started prior to 1980.[64] This can be attributed to the accessibility of drug resources and revenues that permits militarily weaker groups to maintain their viability rather than being swept from the battlefield. For example, when the IMU was nearly eliminated because of its support of the Taliban in the battle for Kunduz in November 2001, the IMU was able to regenerate with profits from its links to the heroin trade.[65] Direct participation in segments of the drug

trade creates a strategic link to a resource that used to be filled by a superpower patron. In such a context, government forces that are involved in fighting groups with links to drug crops are doubly disadvantaged—they must hunt guerrillas in unfamiliar territory or locate drug crops in areas of potentially greater violence, which means that casualties are often higher and that training and equipping for operations takes longer.

Segments of the drug-trafficking infrastructure are now part of the strategic equation for many combatants. With drugs now playing the role of an economic engine for many belligerents, it is not surprising that battles for control over aspects of drug trafficking have occurred. As a result, drugs have often deepened conflicts; drugs not only provide another means to continue fighting, but they provide another reason as well. Many violent non-state groups have a vested interest in the ongoing unrest and disorder in their areas so they can secure transportation routes for drugs. Conflicts that have crossed into and beyond the serious level have had frequent clashes over drug supplies, smuggling routes, and transportation resources. Clashes over drug resources, resembling "turf wars," routinely occur among the warring groups in Afghanistan, Colombia, and Myanmar. These conflicts engender a vicious circle where sustaining the conflict becomes more necessary to secure access to parts of a trafficking network because the rise in violence between groups becomes increasingly costly.

These phenomena are not only present in drug producing countries, but in transit countries as well. For example, during the war in Bosnia the police chief of Sarajevo accused a triethnic mafia of prolonging the siege of the city to profit from the black market.[66] Since weapons were traded for drugs and smuggled to both sides of the siege, "the result was to reinforce the siege—and thus prolongation of the war."[67] Because the drug trade is compartmentalized, drug traffickers must compete for limited smuggling routes. Pressure or obstruction on one route translates into advantages for other warring groups who want to ensure their parts of the trafficking network are secure.[68] However, a shrinking demand at one stage of production and distribution because of military activity or actions by another rebel group leads to increased violence among market participants who tend to be heavily armed and willing to use force. It takes considerable political will and equal resources for governments to deal with the actors engaged in drug trafficking who want conflicts to continue.

Proliferation of Small Arms and Dual-Use Technology
Another effect of the influence of the drug trade on warfare and one that is closely related to the protraction of contemporary conflicts is the growing availability of small arms and dual-use technology to greater numbers of violent actors. Drug profits or drugs themselves are used to purchase small arms that "destabilize regions; spark, fuel, and prolong conflicts; obstruct relief programmes; undermine peace initiatives; exacerbate human rights abuses;

hamper development; and foster a culture of violence."[69] The situation in Latin America represents a familiar pattern in many conflicts.

> Colombian insurgents are buying arms from…Central America with drugs to propagate their own ferocious civil conflict. Central America is awash in weapons leftover from Cold War conflicts and they are now being bartered for cocaine from neighboring Colombia, which in turn will be shipped to the U.S. "The drugs trade and the arms trade are the same. They use the same infrastructure," says Rosendo Miranda, chief drugs prosecutor of Panama, across whose slender territory both commodities pass.[70]

In the recent past, the UN has urged governments and regional organizations to provide assistance in combating the global trade and proliferation of small arms and light weapons linked to drug trafficking and political violence.[71]

More violent groups are also acquiring dual-use technology. Sophisticated communication equipment such as mine detection equipment, laser range finders, blasting caps, and digital encryption devices that are used by traffickers to communicate with each other and to monitor law enforcement is now being used by non-state groups to keep track of military countermeasures as well.[72] Thus, many irregular forces have been able to compete with established armed forces, contributing to their ability to stave off defeat and thereby prolonging the conflict. Technology given to legitimate governments involved in counternarcotics operations has also fallen into private hands. Approximately two hundred and fifty sets of night-vision goggles that were sold by Britain to Iran in an effort to help the Iranians monitor the Afghan border were apparently passed on to Hezbollah.[73]

Undermining of Governmental Authority in Weak States
The presence of drug crop cultivation and narcotics trafficking serve the strategic purposes of insurgent groups in particular. The illegality of the trade and the criminality surrounding it promote the internal disorder insurgent groups desire. Such disorder disrupts the legitimate economy, produces more dissatisfaction, and undermines governmental authority. It is also inexpensive to weaken security while expensive for counterinsurgency operations, which try to maintain order in wide swaths of territory, to compensate for the lack of security in a particular area. Thus, it is tempting for the government, its military, or sympathetic paramilitaries to participate in a segment of the drug trade in order to raise funds to quell an insurgency.

Civil society also suffers when disorder, criminality, and poverty become ingrained. Cynicism toward government can lead to resentment, which can foster support for alternative power structures in society. Diminishing governmental authority, and consequently the power to protect citizens and provide modest economic security, contributes to state weakness and failure. The competitive logic of drug trafficking when combined with heavily armed groups also provides more potential for state failure.

> Unless [the combatant] leadership is able to monopolize the means of exchange between a resource supplier and its customers (e.g., vehicles, airports, roads, bank accounts, export authorizations, middlemen, importers), allies and subordinates have the opportunity to become autonomous through commercial or criminal activities based on local resources. The inherent risk of private appropriation can undermine trust between members of an armed group. More generally, this pattern of resource flow is likely to weaken discipline and chains of command.[74]

Such degeneration in the cohesion of an armed group can lead to the creation of swaths of ungoverned spaces, which provide rich environments for various other armed groups to operate freely and further complicate the battleground.

The quintessential ungoverned space is Ciudad del Este in Paraguay that borders Brazil and Argentina. Its porous borders, numerous unguarded waterways, unmonitored ports, airstrips, and weak passport controls have attracted a rich stew of smugglers, counterfeiters, arms dealers, guerrillas, and terrorists. With such a variety of violent actors engaged at all levels of the drug trade and criminality, Ciudad del Este represents a new type of support base for those engaged in violence across the spectrum of warfare. Yet, eliminating this support base has been beyond the reach of both law enforcement and military actions.

Damaging the Licit Economy

Regardless of whether a country is the source of drugs or a transshipment point, drug-financed warfare undermines national sovereignty by corrupting legitimate sectors of a national economy. Drug trafficking requires the participation of numerous professionals to remain profitable. Chemists and doctors are needed to review the purity of a product. Accountants, lawyers, and bankers handle the disposal of drug proceeds through a country's financial system. Transportation systems are also compromised. For example, pilots for Afghanistan's state-owned airline, Ariana, are routinely subjected to demands, at gunpoint, for drug runs.[75]

The need for precursor chemicals to make heroin, cocaine, and ATS also spurs further corruption of legitimate businesses. For example, with processing labs now operating within Afghanistan, smuggling vast quantities of precursor chemicals is a burgeoning trade. Chinese officials confiscated 5,760 tons of acetic anhydride, a chemical needed for heroin production, hidden in carpets destined for Afghanistan.[76] Such seizures are infrequent and inconsistent because customs, law enforcement, and governmental officials are often bribed to overlook the importation and transit of these commodities. Countries in conflict and those bordering them are mostly developing states with already weakened state governments. The creation of a shadow economy further diminishes political legitimacy and accountability, while the entrenchment of corruption undermines economic development by lowering incentives for investment by legitimate businesses.

Undermining Legitimate Agriculture

Beyond the regional effects of drug-financed warfare, legitimate agriculture suffers in those countries where drug crops are grown, thereby lowering prospects for sustainable economic development. Drug crops have a competitive advantage over legitimate crops. Farmers can earn more from drug barons than they can by relying on the workings of a legitimate market. In effect, drug barons can subsidize the production of crops at a higher rate than a government or international organization can with legitimate agriculture. With the profitability of drug crops outstripping that of legitimate crops and with finite arable land in a country, many farmers are compelled to enter the drug trade in order to earn a reasonable living. In addition, warring groups have a greater ability to coerce farmers to grow drug crops whereas governments, businesses, NGOs, and international organizations are morally restrained from coercing farmers to grow legitimate crops. The advantages of economic incentive and physical coercion undermine development projects that may put a country on the track to sustainable economic prosperity.

Human Rights Abuses and Deterioration of Public Health

Irregular forces with access to natural resources, such as drug crops, that are less dependent on external support are more likely to commit atrocities on non-combatants.[77] Coercion of farmers to grow drug crops is one way drug-financed violent groups contribute to greater abuses of human rights. In some narcotized conflicts, children are traded to drug barons as payment to pay off debts when drug harvests fail or are eradicated.[78] Civilians have become integral to these types of conflicts. They form the backbone of a war-making resource and, therefore, are also likely to be targeted by opposition groups. Often caught between two or more violent groups, drug-producing peasants find that their misery is compounded. Much as factory workers were seen as crucial to the war effort in World War II, peasants who cultivate crops, villagers who process drugs, and drivers who transport drug products are viewed by contemporary armed groups in a similar way. This makes them legitimate targets in the calculations of many enemy commanders. Amid violence, exploitation, and death, the distinction between combatant and non-combatant becomes blurred for those people directly involved in the drug trade.

However, a civilian's value is often limited by the unskilled nature of the drug trade, for the hydra-effect does not act as a restraint. Atrocities and abuse committed against a group's own civilian population have been mitigated by another individual's ability to step into a role and replace a loss. Civilian resistance has been limited by the lack of other meaningful work or the terror inflicted on them by multiple groups involved in the wartime economy. The aim in these wars is "the control of people and acquisition of booty more than to control territory in the conventional military manner."[79]

Beyond widespread incidences of extortion, kidnapping, and murder, however, many violent groups involved in the drug trade also participate in the international trafficking of humans. Since transportation networks and transactional relationships are key parts of the illicit drug trade, they are also equally useful for smuggling migrant laborers, sex industry workers, and illegal immigrants. These people are regularly transported by many of the same criminal and violent groups that participate in drug trafficking and via the same narcotics transshipment points. Warring groups in Afghanistan, Myanmar, and the Balkans have been adept at using their drug-smuggling networks to smuggle people.[80] In addition, trafficked people are regularly used as "mules" to smuggle small quantities of drugs on their person, creating another method of getting drugs to market and minimizing a trafficker's exposure to apprehension by law enforcement.[81]

Countries that are used as transshipment points face an additional burden than do source countries. Typically these countries develop "offshoot" markets of users who seek to escape the chronic instability and poverty of their own societies. Rising rates of addiction add to the strain of public health systems within developing countries and contribute to higher rates of infectious disease, such as HIV/AIDS. The spread of the Afghan opium trade via heroin transportation to the large European market has contributed to steady rates of addiction and infection through the desperate countries of central Asia, while the use of West and central Africa as transit points for cocaine bound for Europe has spawned a growing African drug market. Pakistan has a half million chronic heroin users; the prevalence rate among the adult male population is more than 2 percent.[82]

Undermining Legitimate Financial Institutions and Systems

Drug-funded political violence also has a corrupting effect on sectors of the international economy. Similar to profits from an international business, drug proceeds must go through a formal banking system. The British Foreign Office estimates that money laundering transactions account for between 2 percent and 5 percent of global Gross Domestic Product (GDP) or $1.5 trillion per year.[83] The drug trade accounts for the largest share of international money laundering crimes.[84] However, unlike legitimate international business, the source and ownership of these proceeds must be concealed. When a warring group is involved, even greater concealment is needed to not alert authorities. This requires warring groups to engage in additional illegal and corrupting activities, such as invoice and license fraud, bribery of customs officials, creation of shell companies, and the use of underground or illegal remittance systems.[85] Informal ethnic diaspora banking systems like *hawalas* among Arab communities, *fei chens* in Chinese circles, and *hundis* among Indian groups are often used for the specific purpose of evading state scrutiny. They continue to be a source for the transit of drug profits for combatant groups.

Beyond financial institutions, real estate markets are also subjected to the corruption of money laundering. Investing in real estate offers a greater level of opacity since many banks are becoming more scrupulous about their clients. These proceeds undermine the faith that ordinary citizens have in the security of their own finances and can lead to bubble markets while distorting the relative economic and financial stability of a nation.

Contributing to Regional Instability

The vastness of the networks employed to traffic narcotics produces regional instability in many areas. Because illicit narcotics are highly sought, yet compartmentalized, commodities, "regional economic networks are an important avenue of access to global markets, a factor that multiplies the number of economic stakeholders in a conflict, thereby posing an additional challenge for conflict resolution."[86]

Many economic stakeholders, violent and non-violent alike, who lie outside drug producing areas of conflict keep a conflict alive through their participation in the drug trade. Reflecting this reality, rebel groups in Myanmar reportedly were ready to barter heroin with North Korea in exchange for a shipment of light weapons in 1998.[87] Current conflicts in the Middle East are also affected; Iraq's former minister for national security affairs asserted in May 2005 that "drug trafficking rings in Pakistan, Afghanistan, and Iran are trying to operate in the Iraqi area, which has become a gateway for transporting narcotics to neighboring states."[88] Such participation by groups outside Iraq is hamstringing efforts to reduce the level of violence and achieve stability in the country.[89] Countries without active conflicts but border such conflicts also experience increasing rates of violence. Tajikistan border control agents have reported an increasing number of incidents of gunfire exchange across the border with Afghanistan.[90]

Drug trafficking by warring groups can also sustain a corrupt and authoritarian regime. To reach markets, drugs are often transshipped via such a regime, while government agents collect kickbacks for the government. The Castro regime routinely charged vast sums of money for each drug-laden vessel that the FARC and M19 guerrillas docked at a Cuban port.[91] Such schemes earned the Castro government hundreds of millions of much needed dollars.[92] Venezuelan leader Hugo Chavez also relies on the drug-financed FARC to sustain his regime.

Adds a US official, "It's no secret the level of cooperation that the Venezuelan government is giving to the Colombian groups, from the shipment of arms in, to the shipment of drugs out, to the movement of people in and out of Colombia.". . . The FARC and ELN were "instrumental" in the formation and training of a 200-man Venezuelan armed group called the Frente Bolivariano de Liberacion that operates in western Venezuela, according to US officials. The FARC has also provided training to the so-called Bolivarian Circles, an urban organization that Chavez set up to defend and promote his revolution.[93]

Meanwhile, the North Korean regime is actively engaged in the production, distribution, and sale of drugs as part of government policy coordinated by Central Committee Bureau 39. In fact, North Korean military personnel have been used to smuggle drugs for nearly thirty years.[94] North Korean infiltration craft (manned by North Korean Special Operations Forces) have often been found in Japanese waters since the late 1990s to engage in "drug drops."[95] North Korean uniformed personnel have reportedly been involved in the transfer of illegal drugs off the coasts of Japan and Taiwan.[96]

COMPLICATIONS OF THE CONTINUING FLEXIBILITY OF THE DRUG TRADE

The history of the drug trade demonstrates that belligerents have used its profits, flexibility, and adaptability to financially undergird their wartime efforts. Unlike the empires of the past that controlled the monopoly over the licit trade of narcotics, today warring groups are active in trading a variety of drugs and participate in numerous nodes of drug-trafficking networks. From cultivating drug crops, securing transport routes, working in processing labs, and ensuring its distribution to various markets, warring groups have found a reliable and profitable business to fill their war chests. Although the differences among heroin, cocaine, marijuana, ATS, khat, and datura provide different groups with differing opportunities, thereby affecting the intensity level of a traded drug's impact on conflict, they all have effect on the battlefield. Drug-financed warring groups participate in the small-arms and light-weapons trafficking, which make irregular forces more competitive with professional militaries. Warring groups further victimize people via extortion, kidnapping, and human smuggling to maintain control over drug links and ensure profit. They undermine domestic and international financial systems. Furthermore, drug-financed warfare contributes to generating a wartime economy within countries and regions based on criminality and disorder, which chapter 4 explores more thoroughly, and provides transnational terror groups opportunities to generate income.

Such wide-ranging effects on warfare, brought about by the contribution of drug financing, portend an unfamiliar future for policymakers and military leaders. The pressures of the drug trade and its links to warfare have created a reinforcing dynamic that ensures the continued influence of drug financing on warfare in the near future. Insurgents, paramilitaries, and militias are involved in higher levels of violence than organized crime syndicates, meaning it is more difficult to clamp down on the trafficking of illegal drugs. As a result, trouble in enforcement leads to the deepening entrenchment of drug trafficking and an ever-available commodity to be exploited by violent groups. The outlines of this reinforcing dynamic are apparent today—the head of the U.S. Drug Enforcement Administration testified before Congress that "the challenges we face fighting the drug trade in Afghanistan are tough, with conducting law enforcement operations in a war zone."[97]

Further adding to this murky future is the widespread use of drugs by combatants themselves. Consumption of drugs by individual fighters also affects the ways contemporary wars are being waged. The next chapter explores the reasons combatants use drugs, the types of drugs consumed, and the battlefield effects.

3

HIGH AT WAR
Drug Use by Combatants

COMBAT FUNDED BY DRUG PROFITS IS not the only factor that complicates contemporary armed conflicts. Drug use by combatants themselves also contributes to conflict environments that challenge policymakers and military leaders. As previously discussed, drugs are unlike other illegally traded commodities such as oil, diamonds, and timber because drugs can be readily consumed by fighters for combat-related purposes. This chapter examines the reasons combatants consume drugs, the type of drugs they consume, how combatants acquire drugs, and how drugs affect the battlefield. It also examines how some warring groups have encouraged drug use among the ranks and in the society of the enemy in hopes of diminishing their fighting ability.

Similar to drug-financed political violence, the non-medical use of drugs by combatants has a long history. In fact, it appears that all wars have pit belligerents using one set of drugs against those using the same or different set.[1] Although drugs used for medical and recuperative reasons have been commonplace on the battlefield, various societies consumed mind-altering substances before combat. In 1781, a South American Indian militia refused to fight against the Spanish unless they were given coca leaves. Before armed clashes with British, French, and American colonial armies, Native American warriors routinely used *peyote*. The Zulu warriors of Isandlwana cooked a cannabis broth, which emboldened the warriors and made them unpredictable to British troops in 1879. Commanders of European forces, however, were reluctant to permit their own troops to partake in the local drug of choice.[2] While in Egypt, Napoleon noticed the smoking of hashish among the lower classes and forbade it from his troops.[3]

Paralleling the trade of opium to fund European imperial expansion, opium use flourished particularly among the British and French officer corps. As a result of being given morphine to treat their injuries, many American Civil War soldiers became addicted to morphine.[4] In fact, opium and morphine became so closely associated with the military profession that those who became addicted were said to have contracted the "soldier's disease."

Western forces were not the only forces that succumbed to the intoxicating benefits of the poppy; opium took its toll on the forces of the Chinese emperor during the Opium War. Many Chinese soldiers who were fighting to defend the empire against opium were addicted themselves. More than ten years after the First Opium War, the successes of the Taiping Rebellion (whose members touted their sobriety as a virtue) may be explained in part by the nearly 90 percent addiction rate among the Chinese emperor's army.[5]

Cocaine use also has links to modern wars fought by Western militaries. During World War I, prior to a particularly severe attack in Gallipoli, Australian pharmacists were ordered to distribute their cocaine supplies to troops. The media increased the British Imperial Force's fear of cocaine abuse by portraying it as part of a German plan to demoralize their adversary.[6] During World War II, amphetamines were widely used among all sides to keep the fighting men alert. Pills were provided in ration kits, and drug use among American troops averaged one pill per soldier per day.[7] The Japanese synthesized methamphetamine (meth) in an injectable form that was widely used by Imperial Japanese forces in World War II.[8] During the Korean War, American servicemen stationed in Korea and Japan invented the "speedball," an injectable mixture of amphetamine and heroin.[9]

U.S. troops in Vietnam preferred marijuana, but when subject to a sudden marijuana ban, they then turned to a more addictive and more impairing drug: heroin. Discipline problems quickly rose. As one commanding officer lamented two years after the marijuana crackdown, "if it would get them to give up the hard stuff, I would buy all the marijuana and hashish in the Delta as a present."[10]

DRUG USE IN CONTEMPORARY CONFLICTS

Intoxication among combatants continues to be a part of today's conflicts and, as discussed in chapter 1, occurs in minimal, acute, and unrestrained degrees. Regardless of the degree, however, the perceived benefits of combatants consuming illegal narcotics on the battlefield, much like the drug financing of violent conflicts, has few pressures to constrain it. Some argue that drug use by belligerents is part of a universal human drive, which would make prohibition in the conduct of warfare a nearly impossible task.[11] Taking mind-altering substances may seem like a risk for an individual fighter who must be aware of danger and competent enough to defend himself, his comrades, and his equipment. Maintaining a clear mind would seem to be more advantageous than being strung out. However, much like drug use by ordinary citizens in peacetime, "gains generally loom larger than risks [because] gains tend to be immediate" while jeopardy, danger, and consequence are more remote.[12] Individual fears and concerns are often mitigated by the atmosphere of organized violence—the gain of cheating death outweighs the possibility of impairment, illness, or injury in the minds of many combatants who consume drugs.

Additionally, while there are numerous external pressures that constrain an individual's desire to use drugs in peacetime, such constraints are not always present during war. These constraints include social norms, legal controls, expense, and availability along with individual concerns of addiction, toxicity, and the lack of knowledge about a drug. The nature of contemporary wars often mitigates social norms, legal controls, expense, and availability, for attacks focus on the institutions and people who comprise them.

In fact, some of the appeals of peacetime drug use are heightened during war. For example, peer pressure and "turning on" a friend to a drug are more acutely felt in wartime when an individual fighter must demonstrate his bravery and honor. Small group cohesion occurs when individuals experience and survive danger with fellow comrades. Drug use allows an individual to "prove himself" to his comrades and eases his transition into a battlefield context.

Although key restraints are removed and appeals increased, drug use and abuse in wartime still depends on the law of supply and demand. However, supply and demand is distorted because of the type of consumer (a person engaged in armed violence) and the areas a drug is available (conflict zones). Much as there are distinctions in the trafficking of drugs that allow warring groups to participate in certain key nodes, there are distinctions in supply and demand at the level of the individual fighter that are significant to the ways contemporary wars are now being waged.

DRUG DEMAND AMONG COMBATANTS

Drugs are used by individual fighters for four main reasons—stimulation, reward, recruitment and relaxation—and make up a type of "combatant demand."[13] Drugs can stimulate a person's will to fight and to ignore the possibilities of injury and death. The notion of "liquid courage" is not only applicable to the use of liquor, but to the use of other drugs in situations of organized violence. Afghan soldiers who collaborated with Soviet forces against the *mujahedin* were provided hashish in their rations. "When you get high on hashish, you become completely revolutionary and attack the enemy—fear simply disappears."[14] Drugs are often used to fend off the boredom that accompanies being a part of a group that when not fighting is waiting to fight, hiding, or carrying on the mundane duties that are required to keep a combatant group effective. Drugs have been offered as rewards for conducting hazardous or unpalatable operations against civilians. John Mueller describes the phenomenon as "carnival" whereby warring groups take a territory and celebrate by looting medical buildings for drugs and then following up with orgies of rape, torture, and murder of local residents.[15] Recruitment is also aided by the use of drugs and the type of devastation that occurs in internal conflicts. As drug profits alleviate key problems of recruiting, training, and retaining fighters for a combatant leader, the provision of drugs can sway an individual's decision to join the ranks of a warring group. Warring groups also addict children to drugs to force them into combat as child soldiers. The stress of combat can also increase the desire to seek mental escape in a fighter; depressant drugs can alleviate the stress felt by a combatant and help him to avoid reflecting on his circumstances. Members of professional militaries can be prescribed anti-anxiety medications, such as Zoloft, Paxil, and lithium, to achieve the same effects. Sometimes, a rise in the level of violence has altered the drug habits among irregular fighters. The young Hmong fighters of the Pathet Lao were forbidden by social custom to smoke opium, but after the American bombing campaign against their strongholds, many took up the habit to calm their nerves.[16]

There are many ways that the nature of contemporary wars generates the demand for illegal narcotics. Because today's wars are primarily intrastate wars with sharp asymmetries between the sides, the ways demand is generated are different for irregular forces and members of professional militaries.

Drug Demand Among Irregular Forces

Non-professional armed groups, including insurgent organizations, militias, and paramilitaries, largely fight today's civil wars. Unlike drug use by conventional forces in interstate wars, drug use within unconventional forces is not prescribed, administered, or monitored by a centralized government or medical professionals. This has become problematic, for these groups mainly consist of civilians who are neither trained to handle combat stress nor equipped with sophisticated weapons like their professional military counterparts. Without sophisticated weaponry, individual fighters engage in close combat encounters and often the extreme tension of hand-to-hand combat. Drugs provide a means to cope with the physical stress and mental anxiety that are part of such violent encounters. In essence, drugs can compensate for a lack of training and mental discipline that is part of professional military training, and they can increase the probability of winning for militarily weaker groups.

While drugs can compensate for the lack of formal training that members of professional militaries receive, drug consumption can also empower the ways irregular combatants from traditional societies fight. Since traditional societies do not have standing armies, they rely on men of fighting age who display fighting courage, honor, and valor in battle.[17] The consumption of drugs aids in the display of these qualities.

In some conflicts, the widespread presence of civilians on the battlefield is also worsened by warring groups' financial reliance on the drug trade. With the growing wartime financial significance of drug crops and smuggling routes to warring groups, civilians who cultivate drug crops, inhabit valuable agricultural space, or live near transportation routes come to be seen as legitimate targets by opposing groups. Violence against civilians triggers combat stress in non-professional and poorly equipped troops. Often, individual fighters seek to lessen this stress by using narcotics.

The types of equipment used by irregular forces requires little skill. Shooting a gun, planting a mine, and aiming a mortar do not require a combatant to be clean and sober. In contrast to the high-tech weaponry of professional Western militaries and the integrated way they fight, easy-to-use weapons provide little restraint on drug use and intoxication by irregular or untrained forces.

In addition, the emergence of wartime drug markets is assisted by the presence of criminals and addicts in the ranks of irregular forces. Besieged governments have not been averse to letting criminals "earn their freedom" by fighting for their people. Both Slobodan Milosevic and Saddam Hussein emptied their jails of drug criminals and other inmates to fight in paramilitary groups. Moreover, many insurgents and terrorists, who are considered lawbreakers to established authorities, have spent time in prison among drug dealers and abusers. For the former leader of al Qaeda in Iraq, Abu Musab al-Zarqawi, participation in the drug trade was nothing new. Zarqawi even went so far as to recruit drug addicts and dealers to his cause during his time in a Jordanian prison.[18]

Drug Demand Among Professional Soldiers

The longer duration of contemporary conflicts contributes to drug use among members of professional militaries when deployed abroad. Lengthier time in the field or deployed generates personal hardships that are soothed by drug use. Also, conflicts that involve fighting irregular troops in cities, towns, or villages who are not easily distinguished from innocent civilians create anxiety among uniformed soldiers. A drug quagmire can develop in conflicts that are affected by the drug trade—as drug financing contributes to the protraction of conflicts, an atmosphere for the greater demand among troops for drugs is created.

Professional militaries of developed states generally possess better resources to diagnose and address the stress that individual fighters undergo and have access to prescription medication administered by experts.[19] However, such access to professionals, tightly controlled prescription drugs, and monitoring of possible drug abuse does not make professional forces immune to drug abuse. To mitigate this anxiety, prescription drugs can be abused. "Some of [the soldiers] were taking as many as ten sleeping pills and still could not rest."[20] With conflicts growing more protracted and with murkier operational and tactical environments, illegal drugs are more tempting to Western troops. The rate of illicit drug use increased among U.S. troops to an estimated 5 percent in 2005, nearly double the percent measured in 1998.[21] Dr. Thomas R. Kosten, a psychiatrist at the Veterans Affairs Medical Center in Houston, traces drinking and drug use to the stress of working in a war zone. "The treatment that they take for it is the same treatment that they took after Vietnam,"

Dr. Kosten said. "They turn to alcohol and drugs."[22] A protracted conflict can also have repercussions in recruitment that present opportunities for drug use to become problematic. As two simultaneous protracted conflicts against irregular troops continue for the U.S. military and with more service members opting out of continued service, recruitment is becoming a higher priority. However, recruitment is exceptionally difficult in the face of the ongoing unpopular war in Iraq. Similar to the problems with recruitment quality associated with irregular fighters, reducing recruitment standards during protracted wars risk bringing societal drug habits into a professional military.

> As the recruiting climate has grown more difficult, the Army also has increased the number of recruits who require moral waivers because of misdemeanor offenses. Through April, about 15.5% of recruits required some kind of waiver for a misdemeanor offense, *drug or alcohol incident* or medical problem, compared with 12% for 2004 and 15% for 2005 when the Army missed its recruiting goal. (emphasis added)[23]

As the wars in Afghanistan and Iraq continue, the use of moral waivers has increased and led to the acceptance of many more recruits who have had contact with law enforcement and the courts because of drug offenses.

When other types of forces have been sent to conflicts where drugs are available, they have not proven immune from succumbing to drug use themselves. Much like combatants, United Nations peacekeepers are frequently exposed to dangerous, provoking, or humiliating situations and have limited possibilities to express the resulting anger and frustration due to restrictive rules of engagement that encourage neutrality. Self-medicating with alcohol and drugs to calm down or to "take the edge off" has not been uncommon.[24] In Cambodia, the favorite drink among the UN personnel at parties was the "Space Shuttle," which was made "by distilling a pound of marijuana over a six-week period with increasingly good quality spirits. It is a work of love, and the final product is an amber-colored liquid that tastes like cognac. We drink it with rounds of Coke."[25] Members of private military companies, such as Blackwater, have also allegedly been involved in consuming drugs that may have led to committing atrocities.[26]

DRUG SUPPLY IN CONTEMPORARY CONFLICTS

Whether humans are universally driven to mind-altering substances when they are involved in organized conflict or whether war removes many constraints and induces a greater desire for non-medical drug use, a drug supply must somehow be accessible and attained. The combatant's demand for drugs has to be juxtaposed with the availability of drugs to combatants in order for the described effects to occur. Typically, the supply for drugs in today's wars falls into at least one of four categories: traditional, transshipped, looted, and manufactured. These categories are not mutually exclusive to a single conflict since combatants often find access to drugs from numerous sources. Traditional drugs are part of the longstanding cultural practices of the warring group's society and are naturally produced in the territory where a conflict takes place. For example, though the drug khat is part of the social landscape of East African societies, and combatants in Somalia and Sudan now use it as well. Traditional drugs can also be ceremonial by linking the fighter to the traditions of the past and connecting fighters to the mystical. Connections to the mystical are seen as ways to fight honorably or become impervious to injury and death in combat. This has been commonplace in Liberia's civil wars when fighters fortified by marijuana and palm wine donned dresses and wigs, believing that bullets would be confused and misidentify their true targets.

Other drugs are available owing to the presence of a transit route through the territory where a conflict is occurring. Once again, globalization has been a significant factor, because it has made many drugs available to new markets where there are conflicts and valuable transshipment points. Coca, for example, is not grown in Africa, yet combatants who are paid with cocaine by traffickers routinely use it. Such bartering in exchange for securing routes is not uncommon; the Revolutionary United Front (RUF) fighters in Sierra Leone regularly consumed crack cocaine and *brown-brown* (heroin) that were transshipped through their territories.[27]

Drugs can also be attained by looting pharmacies, clinics, and hospitals. Though they are intended for ailments unrelated to combat, they can alter the consciousness of a fighter during combat. Drugs stolen from pharmacies were used as rewards and motivators for the Hutu who committed atrocities against the Tutsi during the 1994 Rwandan Genocide.[28] In Iraq, numerous pharmaceutical drugs, including Captagon (stimulant), Benzhexol (relaxant), and benzodiazepines (sedatives and hypnotics, such as Valium), looted from clinics, pharmacies, and hospitals in the immediate aftermath of the fall of Baghdad are being abused.[29]

Manufactured drugs refers to pharmaceutical drugs prescribed by physicians to members of professional militaries and "home-manufactured" drugs, such as amphetamine-type stimulants (ATS), meth in particular. In Iraq, evidence of meth production and use has been found in insurgent hideouts. Numerous military field commanders have substantiated claims of drugged insurgent fighters from Zarqawi's group; hideouts used by Zarqawi's fighters were frequently found littered with drug paraphernalia, including pipes and needles.[30] A Marine in Ramadi reported that random autopsies of insurgents showed high levels of narcotics use.[31]

TYPES OF DRUGS USED IN CONTEMPORARY CONFLICTS

When the ways drug supplies are made available and the reasons they are in demand are compared, the specific drugs combatants consume can be identified (Table 3.1).[32] Drugs

TABLE **3.1**: Drugs Present in Conflicts

	TRADITIONAL	TRANSSHIPPED	LOOTED	MANUFACTURED
STIMULANT	Marijuana, Hashish, Khat, Mushrooms, Coca	Cocaine, ATS	Pharmaceuticals	ATS, *basuco*
REWARD	Khat	Heroin, Cocaine	Pharmaceuticals	ATS
RECRUITMENT	Marijuana, Khat	Heroin, Cocaine	Pharmaceuticals	Unknown
RELAXANT	Marijuana, Hashish	Heroin, Opium, Marijuana	Pharmaceuticals	Prescribed Medications for Professional Militaries

used by members of a single combatant group can fall in a number of these categories since fighters often combine various drugs. For example, in Colombia many combatants smoke *basuco*, cocaine paste, combined with marijuana and tobacco.[33] In some instances, transshipped drugs are also adopted into the ceremonial practices of a warring group to increase the "high" that is experienced by individual fighters. Cocaine, transshipped via Liberia, became regularly ingested by participants in its civil war.[34] Several drugs, such as heroin, marijuana, and ATS, are used for multiple purposes and are available in numerous contexts. Hallucinogens, including mushrooms, have traditional uses. However, they are also used by troops who do not participate in local practices but merely take advantage of their availability for mental escape. Table 3.2 lists the conflicts where combatants have been known to consume drugs, the supply and demand for drugs, and specific known drugs belligerents consume.

EFFECTS OF DRUG USE ON THE BATTLEFIELD

The law of wartime narcotics supply and demand also affects the ways contemporary wars are being fought. For irregular and professional forces that consume drugs, the degree of effects on the battlefield has varied. The acute and unrestrained degrees of drug use by irregulars on the battlefield are associated primarily with transshipped and looted drugs used for recruitment and rewards. Using drugs for recruitment and reward, in turn, is closely associated with the use of child soldiers, increased unpredictability among irregular fighters, the breakdown of social controls, and the commission of atrocities as well as

TABLE 3.2: KNOWN DRUG USE BY COMBATANTS IN CONTEMPORARY CONFLICTS

CONFLICT	SUPPLY/DEMAND	TYPE(S) OF DRUGS
Bosnia	Transshipped-Reward Looted-Stimulant	Heroin Pharmaceuticals
Colombia	Manufactured-Stimulant Traditional-Relaxant	Basuco Basuco
Haiti	Transshipped-Stimulant	Cocaine
Iraq	Manufactured-Stimulant (AQI) Looted-Recruitment (Sunni insurgents) Transshipped-Stimulant (UK troops) Manufactured-Relaxant (U.S. troops)	Methamphetamine Pharmaceuticals Cocaine Pharmaceuticals
Liberia	Transshipped-Stimulant Transshipped-Recruitment Traditional-Relaxant	Cocaine Cocaine Marijuana
Peru	Traditional-Stimulant	Coca, base cocaine
Philippines	Transshipped-Stimulant	Heroin
Russia	Transshipped-Reward	Heroin
Sierra Leone	Transshipped-Stimulant Transshipped-Recruitment	Cocaine Heroin
Somalia	Traditional-Stimulant Traditional-Reward Traditional-Recruitment	Khat
Uganda	Traditional-Stimulant Traditional-Reward Traditional-Recruitment	Khat

decreased command and control. The minimal degree of drug use among professional military forces is associated with the use and abuse of transshipped and manufactured depressants, which has led to command and control problems and decreased public opinion within their societies.

Whether irregular or professional forces are engaged in drug usage during conflicts, many of the effects cannot be separated. Drugging children to recruit them as fighters breaks down informal social controls and is the first of many human rights violations to come. Protracted conflicts tend to negatively affect public opinion in developed countries even without knowledge of drug abuse among soldiers. Yet, low public approval of military conflicts can make soldiers feel alienated from their country, thereby adding to their desire for drugs.

The Use of Child Soldiers

Roughly 300,000 children are believed to be involved in hostile conflicts, many of whom are drugged by warring groups as a form of recruitment and retention.[35] While the specific number of children pressed into combat via drug addiction is unknown, there are regular reports that child soldiers are drugged to impair their judgment and lower their inhibitions. The experience of one former child soldier from Sierra Leone is representative: "before battles, I was given white powder which was mixed with rice. It made me brave; it made me think I could do anything."[36] Many girls who were press-ganged into becoming members of rebel groups in Uganda and Sierra Leone participated in drug use, terrorist mutilations, and ritualistic murder.[37] In another example, in Iraq, a girl was abducted, taken to Baghdad, drugged with pills against her will, dressed in a suicide belt, and sent to bomb a cleric's office.[38] In Uganda, some 10,000 children have been pressed into service of the Lord's Resistance Army (LRA), drugged, and forced to kill their relatives so they cannot run away and return home.[39]

Increased Unpredictability Among Irregular Fighters

Regardless of the type of drugs and reasons for use, widespread drug intoxication among forces has meant that many fighters do not act in a rational or predictable manner. Combatant behavior is often influenced by an individual's state of intoxication. For example, U.S. Marines reportedly had to change their tactics when notified that the insurgents in Falluja were probably high and thus less likely to be stopped by standard shots to the torso.[40]

Battlefield courage is not the only effect of drug use. Depending on the type and regularity of the drug ingested, drug abuse can lead to long-term behavioral changes that complicate warfare. There are several effects of repeated hard drug use, including increased confusion, agitation, paranoia, and hallucinations. Continued high-level use of hard narcotics, such as cocaine, heroin, and ATS, can alter the brain chemistry of an individual and actually *increase* the sense of fear felt by a combatant. With fear being a natural mental state while fighting a war, increased fear only leads to less control and greater violence. When ex-prisoners, former drug dealers, and junkies fill the ranks of irregular forces and populate the battlefield, standard military operations against strategic installations have taken a back seat to criminal activities supporting individual interests and motivations.

Widespread drug abuse by irregular troops creates a genuine dilemma for their leadership. Much as routine drug use by an individual creates tolerance, requiring ever increasing doses to achieve intoxication or to avoid withdrawal symptoms, leaders cannot necessarily reduce command and control problems by restricting drug use. To do so, would invite more unpredictability and continued coordination problems. As one Afghan soldier, while working with the Soviets, stated, "if the commanders refused to come up with hashish, they would face the wrath of armed soldiers."[41]

Breakdown of Social Controls and Commission of Atrocities

With the lack of government authority across all sectors of a country during a civil war, there are no legal constraints on drug use by rebel forces. In the absence of formal legal controls, informal social controls typically play a major role in regulating psychoactive drug use.[42] However, in many of today's wars, those who exercise social control on drug use are often victims themselves. For example,

> [s]ince ancient times, drugs have probably been part of the "conditioning" of African warriors in very strict ritual settings. Even today, although the social control exercised through the activity by the shamans, witches and other initiates over the use of psychoactive substances has, in many instances, disappeared, these substances are still in widespread use, as was observed, for example, during the conflicts in Liberia and Sierra Leone. Like the grigri, the power to make warriors invisible, leave them unaffected by bullets and so on is attributed to certain substances.[43]

Although social control can also be exercised by families and traditional leaders, they too are often targeted by adversarial groups. Without social controls, fighters are freer to abuse drugs and act in unrestrained ways. Ironically, drugs are frequently used to break social controls. Warring groups generate addiction among vulnerable citizens to fill their ranks and tear them away from familiar social patterns.

Giving drugs to individuals coincides with tactics employed by irregular forces. A common approach is to "tease out someone else's latent prejudices and inflame it with scapegoating rhetoric, mobilize gangs of thugs and criminals and unemployed, arm them, stoke them with drugs and drink, and loose them upon defenseless civilians."[44] Carnival also has a strategic purpose for combatant leaders because it can induce such terror among the local population that they will flee or submit more easily to the new authority. In fact, the promises of carnivals are frequently used as recruitment tools for combatant leaders. Rebel leaders linked to Charles Taylor rallied fighters for his final offensive against supporters and troops of Liberian President Samuel Doe by naming it "Operation Pay Yourself."[45] As a result, campaigns often involve "immiseration and violent population displacement as an essential precondition for asset realization" that is key to maintaining a warring group's cohesion and viability.[46]

Decreased Command and Control Among Irregulars

With informal social controls damaged or eliminated in many conflicts, commanding and controlling intoxicated forces is extremely difficult. The problem is exacerbated because of the already loose structure of many irregular fighting forces; many units are small in number and are not directly under the authority of a large, centralized authority that can definitively establish behavioral boundaries. In such an environment, warring groups can degenerate into criminal gangs whose members fight among themselves over petty drug stakes. Factions of Sendero Luminoso (SL) in Peru routinely deserted when drug supplies were low and would "re-enlist" when cocaine was made available.[47] Some groups within violent organizations go on the prowl for drugs and booty to trade for drugs. Over time, drug use among irregular forces degrades combat effectiveness and leads to internal division and fragmentation. Many Chechen rebels are believed to be regular heroin users who are given doses in exchange for protecting routes through their territory. In fact, their leader was killed by Russian Special Forces because an informer betrayed him in exchange for a dose of heroin.[48]

When drug supplies run low, regular drug users among fighting forces can suffer withdrawal symptoms, which can lead to violence. For example, forensic evidence shows that some of the militants who seized over one thousand hostages in a southern Russian school in 2004 were longtime heroin addicts who were in a state of withdrawal shortly before the violence that claimed more than three hundred lives.[49] Withdrawal can last from a few days, as with cocaine and heroin, to a few months, as with meth, thus varying the length and severity of unpredictable behavior. A common withdrawal effect longtime drug users experience is anhedonia, or the inability to feel pleasure.[50] This causes a disagreeable feeling that can last for weeks, leading many to start taking drugs again. The anhedonia symptoms of meth abuse are particularly acute. Many meth users try to alleviate the effect of the meth "crash" by buffering it with other drugs, such as cocaine or heroin.[51]

Decreased Command and Control Among Professional Soldiers

Professional militaries not only struggle against adversaries who are on drugs, but when their professional forces are involved in protracted wars, they too are susceptible to widespread drug abuse among their ranks. Command and control problems because of drug use can also affect professional militaries. For example, the British Army has confirmed one instance of a major compromise in command and control resulting from drug use among their ranks in the Iraq war. One former soldier claimed that seventy-five men from his company, 60 percent of its strength, regularly took cocaine, ecstasy, or marijuana. "There's guys who have to have two or three lines of coke before they can operate," he said.[52] British officials arrested several soldiers for exchanging their weapons in Germany for $4,700 worth of cocaine, which was later sold to their comrades in Iraq.[53] Willingness to illegally trade arms for drugs represents a significant breakdown in command and control.

Conscript armies are exceptionally vulnerable to drug use for many of the same reasons as irregular forces—their members are not full-time, regularly trained military professionals. As a result, draftees and conscripts have sought drugs as a way to cope with an unfamiliar atmosphere, leading them to behave similarly to irregular troops. Drugged conscripts have been a danger to their own forces; a soldier stationed near the Russian border with Georgia shot and killed eight of his colleagues and wounded five others during a hallucinogenic fit brought on by eating magic mushrooms.[54] Widespread drug problems among conscripts in the Red Army during the Afghanistan campaign resulted in serious discipline problems, including desertion and the stealing of weapons, ammunition, and gas to trade for hashish and heroin. Afghan forces captured many Russian soldiers while they were drugged or seeking to trade their weapons and equipment for heroin or hashish.[55]

The breakdown of command and control in professional militaries because of drug use can lead troops to commit atrocities as well. For example, U.S. troops accused of rape and murder in Mahmoudiya, Iraq, were reportedly abusing alcohol, cough syrup, and painkillers as a way to cope with their dangerous duties.[56]

Decreased Public Opinion Within Developed Countries

The addiction rate of returning troops has been of constant concern to average citizens as well as elites. In November 1971, New York reported nearly 10,000 heroin-addicted Vietnam veterans, which, as discussed in this chapter, was the result of the U.S. military's clamp down on widespread marijuana use by troops.[57] So severe was drug use among American troops in the later stages of the Vietnam War, more soldiers were evacuated for drug problems than for battlefield wounds.[58] Heroin use among Vietnam veterans created societal fears of rising crime and disorder. *Time* reflected the public mood by reporting that "the specter of weapons-trained, addicted combat veterans joining the deadly struggle for drugs [in the streets of America] is ominous…. [T]he Capone era of the 1920s may look like a Sunday school picnic by comparison."[59] The Nixon administration began to fear that the result could precipitate a stronger call for an American pullout from Southeast Asia.[60] The Soviet Union also faced similar fears when draftees returned from Afghanistan with heroin habits.[61]

DRUGS AS A WEAPON

A distinct way that drugs are used in wartime is by combatants encouraging drug use and addiction among the enemy. Rather than combatants themselves ingesting drugs for advantages on the battlefield, some combatant groups have encouraged drug use among their adversaries to undercut their war efforts by demoralizing a nation and introducing criminal activity into its society. As such, supplying the enemy with drugs can be seen as a form of chemical warfare employed against enemy troops and against the adversary's population for tactical, strategic, and ideological objectives. Some argued that Soviet-inspired communism incorporated all three objectives during the Cold War with "the deliberate marketing of drugs and narcotics intended to demoralize US military forces and disrupt the social fabric of the United States....There is also a direct connection between the western drug problem and communist sponsored terrorism and revolutionary warfare."[62] As Ronald Reagan proclaimed, "these twin evils—narcotics trafficking and terrorism—represent the most insidious and dangerous threats to the hemisphere today."[63]Arguments that Soviet interests were served by the drug trade are not without merit. Reports appeared in 1990 that East German Premier Erich Honecher encouraged trafficking as way to undermine NATO. Bulgaria's secret police would barter arms with Middle Eastern terror groups in exchange for drugs that it would send on to Europe and the United States. Before China's break with the USSR, it colluded with Triad groups to move drugs into American military bases in Asia to undermine "imperialist" powers.[64]

Ironically, during the Cold War, the encouragement of drug use among enemy forces was also perpetrated against Soviet forces. The *mujahedin* ran covert supply lines of heroin to Red Army troops in Afghanistan, creating numerous military and political problems for Soviet leaders.[65] Measuring the combat effectiveness of such a tactic is difficult and the results are debatable. Nonetheless, warring groups continue to supply the enemy with addictive drugs as part of their war strategies.

The strategic use of drugs against an enemy population to weaken its society, and thereby weaken its resistance, has also been employed. The Imperial Japanese Army continued to grow and distribute opium in occupied China to subjugate the Chinese population. In fact, narcotics trafficking was one of the charges Japan faced at the Tokyo War Crimes Tribunal. The government of South Africa actively supported its adversaries' efforts to smuggle drugs like Mandrax and ecstasy to communities who resisted apartheid "to determine whether [the drugs] could eliminate their combativeness."[66]

Encouraging drug use and addiction in an adversary's society can also be part of a warring group's ideological campaign. Carlos Lehder, a Medellin drug lord in the 1980s, saw himself as a nationalist resistance leader who believed that selling drugs was part of a campaign against American imperialism.[67] Lehder was fond of telling journalists that cocaine was "Latin America's atom bomb" and that he planned to drop it on the United States.[68] Those terrorist groups listed as part of the Global War on Terrorism, including al Qaeda and Hezbollah, participate in the drug trade not only to raise funds, but as another part of their jihad against the West.[69] In fact, one Hezbollah *fatwa* states, "We are making these drugs for Satan America and the Jews. If we cannot kill them with guns, so we will kill them with drugs."[70] Indicted Taliban drug dealer Baz Mohammed told his followers that exporting heroin to the U.S. was a "jihad in which Americans paid for the drugs that kill them."[71] Likewise, Algerian jihadists are involved in the drug trade for political and religious reasons.[72]

Other violent groups seize upon local drug use as part of their rhetoric to justify violence. The Union of Islamic Courts (UIC) in Somalia publicly executed and flogged people found guilty of drug use. The military discipline represented by the UIC also gave it legitimacy in the eyes of many Somalis. The UIC used disciplined units of fighters in its attacks against the capital. As one local resident observed, "the Courts brought a new style of fighting to Mogadishu. It was military."[73] This was in marked contrast to the warlords, whose militia behaved chaotically, firing indiscriminately and depending heavily on khat supplies.

CHALLENGES FOR CONVENTIONAL MILITARIES

The increasing number of civilians comprising belligerent groups combined with the types and availability of drugs means that the presence of intoxicated combatants will likely be an abiding feature of war in the near term. While drug use by individuals in war complicates conditions on the battlefield, the effects are more far-reaching in an era of globalization. Combatants under the influence of drugs have committed massive human rights abuses against rival groups, creating immense human suffering that affect regional stability. For example, carnival activities in Yugoslavia sent waves of refugees throughout Europe and eventually led to a Western military response to the humanitarian catastrophe unfolding in the heart of Europe.[74]

More significantly, as globalization draws more actors together for purposes that range from development projects to security and stabilization operations and from peacekeeping to humanitarian missions, these actors are more likely to come into contact with intoxicated combatants. While some individuals are seduced by the availability of drugs to join a warring group, others are coerced to join through drugging, which further denigrates human rights standards and undermines the establishment of civil society.

Western militaries will probably continue to deal with the effects of drugs on the battlefield and, in turn, pressure defense establishments to reconsider their battlefield approaches. One way such changes may occur is by understanding the dynamics of asymmetric warfare and the nuances of conducting counterinsurgency operations. The use of drugged combatants by non-state groups lends itself to asymmetric approaches to counter the superior technical firepower and skills of Western militaries. With contemporary war composed of mostly civil wars fought by non-professional armed groups with less sophisticated weaponry, few potential adversaries of the West will wage a conventional, high-tech war because doing so necessitates massive training, logistical, and resource requirements that few groups can produce.[75] Because of its effects on combatant behavior, drug use can narrow the gap between Western militaries' capabilities and those of irregular groups by exploiting the Western legal and ethical regimes under which troops must operate. Enemies may consider the West's humanitarian sensitivity to enemy casualties as an advantage; they "may purposely put their own people in jeopardy if doing so complicates or adversely affects the

West's use of its military power."[76] Increasingly, opponents of Western military forces have sought to present Western troops with moral and ethical quandaries.

These dilemmas were revealed by the British experience in Sierra Leone in 2000. In September 2000, a British patrol was conducting training exercises in Sierra Leone when a rebel force confronted it. The patrol was captured and taken hostage when the patrol leader refused to fire on the enemy force that was comprised of drugged boys of whom the oldest was fifteen and the youngest seven. In response, the British sent paratroopers and the Special Air Service (SAS) to rescue the captured patrol. The SAS response was starkly different—the patrol was successfully recovered with the loss of one British soldier, but estimates on enemy dead vary between 25 and 150 child soldiers.[77] Without adequately addressing the doctrinal issues presented by drug combatants and their associated complications, Western militaries, in particular, leave themselves open to moral conundrums that erode operational effectiveness and place their soldiers in greater jeopardy.

Drugged fighters may operate in unfamiliar and seemingly irrational ways to members of professional conventional forces, yet the standard response to any fighter whether he is sober or intoxicated is the same—a threat to one's force on the battlefield in combat is dealt with by lethal force. This tactic is problematic since the battlefield and combat are no longer the only contexts where professional militaries operate. Since the end of the Cold War, Western militaries have engaged in peacekeeping, stability and security missions, and nation-building activities that were all characterized in the 1990s by the United States as "military operations other than war" (MOOTW) but which are now called Stability, Security, Transition, and Reconstruction Operations (SSTRO). Such operations have lower tolerance of violence and more restrictive rules of engagement. In the face of more constrained uses of force, instructions on how to engage drugged forces in different types of conflicts are still absent from any professional military's doctrine.

The need for a formal doctrine to guide the practices and conduct of professional soldiers is especially acute when wars include children who are recruited through addiction. Professional military leaders with forces involved in the conflict will have to prepare their troops well in advance for possible confrontation. Military operations will require more troop briefings on the possibility of facing not only drugged adversaries but drugged child soldiers. With the potential for violence against drugged children, Western militaries are beginning to realize the effects such a confrontation will have on an individual service member. The Center for Emerging Threats and Opportunities held a seminar for the U.S. Marine Corps and recommended the development of tactics, techniques, and procedures for confronting child soldiers.[78] Although professional militaries are recognizing the problems of combatant unpredictability and unconventional fighting, Western government defense establishments have not strongly grasped the contribution of drugged combatants to conflict narcotization.

However, drugs present other challenges to professional militaries that are being overlooked. As previously mentioned, protracted conflicts fought by conscripts can create conditions that tempt troops to abuse drugs. Drug abuse by professional troops diminishes their combat effectiveness, undermines the health of service members, and erodes the domestic support for the conflict. Unlike professional members of the military, draftees and reservists are drawn directly from society and do not reside in guarded bases and insulated barracks when they are not deployed. As previously mentioned, citizens become especially concerned by the drug habits of returning veterans. One reason for concern is that a greater proportion of the average citizenry has direct contact with conscripts and reservists than with full-time members of the armed forces. When drafted veterans and reservists return from tour, the effects of the war on them and on society at large are more noticeable to the average citizen.

Unlike with the Vietnam era, the U.S. military currently has an all-volunteer force that is primarily designed to compartmentalize protracted conflicts with irregular forces and isolate their effects on society by not relying on draftees.[79] Also, the U.S. Department of Defense has ongoing programs that address combat stress, mental trauma, drug use, and addiction. Yet, because of continuing U.S. military operations in Afghanistan and Iraq and the increased tempo of deployments, especially among National Guard and Reserve troops, military forces are in a stressful situation, which can lead many to abuse drugs.[80] Mental health trauma is on the rise among U.S. ground forces. U.S. Army studies show that more than one third of combat-deployed troops seek mental health care when they return home.[81] Another study showed that 31 percent of veterans returning from Afghanistan and Iraq were diagnosed with mental health and/or psychosocial problems, while 20 percent had "substance abuse disorders."[82] The trend is not encouraging. According to figures from the Veterans Health Administration, 3,057 veterans of the Afghanistan and Iraq wars were diagnosed with drug dependency from 2005–2007, while only a total of 277 veterans were diagnosed from 2002–2004.[83]

While the effects of these elevated numbers on the wider society have yet to be felt, of most concern is that the support structure is too weak to handle such high numbers. Further, mental health professionals are inadequately trained. A survey of 133 military mental health providers conducted from 2003–2005 shows that 90 percent of military psychiatrists, psychologists, and social workers reported no formal training or supervision in four Post Traumatic Stress Disorder (PTSD) therapies recommended by the Pentagon and Department of Veterans Affairs.[84] Depending on the conclusion of the wars in Iraq and Afghanistan, the numbers of returning service members will place additional stress on the military mental health system, and without adequate institutional capacity, illegal narcotics abuse may rise sharply among this group and stoke concerns among the public.[85]

Beyond drug abuse potentially infiltrating the ranks of professional militaries, manufacturing and supplying drugs to the enemy has the potential to be exceptionally dangerous in an era of globalization. Transnational groups act more clandestinely and can more easily produce, access, and smuggle drugs to distant enemies in ways that were not previously possible. Similarly to how the drug trade has been used to fund warring groups, it can emerge as a powerful weapon when wielded in a transnational setting. To wage an ideological struggle, Islamic militants have smuggled drugs to weaken enemy societies while simultaneously gaining funding. Further, they have used their own drug smuggling as a recruitment tool by pointing to drug abuse they have inflicted as an indication of the degeneracy of Western society, justifying attacks against moral corruption.

COMPLICATIONS OF DRUG USE BY COMBATANTS

The presence of drugged fighters and the use of the drugs to attack an enemy's will to fight are not unknown in the history of warfare. Yet, these phenomena coincide with a perceptible change in the nature and type of wars that are occurring—protracted conflicts largely fought by non-professional combatants are taking place in an international system that facilitates the bringing of people and goods into closer and quicker contact. The far-reaching effects of drug use by combatants on human rights and state sovereignty have made many actors in the international arena want to intervene in these conflicts to ameliorate these effects or bring the fighting to a close. Yet, militaries from developed countries are unprepared to face drugged combatants because of the lack of doctrine or policy.

Leaders of professional militaries are beginning to recognize the characteristics and effects of drugged combatants to explain erratic battlefield behavior. For example, United States Pacific Command describes the Abu Sayyaf Group in the Philippines as one that employs "ad hoc strategies and activities that are determined by the mood swings of individual leaders, many with eccentric nicknames reflecting bizarre bandit camaraderie. Discipline is haphazard, and some are addicted to drugs. Still, about 140 hostages have been taken during their last two years of violent kidnapping sprees."[86]

Although militaries from developed countries are beginning to recognize the strategic and tactical effects of drugged combatants, little has changed in the way military and political leaders have conceptualized the role of illegal narcotics and warfare. Drug use and drug-financed warfare are still considered to be more criminal acts than military in their implications and effects. However, as Martin Van Creveld described in *The Transformation of War*, "often crime will be disguised as war whereas in other cases war itself will be treated as if waging it were a crime."[87] In other words, the actions of combatants not only resemble criminal acts, but the combatants themselves share more in common with criminals than professional armies. This is clearly the case in carnival and the use of former convicts in some military forces.

As the illegal drug trade has blurred the line between war and crime, developed states and their militaries have been slow to react to the change. While some militaries may participate in counternarcotics efforts, law enforcement agencies in demand countries still lead in implementing policies to stem the drug flow. This lack of nimbleness on the part of Western governments has led to disastrous effects. Spanish police were keeping one of the Madrid train bombers under surveillance for drug sales while their intelligence services had no clear idea of the plot that was being funded by the sales.[88] These "firewalls" between law enforcement and the intelligence community will continue to plague democracies.

In war zones where there are developing, serious, and critical levels of drug influence at play, law enforcement alone has not been successful—nor have purely military efforts— in bringing violence to an end. Even blended efforts among multiple agencies have not quelled violence in conflicts located in countries such as Colombia, Afghanistan, and Myanmar. Drugged fighters, in combination with drug-financed combatant groups, create significant problems for conflict resolution and any subsequent nation-building efforts. The following chapter examines the reasons many conflicts are so resistant to attempts to end them.

4

NARCOTICS AND NATION-BUILDING
Drug Trade as Post-Conflict Complication

TODAY, THE TWIN PHENOMENA OF DRUG-FINANCED VIOLENCE and drugged combatants pose special challenges for opponents of the drug trade who seek conflict resolution. Drug-financed combatant groups and drugged combatants increase the difficulty of promoting sustainable peace in war-torn societies by reducing many of the familiar dampening forces that have been present in other conflicts while diminishing the effectiveness of measures aimed to reduce ongoing violence. As a result, the face of war is becoming less familiar in many contexts, affecting traditional approaches to conflict resolution. Although agreements have been reached to limit or end several violent conflicts, the drug trade has limited the power of many commitments made by the warring parties.

Combatant access to legal commodities in other resource-driven conflicts, such as oil, timber, diamonds, and gas, can be more easily curtailed through traditional military, diplomatic, and economic actions designed to bring pressure on the parties involved.[1] The three prevailing approaches that have been used in other resource-driven conflicts are to capture resource areas from belligerents, broker an agreement to share revenues between parties, and impose economic sanctions.[2] The diffuse and complex nature of the drug trade, however, makes many contemporary conflicts uniquely resistant to these time-honored conflict resolution measures. They are largely infeasible given the illicit status of narcotics, the ways that drug crops are grown and amphetamine-type stimulants (ATS) are manufactured, the multifaceted manner in which they are transported to market, and the vastness of the international trafficking network that now exists.

For example, there are not enough resources that could be dedicated to capture and hold an entire area where drugs are grown or manufactured and where violent groups operate. Identifying where drug crops are grown is daunting enough. Attacking portions of a drug network infrastructure, including processing labs, transportation nodes, or interdicting shipments, has had minimal impact as a counternarcotics strategy and, therefore, has not been a useful part of any potent coercive military operations. At the wholesale and retail level of distribution, police agencies are overwhelmed by the drug activities and crimes carried out by individuals and groups. Drugs have

> low obstructability.... They can only be blocked with many soldiers and heavy equipment.... Resources that have a lower value-to-weight ratio that must be transported by truck or train—like minerals and timber—are moderately obstructable if they must cross long distances. Resources that are transported in liquid form and travel long distances through aboveground pipelines (i.e., oil and natural gas) are highly obstructable.[3]

Drugs, especially heroin, cocaine, and ATS, have a high value-to-weight ratio and do not necessarily have to travel long distances to meet the next transaction node in the trafficking network.

When it comes to drugs, many external actors, such as countries, international organizations, and aid agencies, involved in conflict resolution cannot endorse the traditional strategy of profit sharing among warring parties as legitimate. Even a national government that takes such a route to end its own internal violence would be in contravention of the current international legal status of the narcotics trade and would be breaking international law.

Economic sanctions against a country to curtail the drug trade's influence on a conflict are counterproductive. If sanctions are not targeted, social and economic conditions may deteriorate within a country, forcing more people into the drug trade or into participating in the ongoing violence. The imposition of trade restrictions on an illegal commodity is also unfeasible, for drugs do not have to face tariffs. Moreover, targeting sanctions against irregular groups is exceptionally difficult. Efforts at "naming and shaming" groups by exposing leaders' connections to the illicit economy, in hopes of eroding their support among their followers, are rarely effective. Many followers either already know about the connections (and even benefit from them) or do not care since the means are secondary to the objective.

Traditional attempts to end resource-driven conflicts miss a critical feature of many conflicts occurring in the shadow of the drug trade: the higher the intensity level of the drug trade's influence on a conflict, the more divorced a conflict becomes from its political objectives. Adding to the intractability of a conflict, drugs can upend political objectives entirely; few political agendas are evident in critical and advanced levels of intensity. In fact, political agendas often evaporate during these conflicts. Many warring groups have "not only lost some of their more comprehensible ideals, but are increasingly turning to smuggling and other criminal activities."[4] It is an open question as to whether the Revolutionary Armed Forces of Colombia (FARC) is now genuinely interested in implementing its leftist political agenda as it was proclaimed in the sixties, or if it seeks to maintain and expand its place as a critical player in the international cocaine trade. Likewise, the Sendero

Luminoso's (SL) commitment to a Maoist vision of political life in Peru, should it somehow prevail, is also murky because of its active and committed participation in coca cultivation. The Afghan insurgent group, Hezb-Islami Gulbuddin, is now a "full-fledged smuggling organization."[5]

As these conflicts continue, many individuals within the warring groups become driven by financial rewards rather than political objectives. Rather than being populated by fighters dedicated to a political outcome, warring groups become filled with opportunists. As such, intense pressures are exerted on combatant leadership to maintain group cohesion or avoid accepting political concessions. Unlike the Cold War when external resources fed from outside powers could be tightly controlled by combatant leaders and distributed to subordinates and allies, today's combatant leaders must concern themselves with preventing the "explosion of the movement because everybody likes to do business and soldiers risk doing more business than fighting."[6] In some cases this has meant deepening a group's participation in the drug trade or other illicit trade as a way for combatant leaders to fully fund their supporters and the families of their supporters, thereby keeping a cohesive organization.

When leaders fully embrace drug running to maintain group cohesion, recruitment suffers and political commitment becomes displaced. Individuals may become more attracted (and more attractive) to the group without having to demonstrate a commitment to the ideological goals of the movement, but show an ability to extract resources from the drug trade to keep the group viable. A type of "bandit rationality" takes over members of the group.[7] Therefore, maintaining a certain level of violence becomes necessary to preserve the benefits for the group while holding little promise of achieving an identifiable political goal. The Islamic Movement of Uzbekistan (IMU), for example, appears to have "a vested interest in ongoing unrest and instability in their area in order to secure the routes they use for the transportation of drugs."[8]

Far from cohesive political movements, many groups are now more akin to armed business ventures. They are now known as much for their activities, such as kidnapping, extortion, assassinations and drug running, as for the political causes espoused by their founders. The FARC, for example, is now often referred to as the "third cartel," after Cali and Medellin.[9] Similar groups, including the IMU, SL, the Taliban, and the United Wa State Army (UWSA), no longer appear to be ideologically inspired, yet they do not state that their goals are to turn their respective countries into full-blown "narco-states" or possess an autonomous region for the sole purpose of producing drugs. This ambiguity over the central direction or goal of their violence makes these groups difficult to defeat in combat or to be persuaded into good faith negotiations.[10]

As detailed in chapter 2, segments of drug-trafficking networks, including farming, provision of precursor chemicals, and transportation, are part of the strategic equation for many combatants in today's violent struggles. Drugs are the economic engine for many belligerents, which, as a result, undermines processes and structures designed to prevent relapses into conflict. For actors who are deeply involved in the narcotics trade as a way to sustain violence, war becomes political power rather than an extension of political power. Therefore, war and violence turn into a natural state of affairs whose benefits are not easily negotiated. A conflict where war is political power and not a means to an objective offers "a more promising environment for the pursuit of aims that are prominent in peacetime.... [K]eeping a war going may assist in the achievement of these aims and prolonging a war may be a higher priority than winning it."[11] The results have been ceasefires used by some combatants to expand drug activities and plan future military operations rather than being used as confidence-building measures for future political negotiations designed to fully resolve the conflict.

Conflict resolution and nation-building are further complicated by intoxicated fighters. Raids and carnival activities degrade unit cohesion and challenge coherent efforts to achieve valuable political or military objectives. A strung-out fighter is not likely to be fully committed to a military goal let alone a more distant political objective. The leadership cannot always guarantee good behavior of all combatants. Command and control degenerates not only during the war; warring groups devolve into criminal gangs whose members fight among themselves or with other groups over petty drug stakes during ceasefires and negotiations.

As chapters 2 and 3 demonstrate, access to drug resources also increases the likelihood that warring groups will abuse the human rights of civilians uninvolved in open hostilities. Widespread drug abuse, child soldier recruitment, and atrocities against civilians breakdown informal social controls that restrict behaviors that are detrimental to civil society, like drug abuse and criminality. Such effects during conflicts mean that dealing with the aftermath of widespread human suffering serves as an additional complication for governments and outside agencies that are involved in implementing the conditions of conflict-resolution agreements. Without coming to grips with atrocities, criminality, and the breakdown in social norms, governments may find that popular discontent will affect newly gained but fragile political stability.

Moreover, the traditional approaches used in other resource-driven wars—seizing of territory, sharing resources, and sanctioning—do not address the consumable nature of drugs by combatants. The low obstructability of drugs works to impede efforts to prevent combatants from gaining access to drugs for consumption as well. A large volume of drugs to supply combatant demand is not required for stimulation, recruitment, reward, or relaxation. Therefore, there is little product to track and trace. Nontraditional drugs that are transshipped through territory where a narcotized conflict is occurring are often bartered for safe passage, arms, or other services and commodities and are likewise difficult to restrict. It is nearly impossible to prevent looted drugs, which are used to satisfy a variety of combatant demands, from being ingested by individual fighters.

In many of today's conflicts, traditional attempts to manufacture political solutions to end the violence are tenuous or completely untenable from the beginning. Drug-financed warring groups combined with drug-fueled violence lessen the ability of policymakers and military leaders to control the magnitude and duration of war. In previous eras, empires or commercial surrogates almost exclusively controlled the drug trade, which meant that governments could more easily manipulate the role of drugs in warfare; their role was more tightly controlled and more closely tied to clear political objectives for war. While the Opium Wars may stand out as a contrary example, they were nonetheless wars whose underpinnings were the commercial interests of the states involved.[12] Although Britain wanted China to open its market, China did not want to cede any sovereignty to European powers. Contrary to many of today's wars, the Opium Wars were not protracted, unrestrained, fought by irregulars, or involved shifting strategic objectives owing to the presence of drugs. In fact, despite the central issue of dispute being the trade of a narcotic, the British and Chinese governments were able to manage the levels of violence in hopes of bringing about their respective political objectives, a quality that many current warring groups do not share.[13]

DRUGS AND THE STATUS OF ARMED CONFLICTS

Table 4.1 reflects the status of contemporary conflicts that have been influenced by the drug trade, while Table 4.2 reflects the status of conflicts that have been influenced by drug use among combatants. Ongoing conflicts are those where no settlement among the warring parties has been reached, and violence continues in varying scope and degrees. Abeyant

TABLE 4.1: STATUS OF CONFLICTS INFLUENCED BY DRUG TRADE

	INCIPIENT	DEVELOPING	SERIOUS	CRITICAL	ADVANCED
ONGOING	Iraq, Palestinian Authority, Spain	Morocco, Philippines, Sudan	Sri Lanka, Turkey (PKK)	Pakistan, Peru, Uzbekistan	Afghanistan, Colombia, Myanmar
ABEYANT	Congo, Nepal, Russia	Algeria, Somalia	Bosnia, Cambodia, Kosovo, Lebanon (Hezbollah), Liberia	———	———
SETTLED	Northern Ireland	Indonesia (GAM), Senegal	———	———	———

TABLE 4.2: STATUS OF CONFLICTS INFLUENCED BY DRUG USE AMONG COMBATANTS

	MINIMAL	**ACUTE**	**UNRESTRAINED**
ONGOING	Iraq	Colombia, Peru, Philippines	Uganda
ABEYANT	Haiti	Bosnia, Congo, Russia, Rwanda	Liberia, Sierra Leone, Somalia
SETTLED	———	———	———

conflicts are those where there are ceasefires between the belligerents or the presence of an intervening force to maintain peace. In this type of conflict, however, ceasefires may breakdown and be re-established, and if a mediating third party departs, violence will probably begin again. Settled conflicts are based on agreements between belligerents to end hostilities or exist in situations where one belligerent has defeated an opponent on the battlefield.

The cases in Table 4.1 reflect how drug trafficking by warring groups can obscure political objectives. Table 4.1 once again demonstrates that the cultivation of coca and opium by combatant groups is linked to conflict endurance exemplified by the cases of Afghanistan, Colombia, Myanmar, and Peru. Yet, because Afghanistan produces over 90 percent of the world's heroin, Pakistan and Uzbekistan, both of which have critical smuggling routes, are finding their conflicts more enduring. The relative newness of ATS as well as the recent participation of warring groups in their production and trade, however, does not present a clear picture of how it influences post-conflict efforts. Possibly, because the processing and trafficking chain is more compressed, there is less infrastructure to serve as strategic targets and, in turn, lower levels of violence. Without the need to cultivate crops, manpower needs are lower, thus ATS drugs are not as integrated into the social and economic fabric of society as drug crops. This may add to pressures to negotiate. However, because ATS drugs are easy to manufacture and because of their added clandestine qualities, activities associated with the ATS trade are likely to escape detection and compliance monitoring. This has enabled a warring group's trade to continue or facilitated a group's transition into organized criminal activities in a post-conflict environment. In Myanmar, Afghanistan's undercutting of the heroin market has forced several warring groups to branch out into the manufacture and sale of ecstasy. Because ATS drugs are a lucrative market and there is an increasing demand for them, the effects of ATS on conflicts require continued examination and vigilance.

Settled and abeyant conflicts demonstrate that groups involved in the wholesale or retail end of the drug distribution chain or are involved in the production and distribution of marijuana, have not had their political objectives affected by their participation. Therefore, such groups can transition into street criminal groups or organized criminal syndicates that are more willing to negotiate an end to the hostilities. They are then able to exert their power in a political system rather than on the battlefield. Marijuana, as discussed in chapter 2, is used as a supplement in other resource-driven conflicts and rarely as a primary funding source. As mentioned previously, such conflicts are more amenable to traditional attempts to resolve the conflict. Turning to marijuana alone as a way to make up for any pressure exerted on the use of legal commodities is not easy given its high weight-to-value ratio, which makes these groups more susceptible to negotiations or battlefield defeat.

As seen in Table 4.2, there are no settled conflicts where there has been widespread use of drugs by warring groups. This is not to suggest a direct causal link—that drug use causes conflicts to continue. The table does suggest that drug use is an influential factor on a variety of issues that complicate efforts to reach ceasefires and political settlements. One explanation is that drug usage appears to be linked to drug-trafficking routes that may reinforce the enduring quality of these conflicts. The exception is the case of Rwanda, which did not serve as a transshipment country for drugs but where looted stimulant drugs fueled the atrocities that occurred.

As demonstrated in Table 4.1 and Table 4.2, the higher the level and degree, the greater the difficulty in generating successful transitions to sustainable peace. Professional militaries and third party negotiators are conditioned to think of an achievable post-conflict environment with concrete and attainable goals and to establish guidelines and actions to meet those goals. Yet, the drug trade affects a conflict's status when it is felt in the four main areas where conflict resolution and nation-building efforts are typically directed at curtailing: the wartime economy, warlordism, local disempowerment, and political instability and personal insecurity. The more the drug trade and drug use contribute to the continuation of each, the less likely a conflict will be settled, while abeyant conflicts teeter between ending and renewing. Although treated separately, these four broad areas are interdependent and are not easily separated. The interdependence of these areas is especially obvious when the influence of drug trade is at a high level and drug use among combatants occurs at a high degree.

Wartime Economy

Greater attention has been paid to the area of wartime economy, or combat economy in the aftermath of the numerous military interventions in the 1990s. A diverse number of actors, including nation-states, North Atlantic Treaty Organization (NATO), Economic Community of West African States (ECOWAS), and the United Nations (UN), along with powerful international financial institutions, such as the World Bank and International Monetary Fund

(IMF), have viewed the ending of violence and the sustainability of peace as linked to curtailing a warring group's impact on a national economy, thereby allowing society to generate a peacetime economy. Ending the wartime economy of a civil war is treated like the economic conversion of national economies in the aftermath of a major interstate war. However, such economic conversion after civil war is much more difficult if a wartime economy defies official attempts at control and permits the continuity of alternative socio-economic arrangements like the black market.

Attempts to convert a wartime economy that is influenced by the drug trade are at the mercy of the dynamics and nature of the drug trade, including the balloon- and hydra-effects discussed in chapter 2. These effects create numerous alternative socio-economic arrangements and vested interests that are outside the parameters of the licit economy. War economies dependent on the drug trade are exceptionally pernicious because they create commercial patterns that are "mercantilist [activities] that [are] largely uninterested in long-term productive investment, involved with the control and apportionment of wealth, dependent on maintaining differences and discrete forms of control for profit, and likely encourages informal protectionism."[14] Governments and outside institutions attempting to pull a nation out of such patterns are often frustrated because even local investments are "short-term speculative ventures designed more to launder money than promote sustained economic growth."[15] Also, those involved in the drug trade want to maintain advantages in the wartime economy by combining their vast resources "with a frightening ability and willingness to use deadly force."[16] This makes reforms undertaken to improve long-term national economic health exceptionally thorny.

Those engaged in conflict resolution and nation-building often overlook the domestic support for the war by groups involved in the drug trade, which exerts internal domestic pressures exist to keep a wartime economy in place. In some conflicts, drug farmers support the initial momentum for rebellion. The tax collected on cannabis in Senegal dates back to the creation of the armed branch of the movement, Attika, when it was mainly the fighters' families who cultivated the drug to support the rebellion.[17]

Crosscutting regional networks and the compartmentalized nature of drug trafficking means that the economic impact of a wartime economy is not isolated to the country in conflict. Economic stakeholders outside the conflict are also linked to the wartime economy, making it more complicated to end the violence. Law enforcement agencies and politicians of neighboring states have been known to benefit from their roles as conduits for the drug trade across their borders. Some neighboring governments rely on the trade to meet other national security interests. For example, Pakistani intelligence agencies and their allies have routinely used drug smugglers to assist in arms shipment to numerous warring groups throughout the region. In return, Pakistani officials have turned a blind eye to their activities.[18] Legitimate actors outside the government, who have little stake in the political objectives of warring groups or who are uninvolved in the directed parts of drug trafficking, are affected by attempts to end nearby violence. Vehicle drivers, security firms, merchants of farm equipment, chemicals, filters, centrifuges, and other items beyond the borders of narcotized conflicts derive benefits. Criminal syndicates are also affected by attempts to create a peacetime economy, for they fear greater scrutiny of their activities by outside monitoring groups. In sum, formal and informal pressures can be exerted on warring groups from the outside to limit their responsiveness to any incentives or sanctions by outside actors interested in ending the violence.

A war economy can be sustained because the ravages of war leave few economic opportunities in legitimate sectors of the economy. While the devastation of roads, the destruction of transportation networks, and the attacks on subsistence agriculture are part of strategic military goals in today's wars, they also serve to eliminate alternatives to drug crops and constrict access to markets for legitimate goods. Few crops in countries where drug crops are cultivated can be transported far without spoiling or damaging because of insecurity and poor roads. By comparison, poppy resin, cocaine paste, and hashish have a long shelf life, making their cultivation an attractive option for many peasants. Afghanistan represents how the enveloping paradox of drugs and armed conflict cripples attempts to stimulate a peacetime economy. Afghanistan's current opium economy finds many of its modern roots in the aftermath of a previous war—the *mujahedin* struggle against the Soviet invasion. The Red Army destroyed the irrigation systems for legitimate farming in many parts of the country, leaving the less water-intensive poppy as the nearly lone alternative crop.[19] Several wars later, though peace is elusive, the opium economy endures.

As revealed in Table 4.1, societies in which drugs are grown and integrated into the local and national economy have greater difficulty ridding their societies of the perniciousness of the drug trade than do societies that serve as mere transit points. Source countries have been unable to generate a peacetime economy and continue to slip in and out of varying levels of violence. In Afghanistan, the opium economy employs 2.9 million, or 12.6 percent, of Afghans, which would translate to 38 million Americans, or the approximate combined populations of Missouri, Illinois, Ohio, and Pennsylvania.[20] Yet, few opium farmers are committed to the cause of a particular warlord; "most of the guys are in it to make a buck."[21]

While conflict resolution and nation-building are somewhat more successful in conflicts that are not as highly influenced by the drug trade, challenges remain. These conflicts usually take place in countries that serve as transit or transshipment points. Transit points, such as those in the Balkans, are only profitable to those who collude with drug traffickers. As a result, drug-trade involvement contributes only marginally to a local or national economy and is, therefore, less enmeshed in the political, economic, and social fabric of an entire country. Sustained interdiction efforts have resulted in lower profits, forcing drug traffickers outside the borders of the conflict to switch routes in order to maintain a certain level of profitability.[22]

However, drug trafficking in transit countries can still provide the economic strength for warring groups to sustain themselves through ceasefires and post-conflict environments. This is the case with the abeyant conflicts in the Balkans. Like the situation in Afghanistan where much of the legitimate economy was destroyed by endless wars, the disintegration of Yugoslavia left few legal avenues to generate income. The Croatian political elite and the Italian mafia worked to wrestle control over the Turkish narcotics trade away from the Belgrade-Kosovo Albanian mafias.[23] When the Dayton Accords failed to address the concerns of Kosovar Albanians, diaspora communities began to increasingly take over heroin trafficking to influence the politics of the society.[24] Bosnia is not a source country for drugs. Nonetheless, several former combatant groups with vested interests in maintaining control over drug routes still seek a weak central government, fragmented political and social landscape, and impoverished towns to keep drug-smuggling routes open to Western Europe and to maintain profits. Arizona Market in Bosnia, which was established with NATO assistance in hopes of generating a free market zone where people from the various ethnic groups could meet safely, is now a "smugglers paradise, where one could find among other, common use goods, untaxed cigarettes and alcohol, illegal drugs, and stolen cars and guns."[25]

Whether a country is a source or transit country, one area of the wartime economy that warrants special concern is the small-arms market. The continuing existence of small-arms trafficking overlaps the broad areas of warlordism, local disempowerment, and political instability and personal insecurity. This is especially true in conflicts where there is a great degree of collusion among warring groups and criminal syndicates. One U.S. State Department representative in Afghanistan proclaimed that "when it came to drug seizures, you would always find guns as well."[26] The drug-trafficking network provides both an ad-hoc and semi-permanent infrastructure to meet numerous weapons demands of intrastate conflicts. Arms merchants can offer enough merchandise as a "hedge" against the possibility of breakdowns in negotiations or add to a group's arsenal as it expands its operations during a ceasefire. Conflicts at the higher levels of drug influence, ceasefires, and additional arms often pave the way for the further expansion of drug activities. Thus, militaries are continually outgunned by their opponents who can secure areas without interference.

Warlordism

The phenomenon of warlordism is closely associated with the perpetuation of a wartime economy. An individual leader or segment of combatant leadership can consolidate the military, political, economic, and social control over a territory or a population to gain personal or political benefits. Such control is beyond the reach of the central government and an element of a combatant group may even separate itself from its central leadership, creating factionalization within the movement. A warlord uses his resources and influence to create, maintain, and protect a type of state within a state. With drug crops, patterns of warlord behavior are easy to establish. In the cases of opium, coca, and marijuana crops, the existence of drug crops in remote areas far from efforts to monitor compliance with provisions of an accord permit a wide latitude for rebel groups to perpetuate conditions of warlordism. With the power of the small-arms market, warlords and their followers are often better armed than government or intervening forces, allowing them free reign to conduct a variety of military and criminal activities. One poppy farmer in southern Afghanistan summed up his situation by proclaiming that "we don't have law. This is a warlord kingdom."[27]

In drug-transit countries with settled or abeyant conflicts, warlordism takes on the configurations of gangsterism where combatants act like mafia bosses and run certain operations with cooperation, willing or forced, from citizens. Towns, districts, transportation, and ports can be under the influence of these combatants who are seeking to exert control over the movement of certain shipments of merchandise. Sectarian leaders with militias at their disposal often fulfill a warlord function in transit countries. In Iraq, drug smuggling appears to be organized by Shiite militia near Iraq's southeastern border with Iran. Pilgrims to Shiite holy sites in Iraq have participated as drug couriers and large quantities of heroin have been known to pass through the cities of Basra and Amara; both are Mahdi Army strongholds.[28] Guy Philippe, a drug kingpin who led a rebel group against the rule of Haitian President Aristide in the 1990s, is still on the run from U.S. law enforcement while continuing to traffic cocaine in the Caribbean.[29]

In post-conflict situations as in the case of Bosnia, such groups have translated their criminal power into political power. The result is "crime-fighting problems overshadow war-fighting problems. Key players in the covert acquisition and distribution of supplies during wartime have emerged as a nouveau riche 'criminal elite' with close ties to the government and nationalist political parties.... [C]riminal capital accumulated during the war has been converted into political capital after the war."[30]

The ways warlords organize their rule over others, particularly farmers, peasants, local townspeople, and villagers, can be categorized in a number of ways: predatory, parasitic, symbiotic, and independent.[31] Each category of warlord interaction with the local community is deepened by the drug trade, thereby making conflict resolution and nation-building challenging. The case of Colombia illustrates each category and demonstrates the complicating role of drug trafficking in its conflict. A predatory relationship involves the direct extraction of wealth from civil society without anything offered in return. When coca crops initially made their appearance in FARC-controlled territory in the early 1980s, the rebels attempted to eradicate their growth and confiscate farmers' profits without offering any compensation, because the FARC leadership believed that the drug crops in their territory undermined its ideological message. A parasitic relationship exists when a combatant group offers "protection" and "security" in return for financial contributions. As coca farming increased in Colombia, the demand for cocaine in the United States exploded and the Colombian government expanded its counterinsurgency efforts. To compensate for its battle-field losses and dwindling finances, the FARC took advantage of coca production and "taxed" farmers in exchange for protection from government counternarcotics efforts and violent drug traffickers. In a symbiotic relationship, the warlord actively works to foster economic activities in his sphere of influence. In Colombia, the FARC has seized territory to convert it to coca cultivation for unemployed peasants as a way to gain support from the local community. An independent relationship is one where a group receives substantial funding from outside sources. Because the cocaine trade is both regional and international, the FARC continues to negotiate prices on behalf of coca farmers with drug traffickers in Peru, Venezuela, and Bolivia while working with diverse violent groups, such as the Provisional Irish Republican Army (IRA), to improve their expertise in guerrilla warfare operations.

When it comes to controlling the population in its territory, warlords have taken a variety of stances toward drug consumption by the local population. Some have used drugs to recruit new followers or maintain loyalty. Drug abuse in Sierra Leone and Liberia has contributed to the extension of conflicts. The profile of a Liberian fighter has become familiar, "a young man between 12 and 20, who is a regular drug user driven by his own poverty spurred by the African warlord's quest for power.[32] Residents in warlord areas are often denied access to intoxicating substances, including alcohol, for the same reasons many combatant leaders allow drugs to be used by their own fighters—drugs give courage to those who resist warlord control. However, warlords will often permit consumption of small amounts of drug crops for traditional purposes so as to not alienate themselves from the local population. Elements of SL, who acted as warlords divorced from their central leadership, permitted peasants to chew coca, but punished them for excessive consumption of alcohol.[33]

Although there is a coercive element to the relationship between warlords and the local population, many people under the control of warlords readily consent to the "governance" they provide, making narcotized conflict resolution more problematic. Such consent is given because of the pressures that contemporary wars place on civilians. In underdeveloped economic areas, people often move to rebel-held areas for employment. Children will also voluntarily join the ranks as either soldiers or drug farmers. During civil wars, the lack of security pushes peasants to maximize risks; faced with the possibility of losing everything in war, they turn to the most profitable crops to generate short-term gains. Thus, cannabis cultivation has attained a scope unknown prior to the 1993 conflict in the agricultural areas around Brazzaville and in the Pool region, which supplies the Congo.[34]

In areas of drug cultivation, rebels and their leaders are also adept at co-opting drug-growing peasants by appearing to be guardians of their way of life. When the government or outside powers seek to eradicate drug crops, their actions appear to be direct assaults on the well-being of drug farmers. Warlords have sought to protect them from harsh governmental eradication measures and excessive use of force. When the Peruvian government conducted vigorous counternarcotics operations in the 1980s, it included arbitrary arrests, confiscations, looting, and other abuses. Coca farmers sought protection from SL; the rebels worked with local coca growers to construct liberated zones and, as their first action in their newly acquired territory, attacked the local office of the government's coca eradication project.[35] Because of this newly formed relationship, the Peruvian government and outside agencies were faced with a dilemma as to where to focus their efforts to quell the violence—the insurgency or drug farmers.

Even good faith efforts to set the stage for negotiations have created conditions that favor warlordism. In November 1998, Colombian President Andres Pastrana withdrew government forces from a 42,000 square kilometer area in the south central region of the country in support of his "peace strategy" to engage the FARC. Rebels demanded the *zona de despeje,* or demilitarized zone, as a condition for negotiations. The FARC used the zone as a major strategic asset while elements of the movement were able to take advantage of the sanctuary to conduct wider drug-running operations and rearmament activities. In fact, coca cultivation in the despeje increased by one third during the Pastrana administration.[36] Moreover, to consolidate many of their military and economic gains, the FARC launched numerous new attacks to open new corridors and allow a freer flow of drugs and arms. Far from reducing violence, the despeje provided the conditions for warlordism and deepening the conflict.

Ceasefires and settlement agreements often include "golden parachutes" for rebel leaders, which are formal guarantees that allow them to not only keep their positions, but to continue their drug-dealing activities in exchange for ending their armed challenges against the government. The case of Myanmar is instructive. In 1989, the government made peace with several rebel groups by allowing them to continue narcotics trafficking in exchange for ending their violent opposition to the government. In fact, one agreement with a group of insurgents included explicit permission to "engage in any kind of business deal needed to sustain themselves" in exchange for "joining hands with the government."[37] Such an agreement nearly formalized warlord control over portions of the country, and governmental military forces are still not allowed to station troops in these areas. In effect, the generals of the Myanmar military government granted their opponents in the UWSA and Myanmar Democratic Alliance Army (MDAA) a high degree of political and economic freedom. After turning himself in, Khun Sa, one of Myanmar's warlords and well-known drug traffickers, was protected by the military junta in Rangoon until his death in 2007 while his children increase his fortune by investing in the regional economy.[38] As previously mentioned, golden-parachute agreements occurred after the fall of the Ne Win government and served as one of eight key events that shifted the international drug trade into the hands of warring groups.

Such agreements increased Myanmar's international isolation and brought about further international sanctions that exacerbated Myanmar's drug problem by denying it outside economic development assistance, which it needed to turn peasants toward legitimate farming.[39]

Conflicts that are heavily affected by the drug trade are not the only ones that are subject to such compromises, for patterns of warlordism can emerge in conflicts that are less affected by the drug trade. In the Casamance region of Senegal, for example, police and military forces are reluctant to increase enforcement efforts against marijuana cultivation and drug-smuggling activities, for they fear hampering ongoing final settlement negotiations.[40] In other situations, members of the government who maintain militias outside the central government's control may also have links to the drug trade as a means to keep their leadership position intact. Such links are not challenged out of fear of increasing widespread and intense violence. For example, there is evidence that the militia belonging to Iraq's Shiite cleric, Moqtada Al-Sadr, is involved in the drug trade—early in the conflict his group was caught with $30 million worth of heroin,[41] and large quantities of Afghan heroin continue to transit through towns under the control of his militia.[42]

In conflicts where other natural resources contribute to fueling violence, if a warlord captures or otherwise controls an area that the government depended on for funding, the government may turn to the drug trade to compensate. When Liberian president Charles Taylor lost control of the gold and diamond mines in Lofa County in 1991, he turned to the export of marijuana for funds.[43]

As discussed in chapter 2, the effects of warlordism are wide-ranging. In situations of conflict resolution and nation-building, warlordism fosters the steady erosion of law and order as well as disintegration of civil society, adding further obstacles to settling disputes peacefully. When unable to confront the warlord militarily or to entice a rebel group to the negotiating table, the government and intervening forces often appear powerless to citizens. Such powerlessness frequently results in deepening relationships between the warlord and the local population. Any deepening can tempt the government to offer rebels a golden-parachute option as a means to end the violence, further entrenching drug trafficking in society.

Because of the strength of the international drug trade, warlords do not merely derive their power from local control over a territory or population. Warlords have their power reinforced by the global demand for illegal drugs. Breaking their ties to other parts of the worldwide trafficking network is nearly impossible. Without severing these connections, conflict resolution efforts are endangered.

Local Disempowerment

The protracted nature of violence in contemporary conflicts creates the conditions for a wartime economy and patterns of warlordism. Both elements lead to disempowerment of those caught in the conflict. Citizens can be caught in the dilemma of joining the wartime economy by participating in the drug trade or refusing, which jeopardizes the well-being of their families. An additional dilemma is foisted upon locals when warlords govern a region—they can remain and ask for their way of life to be spared, or leave for unfamiliar territory and an uncertain future.

Conflict resolution and nation-building efforts often founder on these dilemmas. The ability of the government or outside agencies to break these dilemmas and return a portion of control back to ordinary citizens is constrained by the existence of the drug trade in many conflicts. The drug trade's compartmentalization in regions also complicates the engendering of local empowerment because of the number of external actors and pressures moving to ensure the maintenance of wartime economies. With multiple, well-armed stakeholders, the grip of warlords on peasants cannot often be broken. In fact, in those conflicts with serious, developing, and critical levels of the drug trade's influence, participation in the drug trade and drug use among combatants is the equivalent of local empowerment for many who do not wish to see their traditional livelihoods attacked from the outside. For a considerable proportion of farmers and peasants, drug crops to them are "as traditional as grapes are to the French or olives are to the Italians."[44] Attempts to rein in the wartime economy and end warlordism by controlling drug trafficking often meet heavy resistance from the people such attempts are designed to help.

In transit countries, the grip of warring groups that act more like gangs can be especially tight where there are few legitimate employment opportunities. Youth often become swept up in the drug economy of a transit country. Not only are there few jobs, but schools are often closed during hostilities, meaning children are a ready source of labor. Children have been paid to be lookouts, spotters, couriers, dealers, and even enforcers. A protracted conflict only adds to the allure of the illicit trade. One field commander in Cambodia expressed his fear about the demobilization process: "My men are scared for their future. They don't know what will happen to them or how they feed their families. Most have been farmers and only know war."[45]

When outside agencies and nations seek to fight against the drug trade, local participants, and some national governments involved in the conflict, view outside intervention as a part of the constant struggle between the developed and undeveloped nations, like conditions on financial loans, human rights concerns, and ordinary trade. Many citizens in Colombia closed their eyes to the initial growth of the cocaine industry because they felt the trade would help the country modernize.[46] Government officials trying to end the fighting in highly narcotized conflicts express similar sympathies. Afghanistan's Counternarcotics Minister Habibulah Qaderi said that he knows "[opium] is an illicit economy, but for the time being, Afghanistan is trying to recover from all the problems of these so many years."[47]

High levels of violence in narcotized conflicts can also affect drug use occurring in a society, adding another complication for those involved in conflict resolution and nation-building efforts. As drug-abuse rates often rise along new drug routes and where fighters use trans-shipped narcotics, public health issues emerge as additional issues of concern. Rapid drug use in countries of conflict has led to the rise in the number of cases of HIV/AIDS, hepatitis, and other infectious diseases. This was the case in the countries of Central Asia in the late 1990s. In areas critical to the drug economy, refugee flows have increased as has fighting over drug stakes. Countries surrounding Peru, Colombia, Myanmar, and Afghanistan have experienced rising refugee numbers when violence over portions of the drug infrastructure has occurred. Refugees fleeing the escalating violence of a narcotized conflict also bring drug abuse to host countries. Many refugees face prolonged hardship and are vulnerable to drug addiction. Many refugees either have no job or have very low-paying jobs. They also increasingly have to deal with discrimination that grows over time in a host country. When drug-addicted refugees are repatriated, they create additional burdens. Of Afghanistan's drug users, estimated by the UN in June 2006 to number nearly a million people, "many started taking drugs while living in refugee camps in Pakistan or Iran."[48] Some refugees participate in drug trafficking and smuggling into host countries as a way to earn a living and to support warring groups in their home countries.

The undermining of public health is exceptionally difficult to counter because targets in today's conflicts often include hospitals and clinics as well as their staff. According to a Parliament of Canada report, in many of the conflicts in Africa, "the psychiatrists trained to treat [addicts] can be counted on the fingers of one hand."[49] As a result, many people do not receive care, further degenerating public health and further alienating ordinary citizens. Even in conflicts with an incipient level of drug influence, hospitals and clinics are frequently unable to cope with rising rates of drug addiction, leading many addicts to turn to crime, which results in continued erosion of law and order. Drugs are looted from many health care institutions by fighters and criminals and consumed for combat reasons. To resupply them is to make them a target once again. The rapid growth of drug abuse in Iraq is taxing the already overburdened health care system. Currently, the Ibn Rushd Psychiatric Hospital is the only institution in the country that deals with drug-related disorders, but it only has eight staff members to treat patients and a diminished inventory of pharmaceutical drugs.[50] Many Iraqis point to drug addicts as the initial source of Iraq's now burgeoning crime problem. As Omar Zahed, the head of Iraq police's anti-drug squad, told BBC World Services in October 2003, "[m]ost of our criminals take these tablets before they act. . . . It has caused a huge increase in crime."[51]

Many societies that have experienced conflict involving varying degrees of drug use by irregular troops are leery that combatants may bring back the drug habits they developed on the battlefield. In Sierra Leone, former combatants "dependent on drugs and alcohol may be more resistant to reintegration into society—a critical task in facilitating the transition from war to peace."[52] Members of society are less likely to trust the motives and actions of those outside the community to rekindle a peaceful way forward.

Political Instability and Personal Insecurity

Efforts to create political stability and enhance the personal security of individual citizens are central to converting the wartime economy, isolating warlords, and empowering local citizens. To support these efforts, a bureaucratic infrastructure of a non-corrupt court system, police force, agricultural ministry, labor ministry, and information office is required. To be successful, such institutions need to be staffed by "well-motivated political and military officials" who possess "administrative competence and capability" to carry out political, economic, and social programs.[53] The profound power of the drug economy in many of today's conflicts means that combating political instability and personal insecurity through the creation of institutions designed to bring about sustainable peace are often hampered from their inception. If the infiltration and subversion of a new political system ultimately leads to the use of the judicial system for the ends of rebel groups, in particular, they are well on their way to crippling the entire state.

Drug profits can be used to subvert efforts to build non-corrupt institutions and bring about the conditions for renewed fighting. Police are bribed to provide information about upcoming drug raids, while soldiers are paid to not show up for duty. Prosecutors are bribed not to prosecute and judges not to convict. "Such impunity translates to great power and leaves communities vulnerable to capricious rule."[54]

In Afghanistan, attempts to build sustainable institutions to safeguard the rights of citizens have been jeopardized by the myriad ways that opium has corrupted approaches to end the conflict. Insurgent leaders and warlords lure many newly recruited Afghan soldiers away from dangerous, but needed, counterinsurgency operations by paying them more than they earn from the government. As one British soldier who is training Afghan soldiers lamented, "If you were a lad in the hills and you were offered [twelve dollars] to stay local or you could take [four dollars] and fight miles away from home, which would you do?"[55] Because of the ongoing small-arms trade financed by drug-running elements of the Taliban, the Afghan National Army is poorly equipped by comparison. Fifty percent of the new Afghan National Police force was killed in action in 2006.[56] This has led the Afghan government to pay tribal chiefs to protect towns and villages near insurgent towns, returning the country to a patchwork of warlordism that the new political order was supposed to replace.[57] In other conflicts, professional militaries are compromised by the drug trade and commit acts of violence on other institutions of the government. In Colombia, eleven members of an elite counternarcotics unit were gunned down by members of the national army on the payroll of a drug trafficker.[58]

In transit countries where there are lower degrees of drug use by combatants in the conflict, law and order efforts are jeopardized in post-conflict environments. Much like the funding of a group via drug trafficking, the reliance on, and even the encouragement of, drugged combatants can foster deep and wide-ranging criminal networks. Disarmament does not necessarily mean decriminalization. Criminal links and activities often continue after a conflict and vex the embryonic political life of a society. Warring groups often "decommission" into local mafias.

As a generally accepted part of conflict resolution, ceasefires and the decommissioning of extralegal armed groups are required to set a foundation for greater political stability and personal security. However, decommissioning intoxicated combatants can be perilous because of the effects of intoxication, long-term abuse, or withdrawals.[59] Early efforts to disarm Liberia's warring factions were fraught with danger owing to the widespread drug abuse by the fighters who used a variety of traditional, transshipped, and looted drugs for stimulation, reward, recruitment, and relaxation.[60] UN peacekeepers in the eastern Democratic Republic of the Congo (DRC) demolished four camps belonging to armed rebel militias and seized drugs, uniforms, and women's clothing used for disguises.[61] These problems are exacerbated by the already loose nature of the command structure of many of these forces, and commanders often have little means to limit the amount and type of drugs that their fighters consume.

Drug financing of warring groups also complicates command and control issues for rebels and warlords and lessens their reliability in guaranteeing the parameters of ceasefire agreements. As previously discussed, the drug trade creates numerous opportunities for fighters with various levels of commitment to the movement's cause to earn money by extracting or transporting drugs themselves or to extort money from those who do. As a result, there is "a reduced level of discipline and central control in the armed forces of the party that controls the resource."[62] Elements of SL involved in coca production consistently rejected the codes of conduct set down by the national organization and would desert the movement, "fleeing soon after collecting taxes on the coca trade."[63] The devolution of authority allowed the leadership of these wayward groups to resist efforts by the national movement to constrain their behavior.[64]

The drug trade adds to the degrees of difficulty to successfully achieving political stability and personal security by increasing the number of warring parties, soldiers, and opportunities for "spoilers." By increasing the number of warring parties, "strategies become less predictable, balances of power become more tenuous, and alliances become more fluid."[65] As seen with the cases of SL, the FARC, UWSA, MDAA, and the Taliban, the drug trade creates opportunism for individual leaders, which often leads to the factionalization of the national movement. Myanmar confronted twenty armed groups, made peace with thirteen, but still violently confronts the remaining seven that maintain links to the drug trade in the Golden Triangle. Militias that are started or supported by a government's use of drug profits to combat insurgents also add more actors to the conflict who may not be willing to go along with conflict-resolution approaches or to decommission themselves. Colombia's right-wing United Self Defense Forces (AUC) has actually fought guerrillas over drug spoils and were not willing to accept the peace feelers put out by the Pastrana administration.

The ability to participate in the illegal narcotics trade can increase the number of forces available to a warring group, prolonging a conflict and diminishing the chances of bringing about political stability and personal security. With the explosion of poppy growth generating more profits, the Taliban have been able to launch attacks involving battalion-sized units of one thousand men and receive more local support than they did four years ago.[66] Such an increase in forces along with new sanctuaries in Pakistan contributed to the 200 percent rise in attacks against NATO and Afghan government forces by the end of 2006.[67] The drug trade allowed Khun Sa to maintain a 10,000 man army and resist Burmese military offensives over decades of conflict. The potential for continued violence not only increases, but the attempt to verify and monitor the actions of a numerous belligerents poses greater demands in conflicts. Cheating on agreements can be more successful if there are too few resources dedicated to demobilization.[68] The lack of a deep, sustained commitment to economic recovery occurring alongside the decommissioning of arms has led many fighters and their supporters to cheat on agreements to limit their criminal activities. Many young people who are involved in the conflicts often go to the cities after the fighting ends, and because of lack of employment involve themselves in the trafficking and use of prohibited substances. Those who stay in the villages attempt to improve their economic situation by cultivating drug crops.

The presence of elements seeking to "spoil" any agreement is also strengthened by the drug economy. As mentioned previously, many individual fighters who join insurgent groups in narcotized conflicts are opportunists and did not join the ranks of a warring group for any political cause. Asking them to surrender their weapons as part of a political settlement is fraught with risk. Rather than mere cheating, they actively seek to wreck the parameters of a negotiation or agreement. Government forces can also be unreliable and act as spoilers if members have become corrupted by the drug trade. As they were fighting the insurgency, the Peruvian military gradually joined forces with drug-running criminal organizations and actually reached accommodations with the guerrillas over drug profits.[69] If warring groups and their supporters are not convinced that their security—physical, economic, or social—will be preserved in the future, they will see drugs as one of the guarantors of survival. If one is craving certainty, drug crops, transportation routes, and smuggling can provide a sense of security. Imposing the terms of a settlement on their own forces and supporters becomes harder for commanding officers and is likely to prolong the conflict as a result.

PERSISTENT CHALLENGES TO CONFLICT RESOLUTION
AND NATION-BUILDING DUE TO DRUGS

Even in conflicts with lower levels of drug influence and a minimal degree of drug use among combatants, mafias, transnational criminal organizations, insurgents, soldiers, and police have been engaged in the drug trade as a way to further their respective political or personal interests. Ideology does not tell the whole story of these conflicts. In many cases, it is a question of whether warring groups have the desire or the ability to bring about the conditions for any sort of good faith negotiations that may lead to genuine conflict resolution opportunities.

The inadequacies of traditional conflict resolution and nation-building techniques in such contexts can be attributed to the uncertain position of drugs in approaches to resolve conflicts. Because drugs are unlike legal commodities or familiar resources that are used in war, they are often viewed as a minor concern. Yet, drugs are entirely within the criminal realm and make warring groups more accustomed to operating in the shadows and sinews of the legal economy, which makes understanding the depths of their involvement in the narcotics trade difficult for governments and outside agencies to assess. Even in cases where the depth of a warring group's participation in the drug trade is well-known, the main approach is to stop the killing and treat drug links as inconvenient, but not crucial, to any ceasefire or peace agreement. The dilemma is stark—end violent challenges to governmental authority by accepting a group's drug-dealing activities or attack a group's drug links and potentially prolong the violence. It is easy to understand why golden parachutes have been given to rebel leaders as a way out of the immediate dilemma.

Resolving such a dilemma with a golden parachute does not necessarily tackle the underlying sources of the conflict but deepens the forces of warlordism, sustains the patterns of a wartime economy, disempowers many citizens, and lays the foundation for future challenges to political stability and personal security. Corruption often penetrates governmental institutions when golden parachutes are accepted. Bribes are given to officials to overlook certain plots, while those who cannot afford bribes and live under government control feel unfairly penalized.[70] In these cases, such conditions further muddle the ability to understand the political objectives of warring groups in highly narcotized conflicts, making even temporary cessation of hostilities more difficult to accomplish even in the short term.

In cases where the government and others outside the conflict choose to solve the dilemma through force, politicians often create confusion by arguing over where military efforts should be directed. When Plan Colombia was established, the Colombian government preferred to focus on the insurgency, while the U.S. government, who funded the plan, was leery of involving itself in counterinsurgency operations that were akin "to another Vietnam" and, therefore, wanted to focus on curtailing cocaine production and export to the United States. For the Colombian government, "profits earned by the FARC from narcotrafficking connections certainly played a pivotal role in their ability to sustain operations; Colombian analysis suggested that drug trafficking could not be shut down *if the insurgency were not first defeated*."[71] Afghanistan also stands as an example of militaries and law-enforcement agencies operating at cross-purposes. Gen. James Jones, strategic commander for NATO forces, has stated that "we have kind of a generally accepted mantra that narcotics is not a military problem."[72] He added, "[Y]ou will not see NATO troops burning poppy fields. This is not our mandate."[73] Meanwhile, an official from the U.S. Drug Enforcement Administration said that to be effective in Afghanistan, "we have to work with the military because they have the assets to get us from point A to point B. There are some issues there; [the relationship] could be better."[74]

Counterinsurgency operations can also become easily blurred by counternarcotics activities with little appreciation of the enhanced nuance of the situation. Many scholars are correct when they look at a conflict like the one in Afghanistan and exclaim that countering the booming narcotics industry in Central Asia is "therefore a sine qua non for the success of counterterrorism in the region."[75] For the established authority, to be an insurgent is to be a criminal. Yet, not all criminals are insurgents, and the response to drug trafficking in countries in conflict makes this distinction important. Counternarcotics operations are routinely divorced from the larger policies aimed at ending political violence, creating a type of second front for military forces to fight.

The converse is also the case in other conflicts; military successes can undermine anti-drug efforts. The balloon effect and hydra-effect permit warring groups to avoid defeat. In situations where government forces have achieved, or have attempted to achieve, battlefield victories over insurgent groups and reclaimed territory where drug production supported rebels, drug production was moved and guerrilla leaders went into exile or were replaced. In Colombia, victories reclaiming drug territory from rebels have only led to increases in drug production in other areas of the nation, while increased military operations against the FARC have dispersed the leadership to neighboring countries. Over the last few years, the FARC-controlled area of Putumayo marked a decline in the coca growth from 60,000 hectares to 17,000 hectares because of pressure from the Colombian military. However, the Narino area, which has not witnessed the same military pressure, saw an increase in coca growth from 3,000 hectares to 60,000.[76]

Even in areas where victories have been achieved by professional militaries against drug-financed rebels, the need to gain the allegiance of the local population becomes essential to holding and securing the area. However, to mobilize rural peasants on behalf of government interests, the strategy of the military has been, in some cases, to officially or unofficially acquiesce to the continued peasant drug cultivation practices without the "taxation" placed on them by the insurgent group. However, as the insurgency continues in other areas of the nation, government forces have begun to tax the peasants once again and subject them to arbitrary abuse for their continued support of the rebellion. In such circumstances, peasants are victims of an ongoing cycle of violence that is not easy to break without external intervention.[77]

As seen in chapter 3, UN peacekeeping personnel have consumed drugs while on missions to assist the implementation of peace agreements. Such episodes are an exception and have not affected the overall success of peacekeeping missions. In fact, new research on the influence of outside forces on peacemaking and nation-building suggests that states that have had sustained peacekeeping forces in a country in conflict are more likely to emerge as democracies, while those that have not lapse into autocracy.[78] However, the power of the drug economy can still skew the long-term sustainability of any democratic political arrangements worked out by the warring parties. A democratic form of government offers little protection against the ongoing influence of the drug economy that was present during the conflict. New democracies, and a few established democracies fighting insurgencies as well, are vulnerable to the influence of a drug-financed warring group's penetration and corruption of the state. Formerly excluded voices and new constituencies are able to join the jockeying for political power. Maintaining the allegiance of these new constituencies is crucial to keeping the peace or moving the democratic process forward. Nonetheless, new actors seek to ensure that their interests are met by the new political arrangements and can use newfound outlets in government to thwart policies and actions that are detrimental to their benefits. As seen with the power of the drug trafficking in wartime economies, the economic benefits it provides are difficult to relinquish. In fact, the established government will go beyond offering golden parachutes to rebel leaders and warlords and offer them prominent positions in government. Afghan President Karzai has included an anti-corruption chief who is a well-known drug dealer and several former rebel leaders in his cabinet who have known drug ties.[79] Such inclusion has hampered both counterinsurgency and counternarcotics operations, making his new government seem corrupt and his leadership incompetent.

These types of conflicts blur hard and soft security issues. Yet, soft issues like local economic development, public health, and psychological treatment are given a back seat. Governments in conflicts with higher levels of the drug trade's influence are under political and financial pressures. Few governments that seek to end a war and reconstruct society can balance the ways and means to handle rebels and fund needed social programs. There have been few programs that help child soldiers cope with drug addiction and mental health issues associated with combat, which would help reintegrate them into society. Moreover, the detoxification of children and veterans is not a focus in the search for solutions to the conflict itself.

Routinely perplexing to interveners is the plight of drug farmers whose consent to any agreement is key to ending the influence of a wartime drug economy. Ending drug farmers' dependence on the wartime market has proven to be exceptionally difficult. Crop substitution programs have failed in many areas because of drug baron coercion and the limited profitability of legitimate crops. This added layer of complexity for nation-building operations is evident since persuading drug farmers, who were extremely poor before their participation in drug cultivation, to abandon growing such lucrative crops has proven exceptionally difficult in the conflicts of Colombia, Peru, Afghanistan, and Myanmar. Tragically, many efforts to end conflicts through economic programs only reinforce the conditions of violence or set the stage for a return to violence when outside military forces have left. Market adjustment programs promoted by the World Bank and IMF to build societal economic linkages to the international market tend to create economic incentives for continued participation of warring groups in the drug trade.

> Wages tend to fall, both because of rising employment caused by demand contraction and because of real devaluation that raises the costs of imports. Fiscal entrenchment, in the form of increased taxes and reduced government subsidies, tends to have a regressive effect, because the easiest taxes to raise and collect are often sales and value-added taxes which fall more heavily on lower income consumers.[80]

Such effects of programs on an economic system can spawn economic dislocation, political unrest, and violence, which only reinforce the power of warring groups and warlords who offer consistent payment and relative economic stability. [81]

Most strikingly, international development institutions, such as the World Bank and IMF, interpret the illicit activity of belligerents as a sign that greater economic liberalization is required. Drug trafficking and other criminal activities are seen as a form of popular resistance, patrimonial corruption, and state inefficiency; they are cast as a revolt of the underclass against the problems of underdevelopment.[82] The expansion of economic reform and the lifting of market restrictions remains the solution. As seen, such policies empower warring groups or allow them to transform into organized criminal syndicates. Attempts to monitor the transition of a wartime economy by implementing international observation of tax collection and the establishment of escrow funds within countries of conflict are undermined by the drug economy. Because of its lack of transparency, the drug economy allows many groups in incipient, developing, and serious levels of conflicts to follow a double agenda of peace transition and rearmament, largely without the knowledge of monitoring agencies.

In nations with abeyant or settled conflicts, deciding on how to treat the actions of belligerents in combat is one matter, while their narcotics trafficking activities are another. Though amnesties, pardons, and prosecutions often occur for those who participated in political crimes, organized violence, and drug trafficking, much is dependent on the level of conflict narcotization. Although Truth and Reconciliation Commissions (TRCs), like the one in South Africa that experienced a low level of drug influence on its conflict, focus on activities related to ending or maintaining the apartheid system, drug crimes are routinely ignored. In Colombia's ongoing conflict, however, the decommissioning of 30,000 right-wing paramilitary members included an agreement not to extradite those who were involved in drug trafficking to the United States if they confessed to human rights abuses and gave details of smuggling routes and contacts.[83]

Almost every nation-building enterprise has included programs to construct liberal market democracies and to do so as quickly as possible.[84] The hope is to "shift societal conflicts away from the battlefield to the ballot box, thereby replacing breaking heads with counting heads."[85] Even though many states have made the transition away from high levels of internal violence while accepting many democratic practices and constructing liberal institutions, their governments still remain fragile because of ongoing political links to the drug trade that were forged during the conflict. Newly emerging democratic governments that are transitioning into an abeyant status are still economically and financially susceptible to the dynamics of the drug trade. To build institutions, fund the military, and carry out needed social programs to gain legitimacy and maintain order are expensive propositions for new political actors. Drug trafficking has contributed to the treasuries of many post-conflict governments. Many new democracies emerging after years of violence are also developing countries whose

> governments are often less concerned about the source of foreign exchange and more about political survival.... The great influx of foreign exchange afforded by criminal activity assists economic development and therefore relieves governments of some of the urgency of meeting citizens demands. Some governments are thus increasingly finding that it is easier to look the other way than attempt to cut off the money source.[86]

The history of the illegal narcotics trade and wars of national liberation during the Cold War reveal that many newly independent governments are cash-strapped because of the ravages of war and will, therefore, engage in the drug trade more seriously. After the communists seized power in Laos in 1973, the government increased opium production. One important Thai drug trafficker was issued a Laotian diplomatic passport to facilitate the drug trafficking to the West and was nicknamed "Minister of Heroin" by American counternarcotics agents.[87] The same phenomenon has occurred in conflicts after the Cold War. When the UN troops pulled out of Cambodia, "with its deep water port, and access to Phnom Penh and the waterways of the Mekong, a long-standing history of contraband networks and an administrative infrastructure controlled by ethnic Thai state of Cambodia officials with external business connections, [the province of] Koh Kong [that borders Thailand] has become a major launching pad for the drug-smuggling operations."[88] The drug-trafficking operations were so deep that the government became tainted by accusations that it was turning the country into "Medellin on the Mekong" because of its reputed ties to drug traffickers.[89]

A DIFFICULT HABIT TO BREAK

The unique qualities of drug-influenced conflicts present obstacles to traditional understandings of the source and conduct of wars and how to bring them to an end. Such obstacles to conflict resolution and nation-building, including the dynamics of the drug trade, the number and types of actors that comprise wartime economy, sustain warlordism, weaken local power, and create patterns of political instability and personal insecurity, represent new avenues for scholars, policymakers, and military leaders to explore.

In many important ways, the drug trade and contemporary warfare no longer follow separate and autonomous patterns; they are intertwined, and attempting to separate them into independent spheres for action has not proven successful. Attempts to conduct counterinsurgency operations at the expense of counternarcotics operations, and vice versa, are testaments to the near indivisibility of these spheres in many of today's conflicts. In the cases of coca and opium crop cultivation, armed conflict now appears to be a prerequisite.[90] Since it is unlikely that the drug trade and warfare will evolve in a manner that separates one from the other, it is likely that the number and intensity of these types of conflicts will not diminish in the near future.

Contemporary conflicts contain many warring groups whose involvement in open violence and criminality blur traditional understandings of war and crime, presenting a significant challenge to the sharp lines drawn between law enforcement and military actions. Drug trafficking and drug use are more commonly classified as criminal activity, which is viewed as "a domestic problem; and law enforcement and national security are based on very different philosophies, organization structures and legal frameworks."[91] Counternarcotics efforts are being run by both police agencies and militaries but for different purposes. This dichotomy has often frustrated conflict resolution, while nation-building efforts have fallen between the fissures of the two. Yet, incorporating military calculations has not been routinely incorporated into drug-policy considerations in assessments of how attacking one stage in the trafficking of a drug affects the levels of political violence in a state or region. For example, counternarcotics programs like crop eradication can create conditions for increased violence among warring groups that will try to secure the profit margins of the remaining crops. Cases in Afghanistan and Colombia demonstrate the volatile effects of counternarcotics efforts on violent conflicts. Traffickers change routes and move their product through countries in conflict or that have emerged from conflict, thus affecting stability. Leaders, foot soldiers, smugglers, middlemen, retailers, and even drug farmers are easily replaced. The balloon effect and the hydra-effect have had serious and similar consequences for conflict resolution efforts in Andean countries, the Golden Crescent, and the Golden Triangle.

Conversely, attempts to limit large-scale violence where narcotized conflicts are occurring create effects on regional patterns of drug production and distribution. Military operations can open a society to the pernicious nature of drug trafficking in new and unanticipated ways. The failure of U.S. and coalition forces to establish order in post-Saddam Iraq allowed the country to emerge as a new transshipment point for heroin.[92] Insurgents and militias in Iraq have been able to gain funding by facilitating the product's journey to Europe, thereby fueling the ongoing violence and instability.[93]

Nonetheless, there is room to garner lessons from experiences in these conflicts. By looking at a conflict's unique qualities, outlines of contemporary war are made clearer, allowing for the design of better approaches toward tackling them.

5

SOBER LESSONS FOR THE FUTURE
The Dynamics of Drug-Fueled Conflicts

DRUG-FINANCED WARRING GROUPS AND INTOXICATED COMBATANTS COMBINE to stymie conflict resolution and nation-building efforts. However, few scholars, decision makers, and military leaders have examined, analyzed, and assessed the lessons drawn from the patterns of conflicts that are influenced by the drug trade. Preferring to focus on the drug trade and armed conflict separately, many acknowledge that each creates serious, multilayered, and profound effects on international security. The effects of the drug trade on contemporary wars have also been studied independently, as if the drug trade did not contribute to them in some manner. The proliferation of small weapons and light arms, diminishing of sovereignty, abuse of human rights, corruption of government institutions, denigration of legitimate agriculture, degeneration of public health, and protraction of organized violence are exacerbated by both drug trafficking and drug use by combatants and contribute powerfully to the dimensions of many of today's conflicts. Attempts to place the causes of these effects into discrete categories of drug trafficking or contemporary war would be theoretically unsound and practically infeasible in many cases covered in this book. Amid the study of these phenomena, drug-fueled conflicts have been overlooked or the role of drugs in war downplayed, making it no surprise that few people have looked at lessons to be drawn from these military clashes.

Such wide-ranging and compound effects on war, and by extension international security, that stem from the drug trade's influence have created an unfamiliar international landscape for scholars, policymakers, and military. Chapter 4 reveals that drug-fueled conflicts often produce a wartime economy alongside local disempowerment and steadily diminishing political stability and personal security. Ranks become filled with opportunists rather than dedicated fighters, making war and violence a natural state of affairs whose benefits are not easily subjected to traditional negotiation techniques or coercive strategies. In such conflict environments, understanding what these groups value and the goals they seek becomes increasingly murky, as do the approaches to bring the violence to an end and to begin societal reconstruction. Atrocities committed against non-combatants by ill-trained, irregular fighters are often seen as strategically necessary by their commanders in internal conflicts where the national demography is a central issue, atrocities that are made easier by drug consumption. Although military doctrine and professional military operations are beginning to take drugged combatants into account in narcotized conflicts, these are tactical adjustments that have not been matched by strategic reassessments and reappraisals of the relationship between drugs and warfare. The drug trade and warfare have been pushed into a closer relationship by the lack of the overarching global superpower competition, asymmetrical nature of contemporary wars, changes in the patterns of the drug trade, and increasing pace of globalization. These factors have strengthened the allure of the modern drug-trafficking business and allowed violent political groups to profit from it more directly and more actively than before, while also supplying drugs for the steady demand of combatant consumption. The seemingly intertwined nature of drug trafficking and contemporary warfare demonstrates its strength in situations where conflicts prove highly resistant to political settlements or military victories. As discussed in the previous chapter, drug-financed combatant groups and drugged fighters create significant problems for conflict resolution and any subsequent nation-building efforts, although many view drug-fueled conflicts as variations of resource-driven wars. Thus, traditional and increasingly obsolescent approaches are still influential, while valuable lessons that have been accrued over time are overlooked.

This conceptual gap has had practical consequences, yet this does not mean that there cannot be any clearer understanding of drug-fueled conflicts. Their unfamiliarity does not completely undermine efforts to gain conceptual clarity or doom all attempts to resolve them. In fact, there are numerous lessons that can be learned from these conflicts that suggest various ways to build solid foundations for their analysis and assessment. Creating and implementing better strategies designed to come to grips with them are critical to managing the international security environment of the future.

Although not all drug-fueled conflicts are the same, broad and specific lessons can be drawn. As seen in previous chapters, different drugs, different nodes in drug trafficking, and the different types of drugs consumed still point to lessons that reflect the overarching patterns and trends inherent in cases where the drug trade and armed conflict intertwine. Many of these lessons are "uncomfortable" because of their lack of familiar conformity to the traditional understandings of armed conflict or to their counterintuitive nature for those who have long and deep experience in foreign policy, military operations, international relations, diplomatic history, or security studies. The lessons can be grouped under three broad categories: the dynamics of the intersection, the strategic use of drugs, and responses to drug-fueled conflicts.

THE DYNAMICS OF THE INTERSECTION

Lessons from the drug trade are drawn from the evolving quality of the intersection of drugs and contemporary warfare—what each does to the other and how both affect international security. It is a mutually reinforcing relationship that constantly generates new forms and phases of conflict, which, in turn, creates new drug avenues. The dynamics of such a relationship point to the ways it challenges the conventional wisdom of many people who deal with contemporary armed conflicts.

Diminishing Separation Between Drugs and Warfare

The growing indivisibility of the drug trade and contemporary warfare has had implications for the treatment of conflicts in many contexts. Policymakers continue to try to separate drug trafficking and armed conflict; the separation of the two phenomena has practical consequences. Neither law enforcement nor military efforts alone have successfully ended violence or stemmed the flow of narcotics. The Madrid train bombings, which were funded by drug sales, are one example of the disastrous effects when law enforcement and military efforts are separated. Policy recommendations that are derived from the study of such conflicts still include separate approaches. For example, an influential Parliament of Canada report argues for actions divided under the categories "In the Fight against Drugs" and "In the Field of Conflict Prevention and Resolution."[1]

Some militaries in democracies in the developed world that participate in counternarcotics efforts participate as auxiliary forces and rarely examine the strategic effects of their actions on conflicts. As the United States continues its wars in Afghanistan and Iraq, the military is pulling back from its long-standing commitment to helping interdict drugs entering North America.[2] These efforts are viewed as separate events with military action only affecting counterdrug efforts. While the withdrawal of U.S. troops from their commitment to help interdict drugs will work to the drug smugglers' advantage, it will also probably shape the fighting in several conflicts in Latin America where warring groups might increase production and assist traffickers in finding new routes.

Conversely, counterdrug agencies are finding themselves on the short end of budget appropriations because of seemingly larger demands of counterterrorism. The FBI and U.S. Customs Service, which is now part of U.S. Customs and Border Protection, have redirected their drug enforcement activities to concentrate on terrorism.[3] Rather than seeking ways to integrate efforts that trace terrorist drug finances and interdict drugs, each is divided with financing placed under terrorism and interdiction efforts relegated to law enforcement.

Even attempts to blend efforts among multiple agencies have not quelled violence in ongoing conflicts, such as Colombia, Afghanistan, and Myanmar. These attempts usually run at cross-purposes, with counterinsurgency operating at the expense of counternarcotics activities and vice versa. Part of the lack of success is the temptation for policymakers to look for "cause and effect" phenomena as a way to guide their efforts. For example, James O'Gara, deputy director for Supply Reduction at the White House Office of National Drug Control Policy, argued, "Afghanistan produces opium because some regions remain under attack and lack security."[4] Is it the lack of security, the ravages of war, the underdevelopment of the nation that is the source of Afghanistan's opium economy, or does the opium economy feed the violence? Attempting to pinpoint a single cause, or set of causes, privileges one policy approach over another while downplaying the near indivisibility of drugs and warfare in highly narcotized conflicts. Stability cannot be gained without development, and security is required for development.

Intellectually and practically, hard and soft security issues are still separated by those who examine drug-fueled conflicts and seek their resolution—killing or capturing combatants, agricultural reform, and treatment for drug abuse are not viewed with the same priority or are coordinated by one institution or agency of government. "Democracy and human rights are not big ticket items" when it comes to finding a middle ground between counterinsurgency and counternarcotics plans.[5] As a result, there is little coordination with lower levels of government that are responsible for meeting the daily concerns of citizens. Mayors and local police forces are often excluded from discussions regarding countrywide security and development strategies, yet are also the primary targets in narcotized conflicts.

The situation is further complicated when outside powers intervene. Decision-making becomes more complicated and convoluted, failing to address many issues and creating new, cascading effects. The U.S. five-pillar program in Afghanistan, which focuses on eradication, interdiction, law enforcement, alternative livelihoods, and public information, does not include a macro-economic policy. As such, local criminal groups and warlords have been able to fill the void, once again fueling the resurgence of the Taliban. There are also constant bureaucratic tangles among the North Atlantic Treaty Organization (NATO), the International Security Assistance Force (ISAF), non-governmental organizations (NGOs), and the Afghan government.

Ideology—No Barrier to Drug Trafficking

The ideological tenets of nationalism, liberalism, communism, socialism, and radical Islam do not prevent armed groups from funding their causes through the drug trade or restrain individual fighters consuming mind-altering substances. Desire to stay true to a political cause and fear of being labeled a hypocrite have not served as inhibitions. Although Mao Zedong prohibited his forces from drinking alcohol or consuming opium (an "unpatriotic" habit), he still allowed funds from opium growing and smuggling to fill his coffers. Acts that appear contradictory to a warring group's rhetoric are dismissed as part of what must be done to prevail against an enemy. The Chinese Nationalists openly justified their use of drug profits by stating, "necessity has no law. That is why we deal with opium [because] we have to continue to fight the evil of communism."[6] Groups tied to radical Islam feel similarly; the seemingly theological contradiction of cultivating, producing, selling, and consuming drugs in battle is mitigated by the belief that their actions are harming the enemy by wearing away the morale and will of the adversary's society. As seen in chapter 3, ideology has been used to justify smuggling drugs into an enemy society or to enemy troops in the field as a way to affect an adversary's will. Although these acts have not been proven effective, they offer justification for a combatant group to enter into drug-trafficking activities. What is bad for the enemy is good for the community of faith.

As discussed in chapter 2, rebel groups and terrorists are typically pushed underground because of their desire to alter the nature of the state and must obtain money to buy arms and recruit followers. Because governments systematically attack open sources of funding, criminal schemes like involvement in narcotics trafficking become a last resort for opposition groups. While many political causes fall by the wayside in drug-fueled conflicts of high intensity, warring groups in lower intensity levels generally maintain political cohesion. In those conflicts where a political program is still identifiable, warring groups have nonetheless participated in drug trafficking to remain viable and have justified their criminal schemes as a necessary evil.

Some groups involved in conflicts at higher intensity levels have used ideology to garner legitimacy, and they indulge in the drug trade for purely financial motives. Radical armed groups in Pakistan have a "veneer of Islam" that makes it "very difficult to discredit these parties" as they continue their drug-trafficking activities.[7] "Profit through crime" becomes a greater motivation for the continuation of the movement.[8] As discussed in chapter 4, when participation in the drug trade deepens, political activities of rebel groups decline. The result is that the political consciousness of the masses they purport to guard is also reduced, ripening the environment for warlordism and widespread human rights abuses.

Combatant drug consumption is no longer a large step for many involved in contemporary wars. Some people assume that Islam's theological proscription against intoxication prevents the consumption of narcotics by jihadists who are committed to a "purer" form of Islam. Thus, some people believe that these groups limit their participation to merely trafficking narcotics as part of their cause to undermine their enemies. "Just as 'puritanical' communists of decades past were willing to traffic in narcotics even if they would never allow their legal sale and use, modern self-proclaimed 'jihadis' are proving willing to be traffickers—just not users."[9] However, the cases of the mujahedin in Afghanistan, the Chechen terrorists in Beslan, and the members of al Qaeda in Iraq prove that this assumption is incorrect. Ideology, in some cases, is actually more likely to support both the trafficking and consumption of drugs, while trafficking supports a group's long-term struggle to undermine an enemy's society, consuming drugs supports short-term goals, such as increasing combat courage when facing enemy forces.

Ideologically motivated groups have carved out exceptions or drawn distinctions between their actions and the actions of others—much like elements of Sendero Luminoso (SL) when they forbid drug farmers from consuming liquor but allowed them and the troops to consume coca. Much as engaging in the drug trade is seen as justifiable given the nature of the enemy, committing atrocities against non-combatants is equally acceptable and made easier when combatants are intoxicated. Phenomena like looting hospitals, clinics, and pharmacies and taking advantage of smuggling operations to gain drugs to consume before rampages against civilian populations become more explainable.

A Reason for an Increased Level of Violence

Typically, increased fighting between combatant groups has been interpreted as a signal that the conflict has entered a new phase. However, in drug-fueled conflicts, increased levels of violence can be the product of turf wars over drugs. With drug crops, crop space, smuggling routes, labs, manpower, and expertise forming the war-making backbone of many groups in narcotized conflicts, violence is not necessarily directed at traditional military targets. Violence can be directed over tactical objectives of the drug-trafficking network, or as part of a larger strategic effort to foment disorder to gain advantage in the drug market.

When violence in drug-fueled conflicts has risen, drug-trafficking stakes were often in jeopardy. As covered in chapter 2, no matter the drug, they all require transportation to the next stage of distribution to go to market.

> If at many points along the road each locally powerful rebel, off-duty army officer, or official exacts a charge in an uncoordinated way, then combined extractions can be so high that they make exporting unprofitable: The competitive predation simply kills the activity....If there is no trade, there is no loot. To prevent this, rebel groups will try to create a monopoly of predation, and for this it must generate a monopoly of rebel violence.[10]

To gain this monopoly, a warring group seeks to eliminate another group or seize the needed portion of the transportation infrastructure. Atrocities in Colombia committed by right-wing paramilitaries and left-wing guerrillas were often the products of turf wars over drug spoils rather than military actions that advanced a political agenda. Tactical operations often serve strategic goals that appear more criminal in nature.

As discussed in chapter 3, looting pharmacies, clinics, and hospitals often presages carnival activities. The subsequent atrocities and human rights abuses have occurred when warring groups have swept into enemy territory where civilians were present. Violence has increased when raiding groups form belligerent parties when their supply of drugs is cut off. Withdrawal symptoms affect judgment while prolonged usage increases paranoia. Given these strong physiological symptoms, sharp increases in violence can occur in the short term.

Strategic Targets—Hospitals, Clinics, and Pharmacies

The consumable nature of drugs separates them from how other resource-driven conflicts affect the dimensions of violence. As seen in chapter 3, atrocities against civilians can be part of a warring group's strategy to realize its political goals or part of its desire to protect its financial interests that have little to do with its ideological agenda. Acts of seeming barbarity have important effects for commanders. However, these acts are often facilitated by the consumption of drugs, which are consumed for various uses and often looted from institutions that have stocks of pharmaceutical drugs. Although attacking medical centers to gain access to medical treatment or affect enemy morale are abiding features of modern wars, medical centers are also attacked now because of the need to supply combatant drug demand so they can carry out further atrocities to meet campaign objectives.

ATS Drugs—The Most Fungible Drugs in Warfare

Opium and cocaine cannot be grown anywhere. Marijuana and hashish, while more robust, require large quantities for profit. ATS drugs are becoming the "chameleon drug" that can change based on the environment of a particular conflict. Such distinctions have major impacts on the nature of a narcotized conflict. In reversals of fortune, groups have turned to ATS drugs to supplement other financial schemes of warring groups. ATS drugs are advantageous because of their ability to compensate for reversals of fortune that do not occur as a result of a battlefield defeat or change in the drug trade. Because they can be produced more clandestinely, ATS drugs have been an alternative source of funding when the government or law enforcement has seized finances or uncovered other funding sources. The compressed trafficking network of ATS drugs can also be advantageous because it allows a warring group to collect profits directly and move drugs quickly.

ATS drugs are profitable like heroin and cocaine, but they are geographically boundless. Although ATS drugs are highly compartmentalized, they are not limited to a particular region. The market for them tends to be more localized with fewer middlemen. In order to profit, warring groups are almost forced to participate in the retail level of sales. For example, the Drug Enforcement Administration (DEA) reported that revenue from a methamphetamine trafficking ring run by Middle Eastern nationals in the Midwest of the United States filled the coffers of Hezbollah.[11] Because of the long network trail to bring heroin and cocaine to market, street-level retail sales for warring groups in source countries is highly constrained.

However, ATS drugs do have disadvantages. Because of the compressed nature of ATS trafficking, warring groups must compete more keenly in smaller markets where locals have already set up operations. Participation at the street level has a downside for those involved in their trafficking: the possibility of market saturation if there are many competing ATS pushers. Such street-level participation can lead to a rise in street violence in cities where diasporic communities linked to warring groups in their home countries fight local gangs for control over a small market. This, too, has been mitigated by the fact that ATS drugs, as previously mentioned, only need to generate enough profit to supplement other resources. They are neither the sole revenue source for any warring group nor do they comprise a major share of any warring group's funding. Therefore, violence over ATS stakes has tended to be in the demand countries and has not figured into increasing the level of narcotization of the central conflict.

Streamlining the Drug Trade

The drug-trade supply chain has been integrating because of warring groups' participation near drug crops. Farmers in Colombia, Peru, Myanmar, and Afghanistan are increasingly involved in processing their crops into narcotics. This has been done under the auspices of insurgent groups that have access to expertise, technology, and chemicals to process the harvests the same way criminal middlemen used to. Insurgent groups, who are well armed and in closer proximity to the crops, can better dictate the terms of their participation than criminal groups who had the processing functions outsourced to them. Crop harvests are decreasingly being processed in clandestine labs far removed from the conflict zones. In some cases, the criminal middlemen have been completely cut out of trafficking arrangements, leaving more profits for the warring group.

STRATEGIC USE OF DRUGS

Warring groups, exploiting opportunities made available by globalization, have created the dynamics of the intersection between drugs and warfare. In turn, the connection between the drug trade and armed conflict creates new opportunities for warring groups to exploit. Rather than being a unidirectional arrow, it is a reinforcing relationship that will continue to grow stronger. The various ways combatants have utilized drugs demonstrates the conditions under which warring groups will further their participation in the illicit narcotics trade and how the intersection between drugs and warfare will be strengthened in the future.

Drugs Both Aid and Comprise Asymmetric Strategies

Most contemporary wars are fought by combatant groups who employ asymmetric strategies designed to leverage their military weaknesses to defeat a militarily superior adversary.

Rebels, insurgents, terrorists, and paramilitaries rely on popular support, greater will, the weakness of the adversary's society, and external support to draw out a conflict rather than meeting a militarily superior force in quick, decisive, and open battles of maneuver. Drug trafficking and drug use enable asymmetric strategies.

As seen with cases in Myanmar, Peru, Colombia, and Afghanistan, irregular groups can garner support from peasants by allowing them to grow their traditional drug crops free from government eradication efforts, which encourages them to grow drug crops rather than less profitable crops, negotiate prices with traffickers, as well as transport and protect harvests. Although some conditions of warlordism are difficult for peasants to endure, few options are left to farmers. In transit countries, transshipped drugs offer employment opportunities in areas where the government has been unable to provide meaningful employment or development.

Drugs can also aid the will of a warring group in numerous ways. Asymmetric strategies do not always seek to attack "hard" targets, preferring "soft" targets where civilian casualties are more probable. In such contexts, drug use can stimulate the desire to fight, reward combatants, and ease combat stress. Drug funds can also be used to pay fighters and purchase more sophisticated weaponry, adding to a group's esprit de corps.

As discussed in chapter 3, drug running is used as a way to damage an adversary's morale and society. However, when weaker groups smuggle drugs into an enemy society that is developed, drug smuggling figures into the weaker group's analysis of the enemy's vulnerability. Developed countries are largely democracies, and many rebel and terrorist groups view democracies as inherently unable to sustain a military commitment in a protracted conflict that a group employing an asymmetric strategy wants to provoke. Drug proceeds and drug-stimulated attacks allow a warring group to sustain itself and create conditions that are not palatable to democracies that seek short military engagements with minimal casualties for their forces and low collateral damage. Recruitment of children via addiction is also a way to challenge the moral and ethical boundaries of militaries from developed nations.

Links to drug traffickers can make up for a lack of external support or add to already existing support. Many irregular forces begin a conflict without access to the type of military hardware required to mount a successful challenge against better-armed government forces. The drug funding can provide a group with more weapons and more recruits, which sometimes has outstripped the troop strength and firepower of government forces. Such manning and equipping has often led to ceasefires or golden-parachute agreements. Because of the compartmentalized nature of drug trafficking, warring groups have been able to keep their external support flowing through regional arrangements; the tentacles of a wartime economy reach far beyond the borders of a narcotized conflict. External support from the drug trade can also be used to purchase outside expertise from other violent groups. For example, the Irish Republican Army (IRA) operatives apprehended in Colombia's despeje were reportedly there to teach members of the Revolutionary Armed Forces of Colombia (FARC) how to conduct urban bombing campaigns.[12]

Drugs often enable important aspects of asymmetric strategies and become targets of these strategies as well. Drug crops, crop space, smuggling routes, labs, manpower, and expertise form the contemporary infrastructure of war-making efforts in many narcotized conflicts. Once again, it becomes difficult to categorize attacks against these infrastructure components as "military" or "criminal." Regardless, one result is that opposition groups often target infrastructure components, creating additional human suffering among civilians.

Drug Trade as a Reaction to Asymmetric Strategies

Governments that employ asymmetric strategies to fight irregular forces sometimes sanction participation in the drug trade as a way to "even the playing field." An autocratic government will use the drug trade to pay its military to fend off guerrilla challenges to its rule. Rwandan President Juvenal Habyarimana ran various criminal enterprises, including marijuana smuggling, to maintain and expand his power.[13]

Such participation in the drug trade has proven dangerous and often backfires. When uncovered, governments and militaries have paid a domestic political price and were viewed to be just as bad as their adversaries. Domestic and international support plummeted. When Turkish military support for drug-trafficking paramilitary groups engaged in attacks against the Kurdistan Workers' Party (PKK) was uncovered, this new information provided a propaganda victory for government opponents. Imperial Japan's opium trafficking that funded its operations against Chinese guerrillas was condemned by the League of Nations in the 1930s, and in the aftermath of World War II, 149 Japanese subjects were executed as war criminals for drug-related activities.[14] In addition, many of those involved have been tempted and personally enticed by personal monetary gain to engage in such a strategy. The lucrative nature of drug trafficking has corrupted many military commanders in narcotized conflicts who saw opportunities for personal enrichment rather than as a means to defeat a rebel group. In Afghanistan, Myanmar, Colombia, and Peru, many cases of military involvement in drug trafficking transformed from being a way to defeat an insurgency into military collusion with insurgents to maintain and expand drug-trafficking opportunities.

As drug trafficking has backfired on governments, such support for drug-trafficking activities has also backfired on government troops. In Vietnam, the activities of various covert agencies to support the transportation of heroin throughout Indochina helped supply the drug habits of many Western soldiers. By themselves, the protracted nature of asymmetric strategies presents drug-abuse dangers to government forces. As seen with the forces of France, Britain, the United States, and the USSR, troops use narcotics to deal with the hardships of long, repetitive tours of duty. Troops view drug use as a way to cope with various feelings, including fear, boredom, homesickness, and grief. As seen in chapter 3, abuse on the battlefield often creates anxiety back home about the effects of drug-addicted veterans returning to society. The fear of drug-addicted veterans undermines the popularity of these wars.

A Response to a Reversal of Fortune

Asymmetric strategies aside, warring groups have sought profits from the drug trade to compensate for battlefield losses of other important strategic resources. As mentioned previously, not all conflicts are funded by only one resource. Because of the low lootability and high obstructability of the conflicts, other resources have been more easily captured or blocked by opposition groups. When this has occurred, the loser has begun or increased its participation in drug trafficking. As covered in chapter 2, once Charles Taylor lost important areas of natural resources, he turned to drug trafficking as a way to keep money flowing to his military. Members of the National Union for the Total Independence of Angola (UNITA) did likewise during the 1990s when access to gemstones and oil resources was obstructed.[15] When members of the Khmer Rouge, who controlled access to mining and logging regions, negotiated a ceasefire with the Camdodian government, remaining members of the insurgency began to trade heroin to make up for the loss.[16]

The militaries of developing countries have proven to be especially vulnerable to the lures of the drug trade when the government is unable to pay them adequately. The longer a conflict runs, the more difficult it is for governments to consistently pay, equip, and train their forces. Without seeing battlefield results, outside powers grow wary of financing the government. When outside powers withdraw funds, military effectiveness suffers. In some incidences, underfunded military units have plundered areas under drug cultivation to make up for reduced budgets and lost wages.

The result of military participation in the drug trade, aside from diminished command and control occurring alongside a degeneration of civil-military relations, is growing international disapproval of the government. When militaries of underdeveloped countries are engaged in drug trafficking and fighting an insurgency, developed countries are placed in a dilemma of continuing to support a corrupt regime as well as drug trafficking or withdrawing support and weakening the effort against insurgents. A spiral effect occurs, for when government troops participate in the drug trade to make up for military weakness, less external financial support is provided as a sign of disapproval, which results in deeper military participation in the drug trade. For example, as Peru's poorly paid soldiers sought wealth from the drug trade, external support for the government's war against SL was threatened.

Groups Will Possibly Turn to ATS Drugs

When drug-trade profit is jeopardized, groups have demonstrated a willingness to engage in the production and distribution of other types of drugs. The compartmentalization of drug trafficking makes a warring group susceptible to changes in regional market forces. Changes in supply or in smuggling routes can affect not only a warring group's bottom line, but its ability to maintain its existence. Based on the type of drug and with networks already in place, it has not been very difficult for a group to traffic multiple drugs. In response to growing seizures of Mandrax, rebel groups in southern Africa are entering into cocaine smuggling and ATS drug production. Afghanistan's undercutting of the Myanmar opium industry has forced many groups in Myanmar to manufacture and distribute ATS drugs throughout Asia.[17]

RESPONSES TO DRUG-FUELED CONFLICTS

Reacting to drug-fueled conflicts has unveiled the difficulties conceptualizing them and designing appropriate strategies to end these conflicts or mitigate their effects. The dynamics of the intersection of drugs and warfare and the difficulty in responding to the strategic use of drugs in armed conflicts is vaguely understood. Embattled governments, neighboring states, regional organizations, military alliances, aid agencies, and international organizations have all struggled with the volatile nature of these conflicts. Several policies, programs, and campaigns have worsened the situation or have transformed the nature of the conflict into one where criminality has become the main threat to the national security of the post-conflict state.

Inherited Drug Problems

Outside powers and agencies that intervene in drug-fueled conflicts have been viewed as assuming the responsibility for curtailing drug trafficking and drug abuse problems within the target state. Those in the target state involved in narcotics trafficking begin to watch the actions of the intervening forces to gauge their effects on their livelihoods. Those citizens who are concerned about the levels of drug abuse and its associated criminality begin to place the burden of responsibility on the interveners and the political officials who the interveners support. Afghan President Karzai and NATO forces are increasingly seen as "forlorn figures" who are unable to break the cycle of violence or control opium production.[18]

While citizens are certain in their beliefs about who bears responsibility, issues arise between the interveners and the government of the target state over who is actually in charge of counternarcotics policies and actions. In Afghanistan, there has been constant friction between the United States and NATO officials on one side and the Afghan government on the other over aerial crop eradication. Early crop eradication efforts by the United States were viewed as a slap against Afghan sovereignty by local ministers, while the Afghan government's refusal to allow it made them appear to the United States and coalition nations as weak in the face of the power of drug barons. To interveners and the government, the drug trade,

with its vast regional connections and deep local entrenchment, acts as a nearly independent "spoiler" in conflict resolution and nation-building settings.

While outside powers intervening in drug-fueled conflicts have been viewed as responsible for curtailing the drug-trafficking and drug-abuse problems within the target state,
they are also held responsible for the repercussions in their own societies. Intervening
states have a dual burden thrust on them—they not only typically comprise the largest
component of force on the ground and are held responsible for the drug supply, they are
also mostly from demand countries where drug markets are located. As a result, many in its
domestic political arena believe it has the appropriate means and the sole responsibility of
reducing supply, because the warring state no longer has to rely on the good faith actions of
the local government to clamp down on drug production and trafficking. In 2006, a leading
congressman from the U.S. House of Representatives pressured Secretary of Defense Donald
Rumsfeld over the Afghan heroin issue stating that the U.S. military must do more to "take
out" drug kingpins and heroin processing centers.[19] This action was once again urged in
2007 after President Bush extended the tour of duty for thousands of U.S. forces in Afghanistan.[20]

With the compartmentalization of the heroin trade, Afghan poppy production feeds the
European heroin market more directly; the U.S. heroin market is supplied by Asia and Latin
America. As a result, the calls for more to be done to restrict Afghan drug trafficking have
been louder in Europe. In the United Kingdom, where heroin use in the streets of London is
viewed as a scourge, many politicians wanted the military to take a tougher stand when
British forces go more deeply into opium-producing areas of Afghanistan. In opposition,
Member of Parliament David Davis argued that the consequences of the British government's
Afghanistan policy meant tragedy and death for youngsters finding cheap heroin on the
streets and a rise in drug-related crime and urged tougher action by the British military.[21]

Even when an outside power does not directly intervene in a drug-fueled conflict, financial support can be threatened when a government involved in the fighting exhibits patterns
of collusion with drug traffickers and drug-financed warring groups. The government of
Colombia is the third largest recipient of U.S. military support, but many close associates of
President Alvaro Uribe have been implicated in assisting drug-funded right-wing paramilitaries. This has led to calls in Congress to block a free-trade agreement with Colombia.

Democracy Is Not an Antidote

Just as ideology has not served as a barrier to a group's participation in the drug trade, the
promotion of democracy in countries that have experienced drug-fueled conflicts has not
resolved the violence or ended participation in the drug trade. In fact, new democracies
have proven to be highly susceptible to the infiltration of drug barons. New interest groups,
which were previously locked out of power or gained power from drug activities, often

become part of the political process and manipulate the government apparatus to protect their drug interests. Treasuries that are depleted by years of war need to be filled in order to fund needed economic, social, and political programs designed to revive the nation. Financial institutions often lack transparency and government ministers have been largely unaccountable. For example, many local politicians in new African democracies see cannabis revenues as useful to boost their countries' balance of payments.[22]

Ravaged by years of war, citizens of newly formed democracies carve out their livelihoods through participating in the black market. In nations where autocratic rule has been replaced by democratic institutions, there is often a reduced role for the military. As a result, it often suffers budget cuts and reduced pay, which create conditions for corruption. All of these elements combine to undermine new democratic institutions and practices and set the stage for the return of the conflict.

In fact, instituting democratic practices too quickly may worsen the drug economy. To be inclusive and gain maximum consensus, conflict resolution and nation-building efforts may force golden-parachute scenarios on a country. The insistence on quick transitions to democracy also comes with development and economic-restructuring programs that often involve massive social transformation. Wide-ranging and far-reaching economic, political, and social programs may disempower locals who, as a result, resent (and perhaps resist) new modes of governance, creating opportunities for warlords and drug barons to exploit.

Transformation During Peace

While warring groups engaged in conflicts where drugs are grown can shift their operations, they cannot entirely break out of regional constraints such as climate, altitude, and soil. Thus, the stakes in conflicts supported by drug crops are much higher, and the intensity of violence is much more elevated compared to conflicts that are not drug funded. Cases where the drug trade's influence on a country is less intense occur in countries that are transit points for smuggling operations. Lower intensity levels have moved a conflict to abeyant and settled more easily, because the countries that experienced them were transit countries. While drug crops are geographically fixed in many respects, drug routes are more elastic. As a result of this flexibility, these groups also have been more willing to engage in negotiations to end the political violence associated with their conflicts. One reason they are more willing to negotiate is because they can simply transform into criminal groups or keep their ties to organized crime syndicates while continuing to control routes politically. In El Salvador, former combatants devolved into gangsters who now act as enforcers and dealers for the well-established drug-distribution network, "creating their own inroads and supply chains, and using profits and addiction to recruit new members."[23]

The portion of the drug-trafficking network that these warring groups occupy makes them more adaptable in post-conflict environments. Warring groups in transit countries do not have to guarantee the safety of an entire route, which is comprised of roads, ports, and transport. They merely have to guarantee the safety of particular shipments. They do not have to relinquish large swaths of territory like warring groups in source countries are demanded to do. Furthermore, warring groups in transit countries are not subject to intense monitoring and compliance operations as are warring groups in source countries.

In some cases, when large-scale violence ends, these groups benefit from increased licit trade flows and financial aid from international donors into the country. When the World Bank and International Monetary Fund (IMF) insist on funding programs that are designed to build a society's economic linkages to the international market, they reinforce the power of warring groups and warlords who are already linked to the forces of globalization via the drug trade. Routes used to smuggle narcotics have been put to use to smuggle a wide variety of other legal and illegal commodities. Because drugs are subjected to interdiction further up the manufacturing and distribution chain, warring groups in transit countries have relied on other sources of income generated by criminal activities, such as smuggling consumer goods, cigarettes, and fuel.[24] A group can ostensibly agree to forgo trafficking drugs while continuing to use the routes to smuggle newly introduced goods that are now entering and exiting the country via new roads and new port facilities.

Given the increasing level of pressure for countries to lower trade barriers and speed-up customs transit, more trafficking routes are opening, thus allowing more opportunities for warring groups to put these to use for illicit smuggling activities. Combined with today's technology, this is likely to allow more groups to involve themselves in drug trafficking, but to do so from greater distances. Shipment tracking and storage can be done remotely, the trafficker and the goods "need never to be in the same place at the same time."[25] Hezbollah's cocaine-smuggling routes are in numerous countries where Hezbollah does not operate and has no physical presence. The dispersed network of drug smuggling may actually facilitate moving a conflict of lower intensity toward the abeyant or settled categories. A warring group can surrender certain political ambitions but keep power over certain communities in a conflict's aftermath by distributing economic benefits that are linked to the illicit economy.

However, higher levels of criminality tend to plague the post-conflict government. When traffickers make payments in drugs, domestic demand increases, which creates a rise in street violence and health problems. These become new issues for a generally weak government to tackle and become subject to criticism from regional neighbors.

Aerial Crop Eradication
Because the most narcotized conflicts involve government forces and irregular fighters, and the drug trade cannot be easily separated from warfare, there are shared lessons that can be applied from both counternarcotics and counterinsurgency. Bernard Fall's writings

on counterinsurgency are relevant to narcotized conflicts: "When a country is being subverted it is not being outfought; it is being out-administered...the kill aspect, the military aspect, definitely remains the minor aspect. The political, administrative, ideological aspect is the primary aspect."[26] The history of counterinsurgency has shown that effective military actions in such contexts involve first, "minimum violence through an emphasis on conservative but effective tactics, and, second, [designing] a political program focused on splitting the revolutionary elite from their followers."[27] The killing aspect of counterinsurgency is similar to the crop eradication of counternarcotics: both are ineffective unless they are targeted, conservative in method, and subsumed under a larger political, economic, and social strategy.

In many drug-fueled conflicts, most crop eradication has been accomplished by air. Rather than reducing drug-crop yields and forcing warring groups to make concessions, both drug farmers and rebels have moved their operations and further complicated government efforts. In Colombia, aerial crop eradication and interdiction operations forced insurgents, drug traffickers, coca growers, and gunrunners to Peruvian border villages.[28] Moreover, aerial crop spraying has not only proven to be ineffective in dramatically reducing crop harvests, it has played into the hands of the insurgent groups that have claimed that sickness and birth defects in farming communities were the result of herbicides, which further demonstrates government callousness. While eradication campaigns may prevent a warring group from profiting financially from the drug trade in the short term, they will help a warring group profit politically in both the near term and long term.

In many ways, aerial spraying is the equivalent to strategic-bombing campaigns employed in past conventional interstate wars. Issues of effectiveness and morality arise while the targeted population does not capitulate but resists the actions of the attacker.[29] This has appeared largely true because of the manner in which aerial spraying operations have been carried out. The chemical compound glyphosate is often used in higher concentrations than the manufacturer's specifications, mixed with another chemical so that the herbicide can stick to the drug plants, and sprayed from planes at a great distance as a defensive measure against ground fire.[30] This method has made aerial spraying indiscriminate and not proportional, playing into the hands of warring groups and warlords and resulting in greater resistance to conflict settlement. Peru's Shining Path (SL) guerrillas actively and violently oppose aerial spraying and their propaganda has labeled efforts as "Yankee imperialism" and "bureaucratic capitalism."[31]

Crop eradication can also conceal ulterior motives beyond drug interdiction and military relevance. In a form of ethnic cleansing, the Burmese government sprayed poppy fields using a chemical compound of Agent Orange that killed livestock and contaminated water supplies of a minority tribe group that the government sought to move out of a rebel-controlled area.[32] Aerial spraying can be a hidden employment of chemical weapons under the guise of counternarcotics. In view of human rights violations committed by militaries in certain conflicts, relying on armed forces carries serious risks of increasing the level of violence.

Militaries from Developed States Resist Involvement in Counternarcotics Operations

Many militaries resist eradication schemes, whether they are aerial or manual, for a number of reasons. If the military is responsible for eradicating drugs as the sole component of a counternarcotics strategy rather than as part of an overall military strategy, commanders have demonstrated genuine unease. They fear that their troops may be susceptible to corruption, that the level of drug violence will increase, and perhaps more importantly, they will get the blame if the fight against drugs is not won. The prestige of the institution will suffer and their effectiveness will decline as a result. Eradication programs that are launched in the contexts of conflict resolution and nation-building are also reluctantly accepted by military leaders. Such programs on their own jeopardize the fragile political and social stability of post-conflict societies and may lead to renewed fighting. The hesitation of NATO and ISAF military commanders in Afghanistan speak to this point. Clamping down on drug crops and the drug trade with indiscriminate and disproportional means has only hurt efforts to move a country toward a comprehensive settlement of the conflict. Even more discriminate and proportional means that target the "greedy rather than the needy," or the crops under the control of violent adversaries and not owned independently by poor farmers, merely raise the price of doing business, thereby enticing others to cultivate drug crops.[33]

Political leaders from developed states are also increasingly leery of putting too many of their troops in harm's way. Expanding a military's mission to include crop eradication further thins the number of troops to control areas that military commanders see as more strategically important to winning the war. Additionally, knowledge of how the drug trade operates economically is not necessarily part of the professional competence of many military leaders. Strong-arm tactics like forcible and coercive crop eradication introduce risk into the lower end of the drug trade. Farmers and smugglers can be compensated for increased risk by increasing their pay; this raises the price of the drug, thereby making entering the drug business more profitable.

Crop Substitution

Crop substitution programs are less coercive than aerial spraying and often gain the consent of drug farmers. Actors that promote these programs rely on the expectation that drug farmers would rather grow crops that are legally traded internationally. The hope is that the farmers will give up their illicit crops entirely and undercut key segments of the wartime economy. By doing so, successes can be had in both counternarcotics and conflict-resolution fronts.

Success on either front has been difficult to find for a number of reasons. The types of crops offered have not been profitable, were difficult to grow, and were not part of the local culture. In the Andes, coffee substitution has been tried, but coffee requires expensive fertilizing products that many farmers cannot afford without cutting into their profit margin. Unlike drug crops, which can be transported via private roads and clandestine airstrips, legal profitable crops like macadamia nuts and passion fruit did not have access to the same transportation infrastructure. Familiar problems occurred in Myanmar.

> The replacement crops often produce less income: poppies can grow on unfertilized, non-irrigated and often otherwise agriculturally useless terrain: opium is easily transported and does not deteriorate: the opium market is fairly stable: the harvest is assured a buyer at a reasonably predictable price. There is no other crop in existence to match such criteria.[34]

Poppy production in Afghanistan is similar. The UN imported wheat to Afghanistan at the same time that domestic wheat production was rising. The result was the unintentional crippling of Afghanistan's domestic wheat market.[35] This sent more farmers into the opium trade and further imbedded the opium economy into the life of the nation.

Substitution programs linked to paying farmers for eradicating their drug crops have met with limited success. In some cases, farmers refuse to forgo growing crops for traditional uses that are part of the indigenous culture. In other cases, responding to exchange programs, more farmers begin to cultivate drug crops to receive extra money from such pay-offs. At times, the monetary alternative has not even covered the expenses incurred by farmers who grow crops. Some warlords are also able to undercut the financial incentives by offering more money for drug crops and offset initial start-up costs for farmers just entering drug cultivation.

Such crop substitution programs underestimated the power of warlords and their links to the illicit global economy. Substitution programs are tied to legal crops and subject to price shocks in the global market in ways that drug crops are not. The economic pressures to grow drug crops are not merely the product of domestic forces. The illegality of the drug trade and its far-reaching influence mean the inherent infiltration by actors and the influence of economic dynamics external to the conflict and beyond the control of any single nation-state or constellation of actors in the international system.

Focusing Conflict Resolution and Nation-Building Efforts

The difficulties to reaching comprehensive resolutions to narcotized conflicts show how the drug trade interferes with designing "effective techniques for preventing recurrence of violence in war-shattered states after the initial termination of hostilities."[36] Many of these difficulties lie in the near single focus of the country in conflict and the nature of the post-conflict restructuring efforts. The process of nation-building has included political and economic liberalization, which are inherently tumultuous.[37] Much of this tumult is a reaction by regional players, who are often disregarded by those involved in resolving the conflict, to projects in the target state. All of these factors add to the notion that efforts cannot be directed at only the country where the conflict occurs.

A vast array of actors who are engaged in peacebuilding efforts share a common hypothesis about their efforts: if they can generate the right institutions, staffed with the right people, neighboring countries and outside stakeholders would abide by the final product.[38] In the previous chapter's discussion of wartime economies and warlordism, there are very few actors who share an understanding of "peace and security" that those involved in conflict resolution and nation-building wish to instill. In a globalized world and with the tentacles of the drug trade extending to the far reaches of the international system, a nation-state cannot be sealed off while conflict resolution and nation-building occurs, or in the aftermath of the international community's withdrawal.

The active presence of the drug trade virtually ensures that a state cannot be isolated from outside forces. The international nature of the drug trade makes it exceptionally resilient when it has been dealt serious blows in conflicts. Such blows have spread region-wide. When one country marks success, it is often offset by a neighbor's setback.[39] The balloon effect not only applies to the drug trade, but to nearly all the deleterious aspects of a drug-fueled conflict—arms trafficking, human rights abuse, public health crises, criminal violence, and governmental corruption in neighboring countries are all affected by peacebuilding projects.

Sanctions Distorting Effects

As discussed previously, sanctions that are intended to coerce parties to reduce or end violence in narcotized conflicts have proven ineffective. Because drugs are illegal, there is little more a government or international body can do to restrict their trade. Sanctions against governments involved in counterdrug efforts can induce more parties to enter the drug trade and increase violence.

Like the actions undertaken by warring parties in reversal-of-fortune situations, other sanctions, like arms embargoes, directed at other elements fueling the violence of a narcotized conflict can be undone by the presence of the drug trade. Arms embargoes raise the price of weapons, and drug sales can be used to compensate for their increased price. Similarly, sanctions designed to limit precursor chemicals needed to manufacture drugs have increased the value of these supplies. As a result, sanctions can also increase the criminality of some warring groups. Bribery, extortion, and other criminal acts often increase when sanctions are imposed in narcotized conflicts as a way to make up for shortages of key ingredients.

Local Reactions Against the Drug Trade and Use

Independent of the acts of interveners and outside aid agencies, local groups often seek to curb the drug trade and drug use of combatants on their own. Often, their actions are reactions to the persistent violence that has surrounded the lives of ordinary citizens. In the case of the Union of Islamic Courts (UIC) in Somalia, citizens support warring groups that promise to eliminate the violence directed against them by drug-financed warlords and their intoxicated fighters. In the case of South Africa, former belligerent groups form community associations that also double as vigilante groups. People Against Gangsterism and Drugs (PAGAD) was formed by former members of the Pan-African Congress who opposed the new political, economic, and social contours of post-apartheid South Africa.[40]

While such groups appear to provide order, they actually use unregulated violence. Their legitimacy is not tied to the state, but often challenges existing state structures. Increased criminality linked to impunity can threaten to upend social stability or lead to intense rounds of new fighting.

PROSPECTS FOR DRUG-FUELED CONFLICTS

These lessons are strong reminders that conflict in the post-Cold War era is complex and that the international security environment is filled with greater uncertainty in the near and long term. The dynamics of the intersection between drugs and warfare, the strategic use of drugs, and the various responses to drug-fueled conflicts supply a rich reservoir of understanding from which to draw. These lessons also challenge commonly held ideas about the nature of conflict while reinforcing others.

The lessons grouped under this chapter's "Dynamics of the Intersection" section suggest that the drug trade's power to influence ideas needs to be acknowledged. As such, there will be greater violence directed against civilians because of the various ways the drug trade trumps ideological goals. This means that actors who seek to forestall conflict or prevent atrocities against civilians will be further challenged to develop norms and effective regimes in the face of new economic and military incentives to abuse non-combatants. Attacks on civilians are not entirely part of a new strategic calculus or purely acts of group depravity as commonly believed; they are now a combination of both that is bound together, in many cases, by drug availability and consumption. In fact, separating violence against civilians as strategic or criminal will be increasingly difficult. Rising levels of violence in many conflicts will likewise be difficult to place in easily understood categories of military necessity or opportunistic gain. While the power of ideas and the importance of values remain relevant to constructing approaches to these dynamics, putting them into action in a global environment where the drug trade and armed violence are intertwined will require innovative thinking and bolder actions in the near future.

Among the lessons drawn from the "Strategic Use of Drugs" section are that warring groups engaging in asymmetric tactics incorporate some aspect of the drug trade to further their objectives and governments and militaries will also be tempted to participate in order to offset any political or military disadvantage. Given this context, militaries will have to accept that armed political violence is likely to be linked in one way or another to international narcotics trafficking, while law enforcement will have to presume that drug dealing is surrounded by one degree or another by aspects of warfare. As a result, because drugs are present in asymmetric struggles, militaries need to be circumspect about victories on the battlefield or against the drug trade in narcotized conflicts. These victories are often short lived since they can be easily turned around by the balloon effect and the hydra-effect. Therefore, keeping in mind the strength of the relationship between the drug trade and warfare, judgment of a military campaign's effectiveness may have to include assessments on how the drug trade can compensate and how it will alter the character of the conflict.

There is also a strong crossover between the dynamics of the intersection and the strategic use of drugs. The dynamics of the intersection also provide a warning for policymakers who seek to cut off funding to a warring party that is used to having strong financial backing. These groups can find other ways to use their expertise, territory, and followers to participate in the drug trade and earn capital. A sudden withdrawal of aid or a clamp down on other funding streams may provide short-term gains against a belligerent group, but lay the ground work for a growing relationship with elements of the drug trade.[41]

Because drugs will probably be part of asymmetric campaigns, realizing the differences among drugs becomes important for understanding the ways in which they will affect conflicts. ATS drugs represent the wave of the future for narcotized conflicts. Heroin and cocaine will likely remain in demand in the future, but opium and coca crops will be limited to the countries where they are currently grown and to where there are ongoing conflicts. Synthetic drugs, however, are inherently more flexible and more clandestine. These qualities not only aid asymmetric strategies but complement the transnational nature of emerging violent groups that do not seek to hold territory in the same way as insurgent groups. ATS drugs are not likely to be monopolized by warring groups like plant-based narcotics. Nonetheless, because they are easy to manufacture, they will be increasingly used by combatants for funding and consumption.

The lessons from "Responses to Narcotized Conflicts" indicate that actors who intervene in narcotized conflicts and seek to build liberal democratic institutions with free markets will be confounded by numerous factors that they must be prepared to confront. If there are military forces from demand countries involved in nation-building, domestic opposition will form in their home countries to tackle the drug economy more forcefully. It must be recognized that professional militaries will be reluctant to confront the trade for reasons of institutional culture—militaries are dedicated to winning wars and, in some cases, to winning the hearts and minds of the local population. Tackling the drug economy goes against their training. Yet, when they are ordered to confront the trade, doing so presents few comfortable options that are likely to succeed. If militaries choose aerial-eradication schemes, they will play into the hands of their adversaries and do little to control the trade. They will also be frustrated by the economics of crop substitution programs that require precise calculations and almost immaculate timing.

Crop eradication and substitution programs are not relevant in transit countries that experience lower levels of drug trade's influence on a conflict. Conflicts with lower levels of narcotization tend to be easier when seeking to end open hostilities, for warring groups have many ways to circumvent the parameters of peace agreements. Although the level of organized political violence associated with such a conflict may be reduced in transit countries, they are at the mercy of high levels of criminality. Criminal activity is often sustained and embedded because of the unintentional actions of those seeking to generate institutions and processes that will sustain the peace. Nation-building programs have included economic liberalization projects that seek to create the conditions for competitive free-market processes. These processes are believed to inoculate a society from future outbreaks of large-scale violence. However, the "infection" of the drug trade runs deep and outlives any institutional and economic prophylactic; the habits gained in battle are not easily replaced with free-market, transparently competitive patterns of behavior by the warring parties. Competition for profit during these conflicts predisposes actors toward monopolistic actions that are often supported by violent coercion. In peacetime, such habits are translated into mafia-like schemes rather than entrepreneurial endeavors. Crime in these contexts becomes the continuation of politics and economics by other means.

The frustration in responding to narcotized conflicts is compounded when there is a narrow focus on the country where the conflict is taking place. No matter how well intentioned the efforts are by outside interveners, the countervailing pressures of the drug trade do not permit the isolation of a conflict. External actors, legitimate and illegitimate, will have deep-seated interests in how a conflict is managed and are unlikely to share some of the most basic notions that must be held in common for the long-term sustainability of any peace that is sought. It is worth remembering that, unlike developed countries or countries largely at peace, countries emerging from drug-fueled conflicts have been subjected to international forces that are largely criminal in nature. Post-conflict governments are coming into new forms of contacts with legitimate international actors and global processes that are different and require new sets of negotiated norms that do not happen instantaneously. Tragically, there is not much that can be done to extend the focus of peacebuilding activities far beyond certain parameters of the country in conflict. Not all of the players connected to a drug-fueled conflict can be co-opted or otherwise removed from interfering in a peace process; there are neither enough resources nor a comprehensive level of interest by the required number of actors in the international community to tackle all the external pressures that sustain a drug-fueled conflict. In the nearly one hundred years since the ban of the international trade in narcotics, with all the complimentary legal, regulatory, institutional, and national efforts, the illicit trafficking in narcotics continues. Tackling the wide-ranging and far-reaching linkages of a single narcotized conflict is nearly as daunting.

Together, these lessons point to a shift in how to understand contemporary and future armed conflict. These lessons reinforce what is grudgingly being accepted about the nature of post-Cold War international landscape: internal or intrastate war is increasingly a misleading moniker. The emergence of organized violence no longer needs to anchor political authority and legitimacy in conventional, bureaucratic, or consent-based structures like the nation-state.[42] The drug trade is speeding this process along. It too is neither dependent on nor bound by the nation-state and has over its history been less and less subject to a variety of local, national, and international enforcement capabilities. A warlord, for example, does not need a nation-state with all its institutional apparatuses to generate authority; while civilians, who are both strategic targets and war booty, suffer drug-induced atrocities by the warlord's fighters and do not find security under the umbrella of sovereignty. Yet, warlords and civilians simultaneously have informal international linkages to the globalized economy in the form of the drug trade.

The combination of a powerful transnational force such as the drug trade and localized warring groups adds clarity to notions of a neo-medieval world order as described by Hedley Bull. A neo-medieval world order is one where modern states "come to share their authority of their citizens, and their ability to command their loyalties, on the one hand with regional or world authorities, and on the other hand with sub-state or sub-national authorities, to such an extent that the concept of sovereignty ceased to be applicable."[43] While sharing authority with regional or world authorities connotes institutions, it can be argued that the transnational drug trade and the organizations that comprise it are contemporary analogies, and warring groups from insurgents and terrorists to warlords represent substate authorities. Transnational forms of economic and political power are inextricably linked to highly localized forms of consent and coercion and make the nation-state a consistently contested means of organizing international relations, national security, and human rights.

This has implications for the future patterns of war. If "[p]ower is migrating to small non-state actors who organize into sprawling networks more readily than traditionally hierarchical nation-state actors, [i]t means that conflicts will increasingly be waged by 'networks' rather than by 'hierarchies.'"[44] In fact, warring groups, because of their participation in an internationally traded and consumed commodity such as narcotics, mimic certain aspects of the "statelessness" of transnational corporations in which they can be nearly completely untethered to their home countries. Each function is not "headquartered" in a single country, but is parceled out in separate areas of the globe. Such transnationality means that many warring groups have more in common with each other than they do with their fellow citizens; their affinity for profit-based schemes transcend ideological differences among them.

This is why ATS drugs and transnational terror groups are such a potentially powerful combination and may be a harbinger of new forms of international conflict. It is debatable whether the ideology espoused by Islamic extremist groups represents a coherent political program. Yet, their ideology has not stood in the way of cooperating with a vast array of criminal groups of varying political and religious beliefs, while the transnational quality of both their organizational structure and the contemporary drug trade form a potent match. Although a criminally funded caliphate without a national capital would confound many, it is not out of the realm of the possible. Additionally, the dedication of a group such as al Qaeda and its affiliates to spectacular acts of terrorism along with its use of the drug trade as both a weapon and a source of funding may permit even greater unrestrained violence in the future.

The greater "medievalism" of international relations combined with decentralized, networked actors using clandestine links to the illicit global economy to wage war poses significant challenges to the roles of the armed forces of nation-states in the twenty-first century. As has been previously seen, drug-fueled conflict poses tactical and strategic difficulties for state-supported militaries.

> Traditional or Westphalian states are not prepared to deal with non-governmental dynamics operating outside the domains of state and alliance systems. Doctrine and force structures are designed around traditional concepts of overwhelming conventional force to achieve decisive victory against established state militaries.[45]

This is an unlikely recipe for success against the types of warring groups examined in this book.

The strategic environment of the twenty-first century is a haunting vision that displays an urgent need for approaches. If neo-medievalism holds true and drug-fueled conflicts represent the character of future warfare, new ideas must be conceived, innovative strategies designed, and committed actors engaged to promote a vision of a more hopeful, peaceful, and prosperous international order.

6

SHAKY PATHS FORWARD
Strategies and Approaches in Drug-Fueled Conflicts

PATTERNS OF WAR AND ORGANIZED VIOLENCE DO not occur in a vacuum, meaning that the continuing pace of globalization, the ever-changing pattern of the drug trade, and the supply and demand of drugs for combatants' consumption point to a future where conflicts will be influenced by drugs. There are few countervailing or moderating influences on the intimacy between the illicit narcotics trade and modern forms of warfare. Demand for drugs continues to rise annually worldwide; drug profits are up; technology and transportation innovation continue to provide new avenues for illicit trade and civil wars go on with the battlefield including more civilians and more aspects of civil society.

In the immediate aftermath of the Cold War, the world was not envisioned to be so complicated. With the decline of the superpower nuclear danger and the spread of Western-style democracy into former communist states, a new era of prosperity and peace was heralded as markets opened in new regions of the globe. The hope was that the former communist states, and those allied with the USSR, would integrate into the world economy and burgeoning democratic international institutions and for Third World nations to direct their attention toward economic and political development, leaving the ideological struggle of the Cold War behind. However, the high number of drug-fueled conflicts and their associated effects dimmed this vision and marred beliefs in the hopeful direction of the future.

With the dynamics of the intersection between drugs and warfare overriding many established ideas about the nature of conflict, combined with the growing strategic use of drugs serving to cripple prevailing responses to drug-fueled conflicts, new lenses must be crafted to view the blurry lines of the international security environment with greater clarity. However, just as there are myriad lessons to be gleaned, there cannot be a single panacea that will act to end the intersection of drugs and warfare, stem the strategic use of drugs, or offer comprehensive responses that will gain widespread and deep consensus. There can only be elements of an approach that are more likely to put drug-fueled conflicts on the path to resolution while coping with the broader global patterns that empower the drug trade's effects on warfare. Though traditional perspectives and approaches utilized by scholars, policymakers, and military leaders have not fully incorporated the lessons discussed in the previous chapter, this chapter serves as a way to begin the debate.

If, as this book argues, the drug trade and warfare are increasingly inseparable in many conflicts, a central question is where and how much emphasis to place on the drug trade or violence when assessing which strategies to select and who should implement a strategy. Primarily, the answer depends on how serious one views the level of drug financing of a conflict and the degree of combatant drug use in a particular case. The approaches offered are a selection and represent an outgrowth of strategies that were attempted in the past in various degrees and contexts rather than straightforward and clear-cut arguments for one over another. These strategies have been adapted in ways to tackle the power of the drug trade as it affects conflicts occurring now and in the future. Rather than dealing separately with the drug trade and warfare, these strategies attempt to take both into consideration by assessing the effects of a counterdrug policy when suggesting military force and by accounting for the effects of military operations on the drug trade.

Each strategy seeks to address the broad categories of lessons learned by suggesting that actions be directed toward the dynamics of the intersection, the strategic use of drugs, and the more effective response to drug-fueled conflicts. The general approach of each strategy is to weaken the dynamic by reducing the attractiveness of the drug trade as a funding source and a consumable resource so that warring groups may be weakened, leaving them less resistant to negotiations or more vulnerable to disruption by legal and military elements of power. Each strategy incorporates short-, medium-, and long-term measures that seek to alter the cost-benefit calculations of combatants in ways that induce them to move away from the drug trade and toward peaceful settlement.

Each strategy incorporates the components that constitute the elements of a strategy. According to Arthur Lykke, strategy is the combination of ends, means, and ways.[1] Ends are objectives or goals that, if accomplished, bring about a desired end state. Means are resources that can be committed to the accomplishment of an objective. They can be tangible as in forces, equipment, money, and institutions as well as intangible particularly in the degree of commitment, creativity, and innovation.[2] Ways refer to how a goal can be achieved and with what resources. Additionally, when considering drug-fueled conflicts that have international effects, deciding who out of the myriad of actors in the international security environment, or what combination, should be part of the strategic equation.

The strategies covered are grouped under three broad titles: control, shape, and abstain.[3] Each has ends, means, and ways specific to them. A strategy of control would seek to challenge the global drug trade as a way to remove a strategic resource from the hands of combatants. Dissatisfied with warring groups' influence on the drug trade, a controlling strategy would use the resources of the major powers to control the trade more directly as a way to undercut wars from generating far-reaching effects that may harm their societies. A shaping strategy would also start with the dissatisfaction with the intersection of drugs and warfare, but seek to work through multiple layers of actors to craft norms and regimes to steadily erode the influence of drugs on war and the attendant negative effects on the international system. An abstaining strategy would accept that little can be done at the international level to break apart the intersection of drugs and warfare and would abstain from large-scale projects coordinated by groups of actors at the international level to tackle drug-fueled conflicts. As such, an abstaining strategy would focus on dealing with the source of such an intersection at lower levels of governance while countering the effects. As with any strategy, risks and pitfalls need to be assessed if its recommendations for action are considered for adoption.

The discussion of these three strategies also serves as a way to demonstrate the need for a new multifaceted strategy that draws from a number of actors and approaches. From these strategies, a new approach can be cobbled together that proposes unified and multi-layered actions as an approach to deal with drug-fueled conflicts of today and tomorrow.

A STRATEGY OF CONTROL

A control strategy would take a harder, more aggressive line against the drug trade and abusers within demand countries. Seeing the nexus of the drug trade and warfare as creating emerging strategic threats to the world order on which their power is based, major powers would seek, either in concert with each other or independently, to more directly undercut the power of the international narcotics trade. Those who advocate a control strategy believe that the neo-medieval quality of international relations requires an actor or group of actors to be in control and impose order. Believing that international prohibition, and the treaties that support it, are valuable, those who pursue a control strategy would seek to push the prohibition paradigm as strongly as possible. Although elimination is not possible, pursuing prohibition more strongly as a goal can lead to more robust interdiction and eradication efforts, increasing risk and lowering incentives. According to this strategy, prohibition standards have not been more forcefully applied by nation-states or international bodies and require the leadership of powerful nations to "fix" the intersection between drugs and warfare, confront strategic drug use by combatant groups, and forcefully respond to drug-fueled conflicts.

The ways to achieve this would be mostly within the military dimension, for the undergirding belief is that whoever dominates the international system "will, to a significant extent, dictate to it politically and economically."[4] The combination of military force with greater political will and economic support are all required to deal with the drug trade and its intersection with war. Militaries would be reconfigured and retrained to overcome their institutional resistance to confronting drug trade. They would be organized, trained, and equipped to deal with internal conflicts that are influenced by the drug trade and seek the most appropriate ways to reduce the drug supply and ameliorate the broader effects in the international arena that would damage short-term stability. The major powers would devise methods to remove safe havens and isolate warlords. Warring groups, in drug-producing countries in particular, would be more directly confronted because they are the cause of higher levels of the drug trade's influence on the conflict and create the farthest reaching effects. Governments that collude with drug traffickers would face the same fate as Panama's Manuel Noriega, while groups that actively use the drug trade as a form of chemical warfare against the forces and societies of the developed world would also be heavily targeted.

Military doctrine would be designed to take a hard line against drugged adversaries, and professional soldiers would brook no quarter when facing intoxicated combatants. Believing that little can be done to prevent or deter combatant drug use, the potential to harm the forces prosecuting a control strategy would outweigh the considerations of the possible lack of formal legal controls or social controls over particular fighters. Interdiction efforts would be directed at intercepting or obstructing the supplies of drugs combatants use to get high. Precursor chemicals to manufacture ATS drugs would also be targeted. Interrupting the drug supply for combatant consumption could be used as pressure to gain important concessions. Unpredictability of belligerents, who are either high or suffering withdrawals, would be countered in various ways depending on the parameters of a particular mission. Lethal and non-lethal weapons could be employed to reduce the deadly effects of intoxicated combatants.

Not all actions would be (or could be) undertaken by the major powers. For example, with encouragement, non-governmental organizations (NGOs) would be urged to find solutions within the guidelines of a control strategy and in conjunction with the interests of major powers. Although part of the war-making infrastructure of warring groups, drug farmers would be provided a mixture of incentives and sanctions. In the case of Afghanistan, farmers would be offered a one-time opportunity to sell their opium to the international community with local authorities and councils collectively destroying the opium under the supervision of the international community.[5] Envisioned as a multiyear effort, it would include a rural credit regime for several years as farmers grow alternative crops and be accompanied by more aggressive interdiction and eradication campaigns.[6]

Meanwhile, counterdrug efforts by the military, rather than targeting farms, would be directed at the next stage of the drug-production process. Locating and destroying laboratories and stocks would produce disruption of wholesale markets creating sell-offs, lowering prices, and exposing the product to even greater interdiction.[7] In turn, these actions would also lower the price paid to drug farmers, increase risk to traffickers, and create tension among warring groups, thereby creating the proper conditions for crop conversion initiatives. In fact, if interdiction efforts become sustained and result in lower profits, drug traffickers in particular have been known to switch routes to maintain a certain level of profitability. Denying insurgents and warlord access to resources can shift the military balance in favor of the forces implementing a control strategy.[8] When a significant drop in a warring group's funds occurs, the group becomes vulnerable to pressure, which can lead to outright defeat or a genuine willingness to resolve the conflict.[9] This could pave the way for counterinsurgency programs to generate a peacetime economy, empower locals, and provide sustainable security.

To ensure that military might, political will, and economic largesse are not squandered, improved intelligence across communities would be required. Based on tactical successes of agencies such as the Drug Enforcement Administration (DEA) and JITF-South in Key West, "fusion centers" would be established in each nation that would serve as a clearing house for information on trends, patterns, and cycles related to drugs and warfare. This would require a deep commitment to breaking down institutional and bureaucratic barriers within and between states.

Because the major powers are also demand countries whose societies provide much of the market for narcotics, and hence much of the financing of drug-fueled conflicts, they would also seek to reduce drug use within their own societies. Many ways could be employed, from early childhood education about drug links to groups that threaten national security to harsher criminal penalties for dealers who could be charged with additional crimes such as subversion or treason. Anti-drug messages would not only be tied to individual well-being, but to the safety of one's country. If these statements about how drugs aid and abet the actions of warring groups were ignored, harsher penalties could be applied. As Nancy Reagan argued during her "Just Say No" campaign, "any user of illicit drugs is an accomplice to murder."[10] Some have already extended her logic by recommending the extradition of users and street-level dealers to countries that are fighting drug-fueled conflicts because

> a drug addict who is aware of narco-terrorism could fall under a category of a depraved mind. So could a person who simply wants to use drugs and does not care about the impact his drug use has on others in a foreign country. Such an irresponsible disregard for human life could be considered "extremely negligent conduct" and, therefore, an act of "depraved heart murder."...This falls under the universal theory of extradition.[11]

Hard-line efforts would be especially important with the growing demand for ATS drugs and other synthetic, home-manufactured drugs that are bound to become part of the market in the future. With ATS drugs not agriculturally based, domestic law enforcement would have to become more keenly aware of what warring groups might be operating or profiting from the ATS market in their communities.

Tackling complicit legitimate businesses at home and abroad would also be part of a control strategy. Because money that is collected from drug trafficking must be amassed, laundered, and redistributed, the more transactions that take place, the more vulnerable these groups are to detection.[12] Thomas Fowler argues that disrupting the drug trade, and thereby lessening the financial power of warring groups, lies in disrupting the flow of profits: "interception of laundered money or the flow of money back to the drug barons has much greater promise of achieving the desired goal of making drugs unavailable."[13] However, to be effective, banking and financial institutions will have to end their complicity in the drug trade. Governments must be willing to monitor and penalize businesses that facilitate the flow of financial resources to warring groups.

Expanding the efforts of such government agencies as the U.S. Office of Foreign Assets Control (OFAC), which composes a list of "specially designated nationals and blocked persons" that details individuals, groups, and companies that support terrorism, would need to include those who facilitate the drug use to fund war and aid in the provision of narcotics to belligerents. OFAC also routinely imposes numerous fines on financial institutions that have not blocked the illicit transfers of people or companies on the list.[14]

Risks and Pitfalls of a Control Strategy

A control strategy, while bold and authoritative, is still full of risk, which may lead to significant pitfalls when attempts are made to implement it. The first major risk is associated with a control strategy's central focus on substantially curtailing the drug trade to separate it from war, thereby limiting the influence of drugs on conflict. History has shown that "no belligerent group has been bankrupted by the effort to eradicate drugs."[15] For example, in modern China it was a belligerent group that finally eliminated opium after the victorious Communist Party determined that the drug trade represented a threat to its newly established political, economic, and social order. Direct external interference by major powers to enforce prohibition, however well-meaning and potentially successful, will still run aground on issues of sovereignty.

A control strategy, in many respects, would feed into the dynamics of the intersection of the drug trade and warfare rather than weaken them. A major power or group of powers cannot eliminate all drugs, and any achievement of major reductions would increase the street price, create more profits, and thereby increase the financial incentives to join the drug trade. Introducing risk increases profitability, while creating tension among traffickers and turmoil in a compartmentalized market that may lead to more violence. As seen in chapter 5, when drug spoils are at risk, violence typically escalates within the country and region.

Remembering that all drugs are different, a control strategy focused entirely on plant-based initiatives would fail. As seen in chapter 5, groups could make up for a reversal of fortune by shifting into trafficking synthetic drugs, particularly ATS, that can be home manufactured, and do so by manufacturing it within demand countries, bringing another front of the conflict to the streets of the major powers.

Stiffening domestic penalties for drug offenses by incorporating violations of national security are also very precarious. Currently, over twenty countries can implement the death penalty for drug-trafficking-related offenses; however, even the death penalty has not served as a deterrent. The death penalty has only increased risk and inflated profits or drug routes have merely shifted. In a country like America, linking the War on Drugs to the Global War on Terrorism may create cries of injustice if low-level dealers and users are charged with aiding and supporting the enemy by selling an intoxicant or because of their addiction. Furthermore, extraditing drug dealers and users to countries in conflict would overburden the judicial and penal systems of already struggling governments.

The harsh use of force against drugged combatants, especially against children who were recruited via addiction, may create deeper resentment in countries where drug-fueled conflicts are occurring. Without attending to informal social controls, repeated confrontation with these sorts of forces is likely. Interdicting drugs for combatant use may lead to greater violence and unpredictability when fighters suffer withdrawals, as was the case with the Beslan school terrorists in southern Russia. Additionally, the psychological toll on professional members of the military who confront such combatants will probably be immense. No matter how much training is completed, repeated exposure to high levels of unpredictable fighting and random firefights is highly stressful. More substantial programs, rather than additional doctrine, to deal with this stress will be needed as a way to forestall the conditions that may lead to drug abuse among the ranks of professional militaries.

Attempting to control the actions of legitimate businesses, especially those in the banking and financial sectors, and limit their interactions with the proceeds of warring groups is important. However, investigative and auditing efforts of agencies like OCAF are routinely thwarted by warring groups and criminals. Even the most advanced financial-screening software cannot detect deceit in all instances. Plus, successfully limiting money laundering activities through banks may lead groups to rely more heavily on informal ethnically based financial arrangements that are more difficult to audit.

More broadly, history has shown that governments of major powers are not immune to the seductive quality of the drug trade. In fact, as the patterns of war change to favor more networked actors employing asymmetric strategies, would exceptions to a control strategy be given to strategic partners or proxies? Chapter 5 suggests that governments will use the drug trade to further other national security objectives that they wish to keep hidden from scrutiny because they may be domestically unpopular. Possibly, major powers will undercut their own strategy of control in certain instances. Inconsistent application would invite further risk and likely doom the strategy.

A STRATEGY TO SHAPE

A shaping strategy is designed to work with multiple actors to craft norms and regimes that steadily erode the influence of drugs on warfare and address the attendant negative effects on the international system at the source. Relying more heavily on international institutions and regional initiatives, such a strategy would express its dissatisfaction with the direction of the drug trade by attempting to shape its direction and decrease incentives for warring groups to participate in illegal narcotics trafficking. Those who advocate a shaping strategy believe that the neo-medieval quality of international relations requires international consensus and legitimacy, which can only be expressed through international institutions and regional arrangements. Encouragement of more actors to do more in the face of drug-fueled conflicts is a key ingredient to tackling such a broad and transnational problem. The strategy rests on the belief that legitimate international actors will recognize that without addressing the dynamics of the intersection between drugs and warfare, war will become increasingly complex as well as unpredictable, creating cascading effects that may not be successfully managed.

A powerful first step would be for international developmental institutions to incorporate drug-trade monitoring with the impacts of the illicit global economy on countries in conflict. Currently, the most active international financial organizations do not. According to a senior World Bank economist, the illicit economy and black market "are not issues we deal with,"[16] while International Monetary Fund (IMF) projects in Latin American countries make their economic calculations "as if the drugs industry did not exist."[17] By collecting such information, better tracking of the growing intersection between the drug trade and conflict can become standard practices and lead to refining policy actions for responding to these types of conflicts.

International agreements and conventions that explicitly acknowledge drug-fueled conflicts, outline their detrimental effects on the international system and national authority while engaging in "anticipatory norm creation" would invest many actors with the legitimacy to respond to such conflicts with diverse, yet unified, action.[18] Action through international institutions and conventions, "rather than weighing each international case individually and evaluating the merits of foreign claims against national sovereignty concerns, accession to an international convention would signal a state's recognition that is generally in its interest to cooperate."[19] A new convention may begin with a conference that has a hybrid focus to both update prohibition treaties and the Geneva Convention. It would seek to outline the status of drug farmers in conflicts—are they combatants or non-combatants?

The status of drugged combatants would also be a subject for discussion. For example, how should children recruited via addiction be treated in combat situations? How culpable are members of professional militaries who use the drug trade to fund their actions or gain personal enrichment?

Depending on how these issues are decided, other international institutions might expand their mandates to respond to the dynamics of the intersection between drugs and warfare and to acts committed in drug-fueled conflicts. For example, the International Criminal Court (ICC) could also have jurisdiction over war crimes committed by drug criminals in such conflicts or drug crimes committed by warlords or by warring groups. Those who willfully support the drug activities of warring groups that have gone on to commit atrocities against civilians could be charged as accessories. This would not be unprecedented; as previously mentioned, several Imperial Japanese subjects were executed for war crimes because of their role in drug trafficking in China. Groups actively engaged in drug trafficking to poison enemy forces and societies would also be held up to international legal scrutiny and sanction. Such a commitment would require the harmonizing of legal regimes across state boundaries and thus would require intense domestic political will.

As a corollary, Interpol should be expanded and its links to other police agencies should be strengthened. As an international law enforcement agency, it possesses a firm foundation of institutional expertise on drug trafficking that can provide a deeper reservoir of support for international efforts. It can be another strand in a web of international associations that would be needed to shape the direction of drug-fueled conflict.

Efforts should be made to take advantage of the regional compartmentalization of the plant-based narcotics trade. The Organization of American States (OAS) has an evaluation and tracking system to monitor and assess drug trafficking in the Americas. The Inter-American Drug Abuse Control Commission (CICAD) includes efforts to reduce demand, create incentives for crop substitution, and limit small-arms trafficking. Converting this commission into a higher level, effective policy-coordination forum requires greater political will.[20] In other regions, there is no equivalent regional institution that could host such a commission.

Legitimate businesses in the financial and banking arenas would be required to acquiesce to greater scrutiny. To be granted certain international certifications, compliance with the broad practices of Financial Intelligence Units (FIUs) would be needed to reduce money laundering. FIUs are governmental bodies that "collect, analyze and share financial intelligence and transaction data in an effort to curtail money laundering."[21] In addition, an FIU has an international quality since it can "aggregate disclosures from financial institutions in its country, combine them with information supplied by law enforcement, communicate the combined information to counterpart FIUs in other countries, and forward cases to prosecutorial authorities in the appropriate jurisdiction as necessary."[22] Such institutions would be nurtured in developing countries with grants from the World Bank and IMF.

Such a strategy would also seek to be aware of the cultural aspects of drug crop cultivation among certain indigenous groups. International and regional efforts would be directed at identifying and monitoring crops used in legitimate, traditional ways. While the distinctions between coca and cocaine would have to be clarified, clarification may yield greater results in limiting drug trafficking than current policies. Rather than relying on coercive measures to move drug farmers toward legitimate crops, efforts would be made to legitimize drug crops for pharmaceutical purposes. For example, as proposed by the Senlis Council for the poppy fields in Afghanistan,

> [p]oppy crops can be used to produce medicines such as morphine and codeine, which are high-demand painkillers in a growing global market. The international community should help the Afghan government start a scientific pilot project to investigate further the practical implementation of a licensing system for Afghanistan. Such a system would allocate existing poppy fields for medicinal purposes, offering all stakeholders, from farmers to warlords, an opportunity to profit in a legal economy.[23]

Such a project could be expanded to other countries where drug crops are grown and would also incorporate legitimate business into the search for solutions, offering new incentives.

The international community would have to reexamine its past practices in conflict resolution and nation-building in source countries that would help fight the temptation for warring groups to slip into organized crime, further undermining efforts to achieve a sustainable peace. Rather than seeking to quickly achieve market democratic practices, interveners would focus on "institutionalization before liberalization."[24] Such a program would delay the introduction of democratic and market-oriented reforms until a basic network of domestic institutions was established. It would then have interveners manage the incremental process of democratization and liberalization rather than unleashing "shock therapy" on a war-ravaged and criminally victimized society. With a longer commitment, golden-parachute temptations could be managed and warring groups would be given additional legitimate opportunities to work within the parameters of an accountable government and fair market.

International action would also be directed at helping societies reestablish both formal and informal social control over drug use as a way to limit combatant usage and to strengthen civil society. Policies and actions would be directed at supporting local initiatives and leveraging positive trends in a society's culture. For example, with prodding from the international community, Afghan president Hamid Karzai has gained the backing of important mullahs for his campaign against opium. Fortunately, in Iraq there continues to be a strong cultural undercurrent against drug abuse in civil society. While stigmatization has weakened in the post-Saddam years, it has not entirely gone. These examples demonstrate that more could be done to work within the cultural parameters of countries experiencing drug-fueled conflicts. Informal social controls, not withstanding hospitals, clinics, and pharmacies, would need to be monitored for, and even protected against, looting to limit further combatant intoxication that may lead to atrocities and other human rights abuses.

Risks and Pitfalls of a Shaping Strategy

A shaping strategy carries with it a significant risk—the faith in the power and moral authority of international institutions may be misplaced when confronting the complexity of these types of conflicts. This is primarily because of the seemingly benign conception of what constitutes an international institution and how it challenges the power of sovereignty in a medieval world. Malcolm Waters's assessment is typical of such a nearly sterile definition.

> What is new is, first, that [nation-states] control [the international environment] less and less, while being more constrained by it; second, that they are less and less capable of controlling their domestic environment, the social groups, or the national minorities that are supposed to be subject to their authority; and finally, that their plight is shared, with a vengeance, by international authorities such as the United Nations or the European Community.[25]

This description, while accepting notions of neo-medievalism, still exhibits a strong bifurcation between internal domestic groups and international institutions. The dynamics of the drug trade, the strategic use of drugs in warfare, and the awkward responses demonstrate that such distinctions no longer hold. Warlords, and those who comprise the modern backbone of narcotics trafficking, are part of the international economy where many groups, legal and illegal, act without regard to national boundaries. International institutions are no longer the only entities that span the globe and must compete with transnational actors who have no headquarters but whose power is almost equally expansive.

Additionally, the growing transnational networks of warring groups have a distinct advantage over international fora. With nation-states maintaining their privileged role in international institutions and regional organizations, meaningful solutions to conflict are "at best, watered down in the process of political bargaining between the interests of the underdeveloped world and the interests of immeasurably more powerful developed world."[26] Warring groups and those that enable them are more nimble and, therefore, increasingly powerful.

A shape strategy that seeks to mold the direction of the drug trade and its intersection offers an alternative direction to prohibition. Buying out peasants' drug crops for legitimate pharmaceutical purposes stands out as a potential opportunity to provide adequate incentives to limit farmers' collusion with warring groups. However, it remains unclear whether the global market has an adequate demand for medicines that will match the demand for illicit street use; many pharmaceutical companies are turning to synthetic painkillers that seem to have the same benefits. Additionally, ATS drugs cannot be incentivized in the same way as plant-based narcotics. Finding incentives for those involved in the ATS trade to end their activities that support warring groups are difficult to conceptualize.

As discussed in chapter 4, international efforts to introduce risk and disrupt the illegal trade of a licit commodity have proven difficult enough. Efforts to do the same with a less transparent trade that is not part of the licit global economy would be even more difficult, as history has shown. Drugs can neither be subjected to a certification regime like diamonds and timber nor can they be similarly traced and tracked.

A STRATEGY TO ABSTAIN

At the core of this strategy is the desire to retain successful patterns and policies of the past to restrain the forces of drug-fueled conflict. In doing so, advocates of an abstaining strategy would urge a recommitment to the concept of state sovereignty by passing down responsibility to lower levels of governance while enabling the sources of better governance to flourish. Advocates of an abstaining strategy view the nation-state as the most effective organization to handle international issues, including the intersection of the drug trade with warfare. An abstaining strategy would accept that the intersection of drugs and warfare will be a fact of life in the international security arena and would abstain from large-scale projects to tackle the intersection at an international level. As such, advocates of an abstaining strategy would focus on the source of the intersection at lower levels of governance such as the nation-state and countering the effects of drug-fueled conflict by insulating their own societies. The aim is prophylactic in nature, to prevent the "virus of disorder" from infecting the developed world.[27]

In short, this strategy would seek to prepare developed nations for the effects of these types of conflicts, while countries experiencing conflict would receive assistance to focus on state-building. They would be done in tandem as many developed countries already accept the understanding that lack of governance in the developing world is the source of international instability that affects the societies of the developed world. This strategy believes that there are genuine limits "to what international efforts at state building can accomplish in the absence of revolutionary domestic change"[28] and that state sovereignty is the best antidote to the growing neo-medieval nature of the international relations.

Ideally, a developed nation would assist a state threatened by drug-fueled conflict to build stronger and more responsive institutions of governance as a way to prevent the effects of refugees, drugs, and smuggling from affecting the national interests of developed countries. Rather than focusing on the larger dynamics of the intersection of drugs and warfare, an Abstaining strategy would assess each case of drug-fueled conflict and design responses fitting the intensity level and how a particular case threatens the national interest.

Such a strategy would make "state-building" a greater priority than nation-building. State-building would require little, if any, foreign presence in countries experiencing these types of conflicts. Implementers of an abstaining strategy would seek to build on existing forms of governance and give them more support to effectively tackle warring groups that fund operations with the drug trade or use drugged combatants. Efforts by developed countries would be done from as far away as possible. An abstaining strategy would resemble portions of the realist strategy of "offshore balancing" where nation-states would allow one another to take over the burden of handling crises that have regional consequences affecting them and intervene only when there are threats to their vital national interests.[29]

Developed nations would strive to break down bureaucratic barriers between intelligence and law enforcement to track how street-level drug sales in their societies feed into conflicts that may threaten security interests at home and overseas. Intelligence fusion centers where law enforcement would have access to information would become standard. Across the various agencies that wield the elements of national power, greater efforts would be made to achieve greater interagency unity to monitor, gauge, and assess dimensions of the dynamics of the intersection between drugs and warfare, and offer guidance for responses to drug-fueled conflicts. An interagency process would be needed to harness fully all the elements of a nation's power. Such processes would be useful in an era where there are groups that traffic drugs into these societies to stimulate crime and disorder.

To support such a strategy, developed nations would prepare their own societies and militaries for the new nature of warfare that includes drug-fueled conflicts. Military doctrine would focus on how to train and support local forces of states affected by such conflicts. Relying on the local knowledge and understanding of the state affected, militaries would assist other militaries in designing tactics to deal with intoxicated combatants. Instead of putting a single doctrine into action in all cases, militaries would stress flexible response. Helping to groom independent, non-corrupt officials and offering protection to these officials would be part and parcel of this strategy. Rather than eradication and interdiction, there would be protection for farmers who switch to alternative crops. These people and their families are vulnerable to a backlash from drug lords and insurgents. The development and deployment of "counternarcotics battalions," such as those in Colombia and Afghanistan that seek out drug traffickers, their products, labs and supplies, should also be used to provide protection for cooperative populations who are at the mercy of drug lords and insurgents. Such an employment of military force can also contribute to reestablishing informal social controls over drug use by combatants and non-combatants.

Training police forces in countries where drug-fueled conflicts are ongoing would also figure quite prominently in an abstaining strategy. Bringing these forces to countries such as the United States, France, and the UK already have long-established training programs for foreign police officers. These programs would be expanded, and officers would be given more sophisticated information systems to track drugs. Such programs could be expanded to incorporate the regional neighbors of a country in conflict. Encouraging the sharing of expertise of institutions in other countries involved in drug-fueled conflicts would also prove useful as a way to further contain the source and effects.[30]

Measuring success would focus on how well local communities are able to resist the power of warlords. By examining three areas—mayors, taxes, and teachers—benchmarks would be established. The loyalty of mayors to the central government, along with whether local taxes are received by the central government, as well as the type of education that children are receiving in outlying areas have been standard benchmarks of success in counterinsurgency efforts.[31] These benchmarks are more important in conflicts where competing authority and economic figures can significantly disempower local residents and destabilize a region of a country, putting it beyond the writ of the capital. As such, informal social controls on combatant drug use could be stimulated.

Linking anti-drug efforts to building the state's capacity would yield useful dividends. Importantly, there would be a clear need for a national goal that is implemented by reliable local officials who are not specifically focused on the "drug problem" but on the overall well-being of citizens. Decisions on eradication would be left primarily to local authorities. Lessons from modern China could be used as examples because such a linkage was successful: opium cultivation and addiction were treated as collective and national issues. In fact, at the turn of the twentieth century China shared many features of contemporary conflicts, most notably warlordism. Anti-drug programs in China were linked to the damage that opium caused the health of individuals, to the strength of the state, and to the survival of China itself.[32] Important to China's efforts was the power of the Communist Party and its ability to infiltrate vast areas of the Chinese countryside. As insurgents themselves, the Party knew the importance of working with poor peasants and co-opting landowners. In reality, early successes were achieved not by outside actors, but by the state's ability to negotiate with actors in the private sector.

In many ways, Colombia's Democratic Security and Defense Policy mimics important aspects of China's anti-opium crusade and would appeal to an advocate of an abstaining policy. The Colombian government's policy recognizes the need to place counternarcotics and counterinsurgency strategies under a larger political program to strengthen civil society. Its central goal is "to strengthen and guarantee the rule of law throughout Colombia, through the reinforcement of democratic authority." It seeks to extend the power of the central government to broader portions of the country by investing in stabilizing and securing the lower levels of government and protecting the human rights of citizens from guerrilla and paramilitary abuses. It envisions creating "a new Colombia, one town at a time."[33] In short, the plan stresses that extralegal activities have no place in a democratic nation and places security and military forces under this mission.

Needed in source, transit, and demand countries will be increases in law enforcement and/or treatment facilities where drug abuse rates might rise. Sudden and sharp increases in drug addiction often point the way to new smuggling routes, which often reveal the influence of warring groups. Yet, these too would be based on a case-by-case assessment of the drug trade's level of influence on conflict and its effects on other national interests.

However, if state-building efforts from a distance fail, an abstaining strategy would permit military action in cases where regional powers have failed to contain the effects of drug-fueled conflicts from spreading to other nations. Military intervention to affect the internal balance of power within a conflict would be justified for advocates of this strategy. Rather than seeking to tackle the entire drug portion of the conflict, intervening militaries would target only crops and transit routes of adversaries. They would support proxy groups that also sought to claim victory in a way that would support the containment of the conflict. As such, America's War on Drugs would be recast. Instead of using the military to support interdiction efforts against all drugs, military assets would be assigned to tracking and tracing smuggling routes, labs, and crops of adversarial warring groups, while police and custom agencies would be the main institutions for intercepting drug shipments. For the U.S. Department of Defense, drugs would be a strategic resource with military operations designed around this conceptualization.

Risks and Pitfalls of an Abstaining Strategy

There are numerous risks inherent in an abstaining strategy. The chief risk is the strategy's central thesis, which is also its greatest weakness—the strategy leaves the dynamics of the intersection of the drug trade and warfare relatively untouched. The ends, ways, and means are piecemeal and narrowly conscribed to these types of conflicts themselves, rather than to the overarching dynamic of the intersection of drugs and warfare. Such a strategy does little to circumscribe how the drug trade's growing connection to armed conflict virtually guarantees that the effects of drug-fueled conflicts will continue to be felt in societies untouched by the hostilities. In sum, it does little to tackle the sources of conflicts.

State-building as a component of offshore balancing has advantages of avoiding misunderstandings of local culture that would hamper responses to individual drug-fueled conflicts. However, state-building puts developed governments in a tighter relationship with other governments of the developing world. As seen throughout this book, what would be the response if these governments were found to be relying on the drug trade to prosecute their own operations? Neither military and police forces nor government officials of developing countries have been immune to the seduction of the drug trade. Although Colombia's new policy holds promise, political officials have been stung with accusations of collusion with drug-financed right-wing paramilitaries. Additionally, efforts to reintegrate paramilitary fighters into society have been slow, leading an estimated 2,500 to 3,600 to join "second generation" paramilitary groups, which are often fronts for drug-trafficking outfits.[34] If support and assistance from outside is withdrawn, as seen in chapter 5, governments might turn to the drug trade more deeply.

Moreover, an over-reliance on the military as a lynchpin for state-building in these conflicts may also become problematic in the future. If citizens see, or the military sees, as indispensable to a critical aspect of national security, there might be little to prevent them from intruding into the political arena in the future.[35] Democratic practices may suffer from or be undermined by the strategy of abstaining.

Preparing the government structures of developed nations for the effects of drug-fueled conflicts may also be problematic. For example, interagency attempts may be too unwieldy. Even the lone superpower is having trouble in adapting its government bureaucracy to the new parameters of the War on Terror. It appears to many observers of American politics that "only the Department of Defense is at war, and the rest of the US government is not."[36] Further attempts to create more unity among government departments may not be possible or jeopardize successful practices already in existence.

ASSUMPTIONS AND PRINCIPLES UNDERLYING A SOUNDER APPROACH

These strategies are not mutually exclusive; there is no reason, for example, why an advocate of an abstaining strategy could not also encourage regional initiatives, or why an advocate of a control strategy could not also support a stronger mandate for the ICC. Combining strategies, however, suggests that it may be more beneficial to employ a strategy that is highly flexible, adaptive, and unified. Although these approaches are varied and contain ideas that can be selected in an à la carte fashion, they reveal several baseline assumptions that underpin them and, thus, set the groundwork for another approach. No matter the strategy, certain fundamental positions and actions are critical to implementing actions against the intersection of drugs and warfare and to cope with drug-fueled conflicts.

The first baseline assumption is that the international drug trade is not going to disappear in the immediate or even foreseeable future. The drug trade has been around for centuries, and its global prohibition and illicit status is a small snapshot of the history of mind-altering substances. Illicit narcotics are a "major global commodity, born in the days of empire-building and mercantile expansion, just as cotton, tea, or coffee."[37] The process by which drugs now play an international role in a vast array of economic, political, and security issues is not one that occurred suddenly; it evolved over time and through the efforts, intentional and unintentional, of numerous legitimate and illegitimate actors. To make any serious dent on supply, multiple points worldwide would have to be attacked with near simultaneity. Curbing demand would take a considerable change in the composition of human beings who seek out intoxication as a matter of routine. In fact, there has been only one society that has not engaged in the cultivation or development of intoxicants—the Eskimo.[38] Clearly, since the drug trade's prohibition, the trade cannot be ended with the available resources and the requisite sustained will of the combined actors in the international community.

Even if it were possible to eliminate the global trade or substantially reduce the drug trade as a controlling strategy seeks, the effects might be worse than the problem and still contribute to the types of wars that are occurring in the post-Cold War era. An example of the effects in drug-producing countries highlights these dangers.

If the cocaine industry disappeared tomorrow, the results could be catastrophic, at least in Peru and Bolivia: the evaporation of hard currency reserves, massive unemployment, and increase in crime and subversion in rural areas, a flood of new migrants to the cities and so on. Such a situation could only play into the hands of extremist groups on both the left and right. For example, how long would democracy last in Bolivia if 200,000 dispossessed coca farmers decided to march on La Paz?[39]

The same effects can be anticipated in countries as diverse as Colombia, Afghanistan, and Peru—let alone in transit countries that are struggling in the aftermath of wars. To attempt an all out, global war on the drug trade "would in these conditions be more tantamount to writing a suicide note than embarking on a crusade."[40] Accepting the drug trade's continuing existence may make it easier to contend with its effects that are now seemingly more manageable, more predictable, and perhaps less catastrophic than the alternatives.

Although the drug trade will persist, this does not mean that legalization is a likely outcome. A second baseline assumption is that the illegal status of the international trade of hard drugs produced from poppies, coca, cannabis, and manufactured ATS is not likely to change. While certain national governments of source countries may legalize the growth of certain drug crops and governments of demand countries may decriminalize the use of certain drugs, the international prohibition of the trade will remain. After all, the worldwide norms against illegal narcotics have been the result of an evolution in attitudes of many national leaders, elites, and citizens over generations. This norm has only grown stronger in the decades since the drug trade's prohibition. The drug trade has gone from being seen as the source of domestic disorder in the late nineteenth century, to being viewed as contributing to threats to international order as it is today. It would take a massive and sudden shift in attitudes to legalize commercialization of the narcotics trade. In addition, although the shaping strategy would use more multilateral forums, it is the United States that has played a leading role in the international prohibition of narcotics trafficking. It also has its own domestic War on Drugs that is dedicated to prohibition as the central strategy. The main goal of the U.S. War on Drugs is to "prohibit supply, so that Americans cannot find or afford drugs to use; its secondary aim is discourage those who do consume drugs, mainly by penalizing them."[41] It is highly unlikely that the United States would divest itself of the War on Drugs, then lead an international movement for legalization or strongly support the efforts of others to do so.

The practicality of worldwide legalization would be overwhelmingly difficult as well. Even replacing the current prohibition and enforcement paradigm with one that emphasizes "harm reduction," which judges the harm caused to society by keeping drugs illegal rather than decriminalizing them and possibly lessening the harm, would require nearly unanimous acquiescence by national leaders. If only one country retains harsh measures against the drug trade while others adopt more permissive laws, a type of narcotics-driven security dilemma will be created. Harsh restrictions would not necessarily lessen demand, and, with increased risk, illicit trafficking into a more prohibitive environment would be seductively lucrative. Meanwhile, in nations where drug consumption is legal, "drug tourists" from countries that have harsh measures would likely swamp more permissive states. Governments would be forced to either forgo legalization efforts because they are being undermined or revert to harsher enforcement measures in an attempt to stem the tide of black-market narcotics.[42]

It is doubtful that a worldwide legalization of the trade, even if possible, would eliminate all drug-fueled conflicts. The illicit trade in legal commodities, such as oil, timber, and gems, as well as the black market trade of legal intoxicants like alcohol and cigarettes by warring groups, strongly suggests that legalizing drugs would not be any different. Additionally, not all drugs have the same intoxicating or addictive properties. Would governments permit a multinational company to introduce a brand of methamphetamine into society? Even if certain drugs were legalized and commercialized, governments would probably restrict the level of intoxicating and addictive chemicals in the product. It is possible that a black market for drugs that have higher concentrations of intoxicating compounds than allowed by governments would spring up. Also, with well-established smuggling routes in place, warring groups can turn the networks toward other illicit trade. Human trafficking, for example, is fast becoming a lucrative trade where profits are competitive with illicit narcotics. In fact, many nations have lower penalties for human trafficking and smuggling than for drug crimes, making involvement in human trafficking slightly more appealing.

When it comes to the drug trade, scholars, policymakers, and military leaders have to accept an uncomfortable paradox—that there will always be some presence of the drug trade that exists alongside continued prohibition of its sale and restrictions on its consumption. Prohibition will probably not eliminate all illicit narcotics, yet it is equally unlikely that the international community will accept legalization. There is simply no international political will to do so. As such, strategies designed to deal with the drug trade's intersection with war must take this into account.

Another common feature among the strategies is the acknowledgement of the continuing complexity in the patterns of war. While conventional war among established states fought by professional militaries over primarily political goals is possible, the majority of wars are likely to be smaller conflicts, fought by irregulars over a mixture of political and criminal goals where civilians will be seen as legitimate targets. Labeled as "fourth generation" or "post-industrial" or "post-modern" warfare, the future's most severe and persistent threats will continue to arise not from conflicts between major political entities but from increased discord within states, societies, and civilizations along ethnic, racial, religious, linguistic, caste, or class lines.[43] Contrary to the parameters of an abstaining strategy, wars are likely to continue to slip out of the boundaries of the nation-state and take on more transnational qualities. Networked actors waging asymmetric war will have distinct advantages over more conventional opponents waging pitched battles, forcing all combatants to adapt to a dispersed and often non-physical battlespace. The future configuration of combatant groups will resemble Hezbollah with their dispersed local, national, and international links, more than the heavyset, hierarchical military of the People's Liberation Army of China (PLA).

Patterns of warfare also suggest another assumption—the neo-medieval nature of the contemporary international security environment. The description of the world as neo-medieval is metaphorical. "In no sense is the world going backwards…but authority is based upon 'parceling out.' That is, the creation of zones of authority with overlapping boundaries and, at the same time, no universal center of competence."[44] War and the drug trade will be intertwined against a backdrop of fragmented sovereignty, overlapping allegiances, and untold numbers of actors. The intersection of drugs and war will be, to paraphrase Martin Booth, more labyrinth and more complex, involving more players, more sources, and more diversity than has been previously witnessed.[45]

Certain core principles of success can be generated from which to build the foundations for any feasible strategy. As such, they raise several questions that each strategy must address and are related to the dynamics of the intersection, strategic use of drugs, and responses to drug-fueled conflicts—will a given strategy make the drug trade less appealing to warring groups, lessen the severe impacts upon civilians, reduce combatant usage, and lower future incentives to become involved in the drug trade? Without an answer to these questions, any strategy will be weak from the beginning.

First, a fundamental core principle is the need for closer monitoring of the drug trade's influence on patterns of war, which, in turn, must also be linked to how warfare enables certain aspects of the drug trade. Without paying attention to the mutually reinforcing dynamics of the relationship, strategic drug use may imperceptibly or even radically change, thereby thwarting whatever response is crafted. In short, a strategy must be constantly adapted, for without close monitoring, a newly crafted strategy will be made obsolete before it is even fully formed. Second, as revealed in the risks and pitfalls of each strategy, the illicit nature of the drug trade cannot be peeled away from the licit economy without the acquiescence of legitimate actors who are complicit in the trade. This is why monitoring the intersection of the drug trade and warfare is so critical; without understanding how combatant groups are linked to the "upper world" of legitimate global commerce, they will continue to flourish. Supply and demand lie at the core of the drug trade, but there are layers that cover this fundamental economic principle. "Rarely do belligerents operate resource exploitation schemes on their own, and all require business intermediaries—from local 'barefoot entrepreneurs' to international brokers and multinationals—to access commodity, financial, and arms markets."[46] The drug trade needs banks, business, communications, and transport. Legitimate commercial firms are adept at providing these without a great deal of unwanted (and unprofitable) scrutiny. A telecom entrepreneur summed up the attitude of many businesses that operate in countries of conflict: "they may be Taliban, they may be warlords, who cares? We are apolitical—they are customers."[47] Incentives and coercion cannot be aimed solely at the violent actors and those, such as drug farmers, who are at their mercy.

Third, with the neo-medieval quality of international life and the power of the illicit global economy, a strategy should focus on networks rather than exclusively on actors such as nation-states, rebel groups, militias, or terrorists. Instead of looking strictly at one hierarchical group making rational decisions based on achieving an identifiable political goal, any sound strategy should "seek the network, when attempting to explain, and eventually anticipate and prevent, troubling world developments" like drug-fueled conflict.[48] Looking for links between warring groups and criminal groups, governments and legitimate businesses will go further toward defeating them. While traffickers and warring groups drive the drug trade and warfare, focusing solely on individual groups operating in a geographically bounded area misses larger processes that are at work in a globalizing world. Knowing why some links among actors are "strategic and others tactical, the way they are created and maintained, their life cycle and the distribution of benefits" create a richer and fuller picture for those who are seeking to counter their influence on international security.[49]

NECESSARY STEPS FOR THE FUTURE: A LAYERED APPROACH

With baseline assumptions and core principles established, constructing the outlines of a more successful strategy becomes more feasible, manageable, and sustainable. A layered approach to drug-fueled conflicts may yield better results by adding synergy and flexibility that are absent from the three strategies previously described. Such an approach would seek to develop a network of actors at various levels who would challenge the networks employed by many warring groups that are involved in drug-fueled conflicts. This approach requires a high degree of multilayered cooperation among nation-states, international organizations, NGOs, and local communities to cope with the dynamics of the intersection between the drug trade and warfare, combat the strategic use of drugs, and assist in moving ongoing drug-fueled conflicts to abeyant conflicts to settled.

The layered approach diverges from the control and shape strategies because it does not start with the need to direct the drug trade at the global level as a way to affect its influence on warfare. The strategies of control and shape demonstrate the difficulty in breaking the intersection between drugs and warfare given the international networks that undergird globalization. With the licit part of the global economy vital to the prosperity of many people, illicit activity cannot be easily combated without affecting the smooth operation of legal global trade. Portions of an abstaining strategy have merit because they focus on lower levels of governance, yet the strategy itself misses larger global patterns of the drug trade.

A layered approach would focus on drug-fueled conflicts based on their intensity levels. At the advanced and critical levels of drug-fueled conflicts, the drug trade cannot be separated from these conflicts. These conflicts involve the cultivation and production of cocaine and heroin, and as previously mentioned, war is now a prerequisite for this trade, therefore both should be focused on together. In addition, these drugs are transshipped through areas where there are ongoing or abeyant conflicts where warring groups can secure funding and supplies for consumption. Conflicts in transshipment countries will likely be affected by any reduction in the supply of these drugs from the regions where they are botanically limited to grow. Focusing on the conflicts where opium and coca are grown will, in turn, affect a portion of the broader dynamics of the intersection of drugs and warfare. Unlike the other strategies, the layered approach seeks to attack the process and not the product.

At incipient, developing, and serious levels, the drug trade and conflict can be more easily separated, yet they still cannot be treated as independent. As transit countries, or countries that grow marijuana and where warring groups manufacture smaller quantities of ATS drugs, the potential to move these conflicts into abeyant or settled is more likely. There will still be a need for a comprehensive program that focuses on what peace might do to a combatant group's participation in the drug trade and what counternarcotics efforts might do to the dimensions of the conflict. The degree of drug use among belligerents must also be part of a comprehensive focus and included in disarmament, demobilization, and reintegration schemes. At such levels, stopping the killing while making concessions to combatant groups to ending their participation in the drug trade must be considered. These actions require timely information and intelligence from various sources.

One area where integrated efforts would be useful in tackling the dynamics of the intersection is the monitoring of global drug trends and patterns of conflict. Such monitoring can support better intelligence, which can be applied to tracking more fully the dynamics of drug and warfare intersection, thereby strengthening the ability of numerous actors to assess strategic drug use and appropriately respond to drug-fueled conflict. Indirectly seeking to curtail the intersection of drugs and warfare at the international level does not discount the need for international cooperation. At the multilateral level, the growing interrelationship between drug trafficking and armed conflict does not mean that responses should be similarly intertwined.

Better monitoring is necessary because the shape of the drug trade changes, and as demonstrated throughout this book, when the drug trade changes, so do the effects on warfare. This expanded and integrated monitoring of the drug trade will become more important because warring groups increasingly exhibit transnational characteristics. Their ability to reach out into the global economy for support combined with their ability to reach into deeper parts of civil society makes the focus on the drug trade more critical. As noted previously, ideology has been used to justify smuggling drugs to an enemy's society, while it has not acted as a barrier for groups to enter into drug-trafficking activities.

Monitoring is also needed to keep pace with future changes in the supply and demand of the drug market as well. With ATS being labeled the "chameleon drug" along with Clausewitz describing war as "more than a chameleon," the future of drug-fueled conflict seems poised to become more complex. Yet, the ease with which these drugs can be manufactured may also lead to their demise as a major funding source. Given the wide and growing availability of precursor chemicals and the simplicity of the requisite equipment, few parts of the world are immune to the emergence of synthetic-drug production. As such, many ATS "entrepreneurs" can compete in various domestic markets and dealers do not have to rely on importing these drugs from countries of conflict.

The potential for new plant-based narcotics entering the global market should not be discounted. Although *khat* and *datura* are locally produced and consumed, diaspora communities and overnight shipping services may expand the reach of these drugs in the near future. Additionally, it remains to be seen what plant will be discovered in the future that may offer a uniquely intoxicating effect combined with an ability to be transported in small quantities and over great distances, or how a combatant group can use it as a stimulant, reward, recruitment tool, or relaxant for its own forces.

The expanded monitoring of prescription drugs needs to be considered as well. Prescription drugs are becoming easily available over the Internet and can be diverted to the illegal market. In fact, reducing the diversion of licit drugs is a major priority for the U.S. DEA.[50] Such a new priority is a welcome development given the changing nature of the drug market. For example, numerous white-collar professionals obtain the drug Adderall from online pharmacies to use as a stimulant.[51] A drug prescribed for attention deficit disorder, Adderall is a combination of four kinds of amphetamines that can act similarly to cocaine and other stimulant drugs in people who do not have the disorder. Obtaining drugs like Adderall would not be difficult; pharmaceutical companies in the West routinely sell expired drugs overseas where distribution controls are weaker. This makes such drugs not only commercially available to combatants, but also potentially available to groups that might loot supplies of such drugs during conflicts. This, combined with worldwide shipping expanding to farther reaches of the globe, means that it would be feasible for warring groups to sell prescription drugs on the black market for funding or personal use in combat.

However, the future may find that new drugs entering the market will be fine-tuned to an individual's own neurochemistry and designed to make their use invisible to others—no red eyes, nervous ticks, or lethargy. These too may be home manufactured and have the same advantages in stealth and wealth (if not more) for warring groups.[52]

Bearing in mind the valuable contributions of NGOs, international institutions, and regimes, a layered approach would seek to gain assistance from NGOs that are working on development projects that can provide a useful gauge of how deeply the drug economy is integrated within a particular community and how it is affecting the conflict. Because it is likely that the NGO projects are also jeopardized by drug-fueled conflicts, a certain level of cooperation could be expected. Knowing who is involved in the drug trade and the methods used to transport the product can contribute to tactics designed to sap the economic and social base of an insurgency. Better intelligence from all sources can be decisive in various counterdrug and conflict-resolution efforts.

A networked series of institutions would be needed to fully tackle monitoring efforts. The UN has an Office on Drugs and Crime and there are several regional law enforcement institutions like Europol. However, fusion centers are needed at the international level and not only the tactical level as described in the control strategy. A fusion center would exist in each institution that allowed for the exchange of information and ideas among different international, regional, and local institutions and across different agencies. Such fusion centers would focus on how drug patterns are not only affecting law enforcement, but patterns of organized political violence as well. Because the trade in opium and coca are largely confined to certain geographic regions that do not have strong regional law-enforcement integration, steps should be taken to encourage their development. Marijuana and ATS patterns require lower-level assistance of legitimate governments and NGOs to generate information to share with monitoring agencies in the UN and other regional institutions.

With networked institutions that monitor various aspects of the drug trade and how it intersects with organized violence, intelligence can be empowered more fully. Intelligence provides the who, what, when, and where for both military and law-enforcement operations. Intelligence can serve as a bridge between the military and law enforcement in drug-fueled conflicts as well as enable anticipatory norm creation for agencies across the spectrum of government and among the array of international institutions. Intelligence can also design operations and find tactics for specific drug-fueled conflicts. The arrest and extradition of Baz Mohammad, a warlord supported by the Afghan drug trade, were the product of fused intelligence operations among multinational, national, and local agencies. Such targeting of warlord leaders removes the culture of impunity that is often part of high levels of drug-fueled conflicts.

Combatant drug consumption patterns will also require broader monitoring. Because warring groups can degenerate into raiding parties, which can fracture and increase their violence because of withdrawals and paranoia, it is worthwhile to gain an understanding of the patterns of combatant drug consumption. Understanding the inner workings of combatant groups will require a focus on who is using what drugs, for what purposes, and how they are acquired. As seen in chapter 3, carnival activities have led national decision-makers to use military force to stem the tide of human rights abuses; focusing on the use of psychoactive chemicals by offending combatants can be powerful information for those intervening in a drug-fueled conflict.

Tracking the growing use of methamphetamine among irregular forces must be made a top priority. Because meth is easy to manufacture and does not require a warring group to be located near a traditional drug crop, transshipment point, or smuggling route, meth will likely be a feature in more conflicts. As discussed in chapter 3, meth withdrawal symptoms are particularly acute and prolonged. As a result, meth users alleviate their symptoms by seeking out other drugs such as cocaine or heroin. Thus, combatant demand for other drugs may rise if meth supply is interrupted, leading to outbreaks of violence, such as looting pharmaceutical drugs.

Adversaries who rely on drug trade to finance violence must be viewed as "adaptive competitors" in ways that conventional adversaries are not. Adaptive competitors "address problems, change practices, and create identities in response to knowledge and experience, sometimes improving their performance and aiding their bureaucratic survival."[53] To tackle adaptive competitors, strategies must be designed to make them face disincentives like lessening demand, lowering profit margins, and raising risks.[54] Beyond focusing strictly on the drugs themselves, the process by which these actors interact with the drug trade must be targeted for disruption. To combat drug use in asymmetric strategies and guard against drugs manipulation in reversal of fortune situations, intelligence should be directed in ways that inject risk into combatant calculations. Drug-fueled conflicts have the hallmarks of the merging of armed conflict and economics that "amplifies the degree to which complex conflicts emulate the characteristics of hypercompetitive markets."[55] Injecting risk into combatants' calculations creates uncertainty that can be turned to the advantage of those seeking to win the conflict or coerce the parties into negotiations.

Many links between members of warring groups, among different warring groups, and between warring groups and organized crime is based on a degree of trust. Unlike legal multinational corporations and companies that are accountable to shareholders and that have a judicial system to resolve disputes, criminal and warring groups must rely on trust. The possibility that trust will disintegrate is why the potential for violence permeates illicit transactions. Law enforcement has been good at attacking trust. In the early days of fighting organized crime, civilian law enforcement chose targets of a few select cronies to continually strike. In combination with a disinformation campaign, this created paranoia among the elite as to who was feeding intelligence to the authorities. Paranoia may be even easier to instill if combatants are heavy drug users, making intelligence on the drug habits of belligerents of abiding importance.

Because of the ways drug-fueled conflicts are different from other conflicts, new objectives need to be added to the plans of interveners. Although militaries have resisted participating in counternarcotics operations, nesting these operations in campaign plans from the beginning while training them to reconsider the military objectives in drug-fueled conflicts will reduce military apprehension over time. Smuggling routes through transshipment countries need to be thought of by military planners as crucial lines of support for the enemy. Such routes are not simply incidental to the conflict; in the cases of Uzbekistan and Pakistan, for example, they are instrumental to the perpetuation of violence. Even at lower intensity levels, focusing on smuggling routes can exert pressure on a portion of a warring group, making them more amenable to concessions. Hospitals, clinics, and pharmacies should be added to campaign lists as objectives that need to be secured in an intervention. These facilities are also now a warmaking resource for combatant groups and their looting has contributed to human rights abuses and combatant unpredictability. Attaching as much importance to these facilities as weapons depots, ammo dumps, and campaign headquarters will lead to a decrease in the overall violence in the conflict.

In situations where nation-building and stability operations are mandated, the main goal of government response to conflicts where there is widespread combatant drug use should be to reduce the level of violence through a reduction of drug use. By lowering the demand for drug use, command and control can be strengthened among irregular forces, thus increasing the likelihood of adherence to the parameters of any possible peace accord. Reducing drug use also limits the potential for further atrocities. By focusing on reducing drug use, peace initiatives have a greater chance to flourish, thereby lessening the conditions of intense violence that led many fighters to take drugs.

Detoxification programs should be integrated into demobilization efforts, no matter the degree or types of drugs used by combatants. These programs should not be thought of as a separate programs to be run after demobilization occurs; they should happen concomitantly and include as many members of society as possible, for they will form the basis of informal social controls on drug use. Village elders, mayors, and the displaced must be empowered again—detoxification programs under traditional social norms offer that chance. In many cases, this is not possible given the duration and magnitude of the conflict. In such instances, members of diaspora communities may be able to assist in reconstructing the rough outlines of these informal social controls. While militaries may have their medical corps undertake such detoxification programs, merely providing security for NGOs who do so may be enough. However, these programs need to become part of existing military doctrine on counterinsurgency, peacekeeping, and stability operations.

To train and prepare troops for drug-fueled conflicts, military planners will need to incorporate organized crime task forces in their operations to identify potential sources of black-market activity that might interfere with post-war reconstruction. Airpower leaders will have to be especially aware of attacking targets that may spur black-market activities.[56] Unmanned aerial vehicles, which can stay aloft for days, can provide surveillance, identify smuggling routes, and patrol borders. Ground forces will require specially trained police units to guard against illicit activities coordinated by criminal gangs linked to warring groups, while civil affairs specialists must be up-to-date on the latest anti-corruption techniques to stamp out criminal practices of the old bureaucracy and rebel groups.

While generals' tables are critical venues for designing new strategies, schoolhouses of professional military education traditionally have been places where the free exchange of ideas and wide-ranging adaptations have been examined and discussed before conflicts erupt. By including people from a variety of backgrounds outside the military, today's professional military education can generate greater synergy for the development of strategies and tactics to combat the adversaries of the twenty-first century. If drug-fueled conflicts resemble "hypercompetitive markets," then those who struggle against violent armed groups should develop a type of competitive ethos that is prevalent in the business world as a way to conceive future strategies. Establishing regular conferences and sponsoring research projects on drugged irregulars would also add to the body of knowledge that may be used to develop new doctrine. Following up on the conclusions reached by the Marine Corps Center for Emerging Threats and Opportunities (CETO) to develop tactics, techniques, and procedures for confronting child soldiers should at least be addressed since, as argued, much recruitment of child soldiers is linked to providing them with drugs. Capturing the knowledge of those fielded forces that have encountered drug-intoxicated combatants would also be useful; more focused after-action reviews and activities on lessons learned about the actions of drugged adversaries would be useful in building an increasing knowledge base.

For professional militaries involved in protracted wars and wars that feature encounters with child soldiers, greater institutional support is needed for the military to monitor, treat, and provide long-term care for active-duty troops and veterans. Additionally, not all military installations offer in-patient treatment for drug abuse, forcing many veterans to go untreated. Depending on how the wars in Iraq and Afghanistan conclude, the numbers of returning service members will place additional stress on this system, and without adequate institutional capacity, illegal narcotics abuse may rise sharply among this group and stoke concerns among the public.

By placing the right elements together, a formula for a framework of "1+1+x" could be constructed and implemented when focusing on a particular drug-fueled conflict. This formula means that one international organization, such as the UN, or regional alliance system is needed, as well as at least one major power plus the neighboring nations of the conflict acting in a unified fashion with the goal of lessening the intensity of the drug-fueled conflict. The history of conflict resolution suggests that only with the involvement of international organizations and at least one major power have conflicts been settled.[57] With the balloon-and hydra-effects of the drug trade, cooperation of neighboring countries to the conflict is essential to lessen their effects. A long-term commitment by the 1+1+x parties is also essential. Engendering long-term stability has typically taken five to ten years of involvement by outside parties,[58] and as seen with the history of drug trade, its impact can linger well after the killing has stopped. Enshrining the group as a forum with regular consultation among the parties would help maintain a long-term commitment.

With the strategic-level focus of intelligence on drug trade's intersection within fusion centers, specific actions directed at a drug-fueled conflict can be handled on a case-by-case basis with a 1+1+x formula with varying goals of moving drug-fueled conflicts from ongoing to abeyant, or from abeyant to settled depending on the context. No matter the context, however, continuing efforts should be directed at understanding the networks employed by warring groups involved in the drug trade. Policymakers must be aware of reversal-of-fortune situations where a warring group may shift from relying on other resources to participating in the drug trade, from trafficking one type of drug to another, or from trafficking drugs to other illicit activities such as human trafficking. Counternarcotics efforts should be integrated into the elements of security, economic growth, and governance.[59]

A 1+1+x formula, under the umbrella of a layered approach, would empower numerous options that may be applied to certain drug-fueled conflicts. Where there is a functioning government with some legitimacy among its people yet is struggling against drug-financed rebels and/or drugged combatants, efforts would be directed to support its law enforcement and military institutions. Where there is no functioning or legitimate government in drug-fueled conflicts, the 1+1+x parties may create a type of "neo-trusteeship" and re-engineer the organs of governance.[60] Where there is no agreement on a neo-trusteeship, parties may seek to contain the conflict by empowering the neighboring states and pursue the instituting of safe zones and humanitarian corridors.[61]

RESTORING HOPE: NEW THINKING FOR NEW TIMES

The layered approach is not without risks and pitfalls. To monitor the drug trade more fully to empower intelligence operations against the strategic use of drugs and more effectively respond to drug-fueled conflicts, new patterns of drug trafficking and its influence on conflicts may emerge as a result. As seen throughout the history of the drug trade, efforts to control it commercially or through its prohibition have made it "necessary for smugglers and other criminalized transnational actors to devise such creative and elaborate means to circumvent them. Transnational crimes, such as drug smuggling, are enormously profitable because states impose and enforce prohibitions."[62] This is yet another paradox that will continue if a layered approach is attempted—any success at reducing the drug trade's effects on wars will likely mean that other groups of individuals will be empowered (and enriched) by the ways they devise to undermine the efforts of such an approach, thus providing an incentive to enter the drug trade and to use violence to profit.

To more fully grapple with this paradox, it will be necessary for scholars to lay new conceptual foundations to study the phenomenon of drug-fueled conflicts. For studies of international relations, comparative politics, and military affairs, there are many concepts need to be revisited to include crosscutting ideas such as "geo-narcotics" and "narco-economics." These terms are broader than "narcoterrorism" and "narcoinsurgency" because they include the various actors involved in giving momentum to drug-fueled conflicts while also speaking to the complex, multidimensional, and multidirectional dynamic of the drug trade and warfare. For the U.S. Global War on Terrorism, the implications are that it will be unsuccessful "without integrating both a 'war on drugs' and a 'war on crime.'"[63]

Although many drug-fueled conflicts are nettlesome, especially those at higher intensity levels, attempts to prevent the outbreak of new drug-fueled conflicts must also be seen as worthwhile. Developing and adopting cross-cutting ideas may provide new ways to prevent low levels of violence in countries such as Zimbabwe, Thailand, Haiti, and Guinea-Bissau from reaching higher levels because of the influence of the drug trade. Understanding the dynamics of risk, incentive, and profit in the early stages of a potential conflict would reduce the regional and international security threats that emanate from drug-fueled conflicts. As Jeremy Weinstein observes, "civil war will be less costly for civilian populations if war can be made more expensive and more difficult for insurgent groups to initiate."[64] Focusing on the drug trade's allure for combatants can support policies and strategies designed to make the decision to go to war an expensive and difficult proposition.

Realist, liberal, and constructivist theories of international relations all contend with legitimate actors following rational interests and how these actors interact with one another and the structure of the international system. Drug-fueled conflicts prosecuted by subnational, and in some cases transnational, warring groups slip outside these theoretical approaches. Is a warlord acting in a realist manner when he uses drug crops as funding, while relying on legal companies (who keep the liberal world order humming) to provide transportation to a country whose customs officials are waiting with false manifests (a form of corruption that challenges the "construction" of sovereignty)? Nonetheless, the intersection of drugs and warfare profoundly affects legitimate actors and the structure of the international system.

International relations theory is somewhat helpful in analyzing drug-fueled conflicts. Realism and its emphasis on power and the security dilemma can be useful in understanding when and why warring groups fight over drug spoils. Liberalism can place a needed spotlight on the human rights abuses of peasants, farmers, and child soldiers caught in the spiral of violence associated with these conflicts. Constructivist theories may add a deeper conceptual richness to understanding the evolution of sovereignty created by the intersection of the drug trade and warfare and responses to the intersection.

Likewise, theories of development and social transformation are challenged by the penetrating nature of the drug trade and the new patterns of warfare in the early twenty-first century. This book supports the findings of other studies that examine the "resource curse" where the presence of natural resources can prolong conflicts and increase human suffering. However, this book points to the need to treat drugs as separate and distinct from other resources; the dimensions of the illegal trade of an illegal commodity, the consumable nature of drugs by combatants, and the compartmentalization of the trade generate political, economic, and social pathologies that are less susceptible to traditional conflict resolution techniques or coercive measures. Can building institutions and a civil society be accomplished in ways that are sustainable when drugs permeate the economic, social, and political fabric of a nation?

This book also indicates that the importance of thinkers, such as Clausewitz, in the field of military theory must be reexamined given the nature of drug-fueled conflicts. These conflicts seem to possess much of the unrestrained violence, fog, friction, and chance of what is considered to comprise war but have no political agenda to justify such violence. Is it war when opposing groups target drug farmers or if a road is attacked to secure it for a drug shipment that will enrich the members of a single group rather than to achieve an identifiable military objective? If war is the extension of politics, perhaps there is the need to expand the definition of war and redefine the meaning of politics to account for new patterns of organized violence in the early twenty-first century.

Military and strategic thinkers of the past still yield valuable insights to the nature of organized war by preparing national and military leaders for the changing guise of warfare with time-tested concepts. This book adds credence to other works that have found that contemporary warfare requires theories and concepts to be more adaptive. As a result, scholars in the field must show greater flexibility in applying the canon of military thought to modern warfare.

Missing from each discipline is the role of intoxicated combatants. The non-medical use of drugs has a long history, yet its effects are largely overlooked. Academic theories all presuppose that combatants are rational actors pursuing conflict for a specific purpose. However, as seen in this study, belligerents cannot be presumed to be "clean and sober" when they make decisions regarding war and peace. Atrocities are seen as the results of bad leaders, morally corrupted fighters, or internal security dilemmas. While they appear to be reasonable causes, they leave room for alternative explanations as well as for future directions for research. The role of the seeming "irrationality" of the ways that contemporary war is being waged needs to be taken into account.

The paradoxes and ironies of the drug trade combined with the complexity and ferocity of contemporary warfare challenge people who are dedicated to building a more secure, prosperous, and peaceful world. Yet, to leave the intersection between drugs and contemporary war unexplored is to surrender the future to greater violence by those who seek to poison many lives and societies. The international drug trade is controversial on its own. When coupled with a discussion of its ties to warfare, the controversy grows exponentially. With the discussion over what to do about the intersection of both, controversy has the potential to lurch between alarm and resignation. What H. B. Morse, an early scholar of China's opium trade, wrote about opium is as applicable to any study about drugs intersecting with war.

> Opium is a thorny subject to handle for any writer. If he is a partisan of the opium trade, his tendency is strong to leave the ground with which he is familiar, that of commercial dealings and statistics, and try to demonstrate the innocuousness of the drug as smoked by the Chinese—to compare it to the relatively harmless ante-prandial glass of sherry. If his mission is to denounce the opium traffic, he invariably seems impelled, by an irresistible inclination, to leave the high moral ground on which he is unassailable, and descend into the arena of facts and figures, with which he is not likely to be so familiar, and among which his predisposition will lead him to pass by or to misinterpret those which make against his case.[65]

Finding a balance in tackling conflicts that occur in the shadow of the drug trade is a challenge itself. Hopefully, however, this book represents a healthy step in the right direction.

NOTES

CHAPTER 1: HAZY SHADES OF WAR

1. James Corum and Wray Johnson, *Airpower in Small Wars: Fighting Insurgents and Terrorists* (Lawrence: University of Kansas Press, 2003), 5.
2. Philippe Le Billon, "The Political Ecology of War: Natural Resources and Armed Conflict," *Political Geography* (June 2001): 563; and Michael L. Ross, "Oil, Drugs and Diamonds: The Varying Roles of Natural Resources in Civil War," in *The Political Economy of Armed Conflict: Beyond Greed and Grievance*, eds. Karen Ballentine and Jake Sherman (Boulder, CO: Lynne Rienner Publishers, 2003), 52.
3. Paul Collier, "Development and Conflict," presentation given at the Centre for the Study of African Economies, Department of Economics, Oxford University, October 1, 2004. In addition, the U.S. Department of State publishes an annual International Narcotics Control Strategy Report where there has been "no exception to this phenomenon: wherever substantial amounts of narcotics were produced, terrorists or rebel groups were taking advantage of drug profits" from Jonathan Winer and Trifin Roule, "Follow the Money," in *Natural Resources and Violent Conflict: Options and Actions*, eds. Ian Bannon and Paul Collier (Washington, DC: The World Bank, 2003), 210. Even those who have tracked the rising intersection of drugs and armed conflict speak of it as coincidental—"Some countries have the *misfortune* to house not only one or more major drug operations but also insurgencies or guerrilla operations of one kind or another." [emphasis added] from Ivelaw Griffith, "Post-Cold War Geo-Narcotics," *International Journal* (Winter 1993–1994): 21.
4. Douglas J. Davids, *Narco-Terrorism: A Unified Strategy to Fight a Growing Terrorist Menace* (New York: Transnational Publishers, 2002), xiii.
5. "Afghanistan's Opium Survey 2006," United Nations Office on Drugs and Crime, 3. The

2007 opium harvest in Afghanistan was a record with a 34 percent increase from the previous year with its export value up 29 percent. As a result, opium is now estimated to equal more than half of the country's legal gross domestic product. Amir Shah, "Afghanistan Warns of 'Tsunami' of Opium," *Atlanta Journal-Constitution*, November 1, 2007.

6. Susan Milligan, "Drug Use Seen on the Rise in Iraq," *Boston Globe*, August 28, 2003.

7. For $150 billion estimate, see "Stumbling in the Dark," *The Economist*, July 28, 2001. For $500 billion, see *The Illicit Global Economy and State Power*, eds. H. Richard Friman and Peter Andreas (New York: Rowman and Littlefield, 1999), 2.

8. Jeffrey Robinson, *The Merger: The Conglomeration of International Organized Crime* (New York: Overlook Press, 2000), 337.

9. "Colombian Report Shows FARC is World's Richest Insurgent Group," *Jane's Intelligence Review* (September 2005): 12–17.

10. David Rohnde, "Afghan Symbol for Change Becomes a Symbol of Failure," *New York Times*, September 5, 2006.

11. For example, Daniel Deudney, "Environment and Security: Muddled Thinking," *Bulletin of Atomic Scientists* (April 1991); Stephen Walt, "The Renaissance of Security Studies," *International Studies Quarterly* (June 1991); and Edward Kolodziej, "Renaissance in Security Studies? Caveat Lector!" *International Studies Quarterly* (December 1992).

12. Taylor B. Seybolt, "Major Armed Conflicts," in *SIPRI Yearbook 2005* (Oxford: Oxford University Press, 2006), 121.

13. Indra de Soysa, "The Resource Curse: Are Civil Wars Driven by Rapacity or Paucity," in *Greed and Grievance: Economic Agendas in Civil Wars* eds. Mats Berdal and David Malone (Boulder, CO: Lynne Rienner Publishers, 2000); David Keen, "Incentives and Disincentives for Violence," in *Greed and Grievance*.

14. Paul Collier, "Rebellion as Quasi-Criminal Activity," *Journal of Peace Research* (December 2000): 852.

15. John Mueller, *Remnants of War* (Ithaca, NY: Cornell University Press, 2004), 86.

16. Azar Gat and Zeev Maoz, "Global Change and the Transformation of War," in *War in a Changing World*, eds. Azar Gat and Zeev Maoz (Ann Arbor: University of Michigan Press, 2001), 3.

17. Peter Spiegel, "Fear of Fighting and Economic Ruin Hold Back Bid to Stamp Out Opium," *London Financial Times*, January 4, 2005.

18. Collier, "Doing Well Out of War" in *Greed and Grievance*.

19. David Keen, "The Economic Function of Violence in Civil Wars," in *Adelphi Paper 320* (Oxford: Oxford University Press, 1998), 11.

20. Ibid., 15.

21. David Courtwright, *Forces of Habit: Drugs and the Making of World History* (Cambridge, MA: Harvard University Press, 2001), 65.

22. Ibid., 69.

23. These conventions complement the Hague Convention of 1912 and are mutually reinforcing. They are the Single Convention on Narcotic Drugs, 1961; the Convention on Psychotropic Substance, 1971; and the Convention Against the Illicit Traffic in Narcotic Drugs and Psychotropic Substances, 1988.

24. Guy Gugliotta and Jeff Leen, *Kings of Cocaine* (New York: Harper and Row, 1989), 257, 280.

25. Loretta Napoleoni, *Modern Jihad: Tracing the Dollars Behind the Terror Networks* (London: Pluto Press, 2003), 40–41.

26. William B. McAllister, *Drug Diplomacy in the Twentieth Century: An International History* (New York: Routledge, 2000), 218.

27. Dan Baum, *Smoke and Mirrors: The War on Drugs and the Politics of Failure* (New York: Little, Brown and Co., 1997), 48–50. Nixon eventually reversed decades of military policy and ordered that drug use no longer be considered a crime under the military code of justice. Baum, *Smoke and Mirrors*, 52.

28. Scott MacDonald and Bruce Zagaris, "Introduction: Controlling the International Drug Problem," in *International Handbook on Drug Control*, eds. Scott MacDonald and Bruce Zagaris (Westport, CT: Greenwood, 1992), 7–11.

29. Mats Berdal and David Malone, eds., *Greed and Grievance*, 13.

30. Tony Perry, "Fallouja Insurgents Fought Under Influence of Drugs, Marines Say," *Los Angeles Times*, January 13, 2005.

31. Steven Montblatt, "Terrorism and Drugs in the Americas: The OAS Response," *Americas Forum* (February–March 2004), http://www.oas.org/ezine/ezine24/Monblatt.htm.

32. Alexandra Guaqueta, "The Colombian Conflict: Political and Economic Dimensions," in *The Political Economy of Armed Conflict: Beyond Greed and Grievance*, eds. Karen Ballentine and Jake Sherman (Boulder, CO: Lynne Rienner Publishers, 2003), 91.

33. Peter W. Singer, *Corporate Warriors: The Rise of the Privatized Military Industry* (Cornell: Cornell University Press, 2003), 65.

34. This table builds from the concepts of David C. Jordan on "narcostatization" indicators, see David C. Jordan, *Drug Politics: Dirty Money and Democracies* (Norman: University of Oklahoma, 1999), 120–121.

35. Alain Labrousse and Michel Koutouzis, *Géopolitique et Géostratégie des Drogues* (Paris: Economica, 1996), 32.

36. Svante E. Cornell, "Narcotics, Radicalism and Armed Conflict in Central Asia," *Terrorism and Political Violence* (Winter 2005): 630.

150   **DRUGS** and Contemporary Warfare

37. Sharon Behn, "Al Sadr Militia Pumping Up with Drugs," *Washington Times*, October 5, 2004.
38. "Southern Discomfort," *The Economist*, April 7, 2007.
39. "That's All They Needed," *The Economist*, December 8, 2007.
40. Gail Wannenburg, "Organized Crime in West Africa," *African Security Review* 14, no. 4 (2005): 7.
41. Ilene Cohn and Guy S. Goodwin-Gray, *Child Soldiers: The Role of Children in Armed Conflict* (New York: Oxford University Press, 1994), 26–27.
42. James Pettifer, "Asylum Seekers: Time for a New Approach," Conflict Studies Research Center—United Kingdom Ministry of Defence (September 2004): 3.
43. Stephen John Stedman, "International Implementation of Peace Agreements in Civil Wars," in *Turbulent Peace: The Challenges of Managing International Conflict*, eds. Chester A. Crocker, Fen Osler Hampson, and Pamela Aall, (Washington, DC: United States Institute of Peace, 2001), 741.
44. Guaqueta, "The Colombian Conflict," 98.
45. Parliament of Canada, "Conflicts, Drugs and Mafia Activities," *Contribution to the Preparatory Work for the Hague Peace Conference May 11–16, 1999*, March 1999, http://www.parl.gc.ca/37/1/parlbus/commbus/senate/com-e/ille-e/presentation-e/labrousse2-e.htm.

CHAPTER 2: DRUGGING THE BATTLEFIELD

1. Michael Renner, "The Anatomy of Resource Wars," *World Watch Paper* 162 (Washington, DC: World Watch Institute, 2002), 13–14.
2. Carl A. Troki, *Opium, Empire, and the Global Political Economy: A Study of the Asian Opium Trade* (New York: Routledge, 1999), 8.
3. F. W. Diehl, "Revenue Farming and Colonial Finances in the Netherlands East Indies" in *The Rise and Fall of Revenue Farming (Studies in the Economics of East & South-East Asia)*, eds. John Butcher and Howard Dick (New York: St. Martin's Press, 1993), 208.
4. Hakiem Nankoe, Jean-Claude Gerlus, and Martin J. Murray, "The Origins of the Opium Trade and Opium Regimes in Colonial Indochina," in Butcher and Dick, eds., *The Rise and Fall*, 189.
5. Trocki, *Opium, Empire, and the Global Political Economy*, 59.
6. Jack Beeching, *The Chinese Opium Wars* (New York: Harcourt, Brace, Jovanovich, 1975), 73.
7. Timothy Brook and Bob Tadashi Wakabayashi, "Opium's History in China" in *Opium Regimes: China, Britain, and Japan, 1839–1952*, eds. Brook and Wakabayashi (Los Angeles: University of California Press, 2000), 17.

8. Pu Yi Aisin-Gioro, *From Emperor to Citizen: The Autobiography of Aisin-Gioro Pu Yi*, trans. W. J. F. Jenner (Oxford: Oxford University Press, 1987), 384.

9. Brook and Wakabayashi, *Opium Regimes*, 17.

10. Alfred W. McCoy, *The Politics of Heroin in Southeast Asia: CIA Complicity in the Global Drug Trade* (New York: Harper and Row, 1972), 96. Additionally, French opium monopoly in Indochina was a lynchpin of Ho Chi Minh's anti-colonial propaganda.

11. Shi-wen Tuan, "China's Forgotten Soldiers," *Weekend Telegraph*, March 10, 1967.

12. McAllister, *Drug Diplomacy in the Twentieth Century: An International History* (New York: Routledge, 2000), 253.

13. Moisés Naím, *Illicit: How Smugglers, Traffickers, and Copycats Are Hijacking the Global Economy* (New York: Doubleday, 2005), 19.

14. Sue Williams, "The Globalization of the Drug Trade," *Sources* (April 1999): 5.

15. Williams, "The Globalization of the Drug Trade," 5.

16. Paul Stares, *Global Habit* (Washington, DC: Brookings Institution, 1996), 5–6.

17. UN General Assembly Special Session on the World Drug Problem, June 8–10, 1998, *Money Laundering* (New York: UN, 1998), 3.

18. Alain Joxe, "Narco-stratégie: de l'île de la Tortue à l'espace Mondial," in *La Planéte des Drogues, Organisations Criminelles, Guerres et Blanchiment*, eds. A. Labrousse and A. Wallon (Paris: Édition du Seuil, 1993), 75.

19. Ian Bannon and Paul Collier, eds., *Natural Resources and Violent Conflict: Options and Actions* (Washington, DC: The World Bank, 2003), 4.

20. Chris Mathers, *Crime School: Money Laundering* (Buffalo, NY: Firefly Books, 2004), 121.

21. Phil Williams, "The Nature of Drug-Trafficking Networks," *Current History* (April 1998): 155.

22. Michael Kenney, *From Pablo to Osama: Trafficking and Terrorist Networks, Government Bureaucracies, and Competitive Adaptation* (University Park: Pennsylvania State University Press, 2007), 26.

23. Phil Williams, "Transnational Criminal Networks," in *Networks and Netwars: The Future of Terror, Crime, and Militancy*, eds. John Arquilla and David Ronfeldt (Santa Monica, CA: RAND Corporation, 2001), 69.

24. Ibid.

25. Williams, "The Nature of Drug-Trafficking Networks," 159.

26. Le Billon, "Fuelling War: Natural Resources and Armed Conflict," *Adelphi Paper 373* (London: Routledge, 2005), 44.

27. David Kaplan, "The New Business of Terror," *US News and World Report*, December 5, 2005.

28. Deborah Charles, "Feds Bust Colombians in Drugs-for-Guns Deal," *Reuters Wire*, November 6, 2002.

29. United Nations Office of Drugs and Crime, *World Drug Report 2007* (New York: United Nations, 2007), 9.

30. Eva Bertram, Morris Blachman, Kenneth Sharpe, and Peter Andreas, *Drug War Politics: The Price of Denial* (Los Angeles: University of California Press, 1996), 13.

31. Mark Kleiman, "Illicit Drugs and the Terrorist Threat," Congressional Research Service, April 20, 2004, 10.

32. Naím, *Illicit*, 77.

33. Chris Harmon, *Terrorism Today*, 2nd ed. (New York: Routledge, 2008), 76.

34. Roughly 350 person days are required to work one hectare of poppy.

35. Harmon, *Terrorism Today*, 76.

36. Robert Charles, "The Afghan Dilemma," *Washington Times*, April 26, 2005.

37. Michelle Garcia, "Alleged Afghan Drug Kingpin Arrested by DEA in New York," *Washington Post*, April 26, 2005.

38. During the Cold War, opium was transported to labs run primarily by organized crime in Pakistan. Pakistani organized crime along with Taliban and Afghan warlords run numerous cross-border operations to support the regional drug trade.

39. International Narcotics Control Board, "Iraq Emerging as a Transit Country for Drugs, INCB President Says," press release, May 12, 2005.

40. James A. Inciardi, *The War on Drugs III: The Continuing Saga of the Mysteries and Miseries of Intoxication, Addiction, Crime, and Public Policy* (Boston: Allyn and Bacon, 2002), 137.

41. Jorge Osterling, *Democracy in Colombia: Clientelistic Politics and Guerrilla Warfare* (New Brunswick: Transaction Press, 1989), 299.

42. German Giraldo Restrepo (colonel, Colombian National Army), interview, U.S. Army War College, Carlisle Barracks, PA, March 24, 2006.

43. Juan Forero, "U.S. Indicts 50 Leaders of Colombian Rebels in Cocaine Trafficking," *New York Times*, March 23, 2006.

44. United Nations Office on Drugs and Crime, *Annual World Drug Report 2007*, 13–16.

45. Ken Dermota, "Snow Job," *The Atlantic* (August 2007): 24.

46. United Nations Office on Drugs and Crime, *Annual World Drug Report 2006* (New York: United Nations, 2006), 18.

47. Indoor growing of marijuana increases the potency of its intoxicating compound, THC. Dozens of marijuana plants spaced closely together and grown under thousand watt lights will yield three pounds of marijuana in two months. See Michael Pollan, *The Botany of Desire* (New York: Random House, 2001), 136. However, there is no evidence that any warring groups have utilized this technique to grow marijuana.

48. Prakash Dubey, "Maoist Rebels Sell Looted Petrol to Raise Funds," March 7, 2006, www.asianews.it/view.php?l=en&art=5570. According to the U.S. Department of State,

before they switched to other criminal activities, Maoist rebels in Nepal were known to have called on farmers in certain areas to increase cannabis production and levy a 40 percent tax on cannabis production. *International Narcotics Control Strategy Report 2005*, http://www.state.gov/p/inl/rls/nrcrpt/2005/vol1/html/42366.htm.

49. United States Office of National Drug Control Policy, *Marijuana Fact Sheet 2004*, http://www.ondcp.gov/publications/factsht/marijuana/index.html.

50. United Nations Office on Drugs and Crime, *Ecstasy and Amphetamines Global Survey 2003* (New York: United Nations, September 2003), 67. Among the report's findings were that, between 1995–2001, the abuse of ecstasy spiraled 70 percent; abuse of methamphetamine grew 40 percent. By contrast, cocaine and heroin abuse worldwide grew less than 1 percent each.

51. David Courtwright, *Forces of Habit: Drugs and the Making of World History* (Cambridge, MA: Harvard University Press, 2001), 65.

52. Peter Swartz, "The War on Drugs," *Foreign Policy* (September–October 2005): 51.

53. Douglas J. Davids, *Narco-Terrorism: A Unified Strategy to Fight a Growing Terrorist Menace* (New York: Transnational Publishers, 2002), 31; and Dale Fuchs, "Spain Says Bombers Drank Water from Mecca and Sold Drugs," *New York Times*, April 15, 2004.

54. In many respects, this mimics the pattern of the global trade in cocaine. Before World War II, the cocaine trade remained small due to few experts with the technical skill to turn coca leaves into cocaine hydrochloride residing in areas where coca was cultivated. Also, coca leaves were too bulky to smuggle to the areas where such expertise existed. However, after World War II, an embryonic capability to produce coca paste developed in Peru with the use of chemicals that had become more widely available. This paste was then transported to labs in Mexico and Cuba and processed into cocaine for the U.S. market. See Paul Stares, *Global Habit*, 23.

55. Shona Morrison, "The Dynamics of Illicit Drugs Production: Future Sources and Threats," *Crime, Law and Social Change* (1997): 131–132.

56. Pierre-Arnaud Chouvy and Joel Meisonnier, *Yaa Baa: Production, Traffic and Consumption of Methamphetamine in Mainland Southeast Asia* (Singapore: Singapore University Press, 2004), xvii.

57. Ibid., 25.

58. Jim Arroyo (special agent, Drug Enforcement Administration, New York Field Division), presentation to the U.S. Army War College, October 15, 2005, New York City, NY.

59. Ibid.

60. Philippe Le Billon, "Fuelling War: Natural Resources and Armed Conflict," in *Adelphi Paper 373* (London: Routledge, 2005), 38.

61. Interestingly, Mexico's Ejército Zapatista Liberación Nacional (EZLN), which fought a short conflict with Mexico's government, did not participate in the drug trade despite

Mexico's vibrant marijuana export to the United States. See Chris Dishman, "Terrorism, Crime and Transformation," *Studies in Conflict and Terrorism*, fn.19, 47. The EZLN received licit external financial support and likely did not want to jeopardize such support by engaging in the harvesting and trafficking of marijuana that would have required crop space to protect and additional manpower.

62. Thomas Sanderson, "Transnational Terrorism and Organized Crime: Blurring the Lines," *SAIS Review* (Winter–Spring 2004): 49–61.

63. The DEA uncovered meth labs run by members of Hezbollah in the rural western United States during Operation Mountain Express. See Sanderson, "Transnational Terror and Organized Crime," 52.

64. Paul Collier, Anke Hoeffler and Mans Soderbom, "On the Duration of Civil War," Policy Working Paper 2861, (World Bank, 2001).

65. Svante E. Cornell, "Narcotics, Radicalism, and Armed Conflict in Central Asia: The Islamic Movement of Uzbekistan," *Terrorism and Political Violence* (Winter 2005): 632–633.

66. Xavier Bougarel, *Bosnie: Anatomie d'un Conflit* (Paris: La Découverte, 1996), 126.

67. Peter Andreas, "The Clandestine Political Economy of War and Peace in Bosnia," *International Studies Quarterly* (June 2004): 39.

68. Kleiman, "Illicit Drugs," 10.

69. United Nations Department for Disarmament Affairs, "Small Arms and Light Weapons," April 24, 2006, http://disarmament.un.org/cab/salw.html.

70. Andrew Bounds and James Wilson, "Colombian Rebels Trade Drugs for Arms," *Financial Times*, May 16, 2002.

71. United Nations, *Report of the United Nations Conference on the Illicit Trade in Small Arms and Light Weapons in All its Aspects*, New York, July 9–20, 2001.

72. Sanderson, *Transnational Terrorism and Organized Crime*, 52.

73. Bob Graham and Michael Evans, "How War on Drugs May Have Helped Hezbollah," *London Times*, August 21, 2006.

74. Le Billon, "Fuelling War," 46.

75. Eric Ellis, "Afghanomics," *Fortune*, October 6, 2006, 57.

76. Institute of War and Peace Reporting (IWPR), "The Killing Fields of Afghanistan," *Afghan Recovery Report* no.16, June 26, 2002.

77. Jeremy Weinstein, *Inside Rebellion: The Politics of Insurgent Violence* (New York: Cambridge University Press, 2007).

78. Rachel Morarjee, "Drug Lords Reap Human Rewards of Poor Afghan Opium Harvests," *Financial Times*, May 10, 2006.

79. Stephen Ellis, "Liberia 1898–94: A Study of Ethnic and Spiritual Violence," *African Affairs* (Fall 1995): 185.

80. United Nations Office on Drugs and Crime, *Trafficking in Persons Global Report* (April 2006).

81. In fact, in many countries, the penalties for smuggling people are lower than the penalties for smuggling drugs.

82. Svante E. Cornell, "Stemming the Contagion," *Georgetown Journal of International Affairs* (Winter/Spring 2005): 24.

83. Misha Glenny, "Boomtime for Mafias," *The Economist: The World in 2007*, January 1, 2007.

84. Peter Reuter and Edwin Truman, *Chasing Dirty Money* (Washington, DC: Institute for International Economics, 2004), 32–33.

85. Bannon and Collier, *Natural Resources*, 170–171.

86. Karen Ballentine and Jake Sherman, eds., *The Political Economy of Armed Conflict: Beyond Greed and Grievance* (Boulder, CO: Lynne Rienner Publishers, 2003), 9.

87. Bertil Lintner and Shawn W. Crispin, "For US, New North Korea Problem," *Wall Street Journal*, November 18, 2003.

88. Foreign Policy Council, *Eurasia Security Watch* no. 86 (Washington, DC: Foreign Policy Council, May 18, 2005).

89. Paul R. Kan, "Drugging Babylon: The Illegal Narcotics Trade and Nation-Building in Iraq," *Small Wars and Insurgencies* (June 2007).

90. E. Aksakova, "Tajik Border Guards Seize at least Two Tons of Drugs," U.S. Embassy, Dushanbe, December 7, 2006.

91. "The Cuban Government Involvement in Facilitating International Drug Traffic" (Washington, DC: U.S. Government Printing Office, 1983).

92. Loretta Napoleoni, *Modern Jihad: Tracing the Dollars Behind the Terror Networks* (London: Pluto Press, 2003), 41.

93. Linda Robinson, "Terror Close to Home: In Oil-Rich Venezuela, A Volatile Leader Befriends Bad Actors from the Mideast, Colombia and Cuba," *U.S. News and World Report*, October 6, 2003. http://www.usnews.com/usnews/issue/031006/usnews/6venezuela.htm (accessed October 9, 2003).

94. Bruce Bechtol, *Red Rogue: The Persistent Challenge of North Korea* (Washington, DC: Potomac Books, 2007), 87.

95. "North Korean Ship Sunk," *Association of Former Intelligence Officers*, December 24, 2001, http://www.afio.com/sections/wins/2001/2001-50.html.

96. Russell Smith, "North Korean Heroin," *NewsMax.Com*, May 7, 2003, http://www.newsmax.com/archives/articles/2003/5/7/30830.shtml.

97. Jerry Seper, "DEA Says Afghanistan's Heroin Begets Violence," *Washington Times*, June 29, 2006.

CHAPTER 3: HIGH AT WAR

1. Ronald K. Siegel, viii.

2. Alcohol was the preferred drug of choice among European troops during the colonial era. As American and British forces faced each other over the independence of the colonies in 1776, both militaries included in their respective doctrines that men could not be expected to fight without their regular rations of rum. Presaging contemporary episodes in today's conflicts, the British routinely sought to destroy General Washington's stores of rum as a way to affect American morale. See Ian Williams, *Rum: A Social and Sociable History* (New York: Nation Books, 2005).

3. The word "hashish" is apocryphally associated with the corruption of the word "assassin." The Assassins of the eleventh century were said to have been recruited after long smoking sessions of hashish. See Michael Pollan, *Botany of Desire: A Plant's-Eye View of the World* (New York: Random House, 2001), 172–173.

4. Matters were made worse by the fact that morphine and opium were cheaper than alcohol and widely available in the United States at that time. See Paul Gahlinger, *Illegal Drugs: A Complete Guide to Their History, Chemistry, Use, and Abuse* (New York: Plume, 2001), 26.

5. W. Travis Hanes III and Frank Sanello, *The Opium Wars* (Naperville, IL: Source Books, 2002), 171.

6. Dominic Streatfeild, *Cocaine: An Unauthorized Biography* (New York: Picador, 2001), 155. Reflecting the change in societal attitudes toward narcotics more generally at the beginning of the twentieth century, drug use by soldiers was viewed as damaging to the war effort and disruptive among the troops. These attitudes were strengthened when returning veterans in Europe and America sought out cocaine to "cure" their addiction to morphine and heroin acquired after treatment of their war wounds. In fact, drug-addicted veterans in the United States often scrounged for junk metal to pay for drugs, earning them the nickname "junk men" and then simply "junkies." See Paul Gahlinger, *Illegal Drugs*, 60.

7. Bruce Eisner, *Ecstasy: The MDMA Story* (Berkeley, CA: Ronin, 1994), 127.

8. This liquid form allowed the body to more quickly absorb the drug than amphetamine pills, but was more addictive. The addictive quality of the drug was felt particularly acutely in Japan when returning soldiers arrived home and methamphetamine supplies stored for military use became available to the public at the conclusion of the war.

9. L.A. Young, L.G. Young, M.M. Klein, and D. Beyer, *Recreational Drugs* (New York: Berkeley Books, 1977).

10. Edward Brecher, *Licit and Illicit Drugs* (New York: Little, Brown & Co., 1972), 189. In addition, with the current "zero tolerance" of drug use and possession by the U.S. military combined with more frequent deployment rotations, troops have resorted to unorthodox ways to achieve intoxication. There have been episodes of troops using over-the-counter cough and cold medications like Nyquil to get intoxicated.

11. Mary Midgley, *Beast and Man: The Roots of Human Nature* (Ithaca, NY: Cornell University Press, 1978); Thomas Stephen Szasz, *Ceremonial Chemistry: The Ritual Persecution of Drugs, Addicts, and Pushers* (New York: Anchor Press, 1974).

12. Robert MacCoun and Peter Reuter, *Drug War Heresies: Learning from Other Vices, Times, and Places* (New York: Cambridge University Press, 2001), 85.

13. These descriptions do not match the clinical and pharmacological descriptions of the physiological and psychological effects of these drugs. For example, although marijuana is clinically classified as a "depressant" and is used by combatants to relax, it is also used as a stimulant in terms of motivating an individual to engage in combat. The term "relaxant" also refers to a combatant's desire to find an escape rather than to the strict physiological effects.

14. "Afghan Soldiers Report Getting Hashish Rations," *St. Louis Post-Dispatch*, May 25, 1989.

15. John Mueller, *Remnants of War* (Ithaca, NY: Cornell University Press, 2004), 92–93. Using drugs as a reward is not exclusively a part of irregular forces. Some government forces have also turned to narcotics to reward troops who conducted unpalatable missions. It was widely reported that Zimbabwean army commandos had smoked a special grade of marijuana for the special mission that included the arrest and torture of government opposition members. See "Police Witness Details of Brutal Assault," *The Zimbabwe Times*, March 15, 2007, http://www.the zimbabwetimes.com/index.php?option=com_content&task=view&id=627& Itemid=44.

16. Martin Booth, *Opium: A History* (New York: St. Martin's Griffin, 1996), 269.

17. Richard H. Shultz Jr. and Andrea Dew, *Insurgents, Terrorists, and Militias: The Warriors of Contemporary Combat* (New York: Columbia University Press, 2006), 262.

18. Jean-Charles Brissard and Damien Martinez, *Zarqawi: The New Face of Al-Qaeda* (New York: Other Press, 2005), 49.

19. Rick Rogers, "Some Troops Headed Back to Iraq are Mentally Ill," *San Diego Union Tribune*, March 19, 2006..

20. Kelly Kennedy, "Kennedy Stories," *Army Times*, December 17, 2007, www.armytimes.com/news/2007/12/bloodbrothers3/.

21. Paul von Zeilbauer, "For U.S. Troops at War, Liquor is Spur to Crime," *New York Times*, March 13, 2007.

22. Ibid.

23. Greg Jaffe, "Army's Recruiting Push Appears to Have Met Goals," *Wall Street Journal*, July 10, 2006.

24. Lars Mehlum, "Alcohol and Stress in Norwegian United Nations Peacekeepers," *Military Medicine* (October 1999): 9.

25. Kenneth Cain, Heidi Postlewait, and Andrew Thomson, *Emergency Sex: And Other Desperate Measures* (New York: Miramax Books, 2004), 77.

26. "Suit Alleges Blackwater Defiance, Drug Use," CBS News, November 27, 2007, cbsnews.com/stories/2007/11/27/national/printable3546518.shtml.

27. Martin Boas and Anne Hatloy, "Alcohol and Drug Consumption in Post War Sierra Leone—An Exploration," Institute for Applied International Studies (Norway), 43–44.

28. Mueller, *Remnants of War*, 89–92.

29. United Nations Office on Drugs and Crime, *Addressing Organized Crime and Drug Trafficking in Iraq: Report of the UNODC Fact Finding Mission* (2005), 13.

30. Interviews conducted by the author at the U.S. Army War College, January 6, 2006. Interviewees wish to remain anonymous.

31. Anonymous Marine, "A Marine Reports from Iraq," *Washington Times*, November 22, 2005. The production of methamphetamine requires certain chemicals with an essential ingredient, pseudophedrine, which is found in commercial decongestants such as Sudafed. Obtaining the needed amounts of pseudophedrine to create methamphetamine requires access to pharmacies or other places where the drug is available, which in turn often necessitates burglary, robbery, or looting. See also Robert Looney, "The Business of Insurgency: The Expansion of Iraq's Shadow Economy," *The National Interest* (Fall 2005): 70–71.

32. Not included in this table is liquor, which is almost always added to the mix of narcotics to intensify the desired effects.

33. Most telling about the use of *basuco* by Colombian guerrillas is that no one smokes paste except those involved in cocaine production. Coca paste is a precursor to the production of cocaine.

34. *Jane's Sentinel Security Assessment—West Africa*, December 2005.

35. Amnesty International, *Child Soldiers: A Global Issue*, http://web.amnesty.org/pages/childsoldiers-background-eng (accessed July 19, 2006).

36. Amnesty International, "War Children Tell Their Story," *Amnesty Magazine* (November–December 2000): 3.

37. Susan McKay, "Girls as 'Weapons of Terror' in Northern Uganda and Sierra Leonean Rebel Fighting Forces," *Studies in Conflict and Terrorism* (April 2005): 386.

38. Brian Bennett, "Stolen Away," *Time*, May 1, 2006.

39. Kasaija Phillip Apuuli, "The ICC Arrest Warrants for Lord's Resistance Army and the Prospects for Peace in Northern Uganda," *Journal of International Criminal Justice* (2006): 180.

40. Tony Perry, "Fallouja Insurgents Fought Under Influence of Drugs, Marines Say," *Los Angeles Times*, January 13, 2005, 1. The Marines who were engaged in the fighting were ordered to target the heads of the insurgents since "body shots were not good enough."

41. "Afghan Soldiers," *St. Louis Post-Dispatch*, 1989.

42. MacCoun and Reuter, *Drug War Heresies*, 99.

43. Parliament of Canada, "Sub-Saharan Africa Facing the Problems of Drugs," April 2001, http://www.parl.gc.ca/37/1/parlbus/commbus/senate/com-e/ille-e/presentation-e/labrousse1-e.htm.

44. Bill Berkeley, *The Graves Are Not Yet Full: Race, Tribe, and Power in the Heart of Africa* (New York: Basic Books, 2001), 140.

45. Stephen Ellis, *The Mask of Anarchy: The Destruction of Liberia and the Religious Dimension of an African Civil War* (New York: New York University Press), 108.

46. Mark Duffield, "Globalization, Transborder Trade and War Economies," in *Greed and Grievance: Economic Agendas in Civil Wars*, eds. Mats Berdal and David Malone (Boulder, CO: Lynne Rienner Publishers, 2000), 81.

47. Jeremy Weinstein, *Inside Rebellion* (New York: Cambridge University Press, 2007), 155–159.

48. Stephen Lee Meyers, "Top Chechen Rebel Dies in Russian Raid," *International Herald Tribune*, June 18, 2006, http://www.iht.com/articles/2006/06/18/news/chechnya.php.

49. Healthcare Customwire, "Beslan School Attackers Were Drug Addicts," October 17, 2004. In addition, an effect of heroin withdrawal is insomnia, which may have contributed to stress and unpredictability of the Beslan hostage takers.

50. Although little study has been conducted on the presence of anhedonia among combatant forces, its presence may explain why individual fighters continue to wage war since fighting allows continued access to the desired drug (or to other drugs that may offer relief).

51. Narconon, "History of Methamphetamine," 2004, http://www.friendsofnarconon.org/drug_education/drug_information.

52. David Leppard, "Soldiers in 'Guns for Coke' Scandal," *Sunday Times*, September 24, 2006.

53. Mary Jordan, "British Soldiers Allegedly Traded Guns for Cocaine," *Washington Post*, September 25, 2005.

54. Mark MacKinnon, "Russian Forces Jittery Even on Army Base," *Toronto Globe and Mail*, November 30, 2002.

55. Arthur Bonner, "Afghanistan's Other Front: The World of Drugs," *New York Times*, November 2, 1985.

56. "Stress Sent Soldiers to Drink and Drugs, Colleague Testifies," CNN.com, August 8, 2006, http://www.cnn.com/2006/world/meast/08/08/iraq.mahmoudiya/index.html.

57. Booth, *Opium*, 272.

58. Gahlinger, *Illegal Drugs*, 207.

59. "The New Public Enemy No. 1," *Time*, June 28, 1971.

60. Ibid.

61. Stephen Handleman, *Comrade Criminal: Russia's New Mafiya* (New Haven, CT: Yale University Press, 1995), 190.

62. Joseph D. Douglass Jr. and Neil C. Livingston, *America the Vulnerable: The Threat of Chemical-Biological Warfare* (Washington, DC: Health and Company, 1987), 4.

63. Streatfeild, *Cocaine*, 350.

64. Joseph Douglass Jr., *Red Cocaine: The Drugging of America and the West* (Atlanta, GA: Clarion House, 1990), 2.

65. Artyom Borovik, *The Hidden War: A Russian Journalist's Account of the Soviet War in Afghanistan* (New York: Grove Press, 1990), 46, 183–184, 272–273.

66. Parliament of Canada, "Conflict, Drugs and Mafia Activities," (1999), 16.

67. Gugliotta and Leen, *Kings of Cocaine*, 149. See also Bruce Porter, *Blow: How a Small-Town Boy made $100 Million with the Medellin Cocaine Cartel and Lost It All* (New York: St. Martin's, 1993), 180–181.

68. Streatfeild, *Cocaine*, 354–355.

69. Andrew Zachrel (Army major, 9th Psychological Operations Battalion, 4th Psychological Operations Group, Afghanistan), interviewed by Air Force Maj. Mark Gaubert, March 28, 2004.

70. Fatwa quoted in Rachel Ehrenfeld, *Funding Evil—How Terrorism Is Financed and How to Stop it*, (Chicago: Bonus Books, 2003), 143–145.

71. Chris Harmon, *Terrorism Today*, 2nd ed. (New York: Routledge, 2008), 91, note 16.

72. Ibid., 77.

73. "Somalia: The Challenge of Change," IRIN News, February 23, 2007, http://www.irinnews.org/report.aspx?reportid=59567.

74. Mats Berdal and David Malone, op cit.

75. Charles Dunlap Jr., "Preliminary Observations: Asymmetric Warfare and the Western Mindset," in *Challenging the U.S. Symmetrically and Asymmetrically* (Carlisle Barracks, PA: U.S. Army War College Strategic Studies Institute, July 1998), 5.

76. Ibid., 8.

77. P. W. Singer, "Caution: Children at War," *Parameters* (Winter 2001–2002): 40.

78. United States Marine Corps, *Child Soldiers: Implications for U.S. Forces Seminar Report*, (Quantico, VA: Center for Emerging Threats and Opportunities, September 23, 2002), http://www.ceto.quantico.usmc.mil. The lack of doctrine confronting child soldiers is not unusual among Western militaries. The British and Canadian militaries continue to have doctrine that deal with specific rules of engagements in contexts that may or may not include the presence of young combatants.

79. For a more thorough discussion of the differences between volunteer forces and conscripts and their effects on society at large, see Gil Merom, *How Democracies Lose Small Wars: State, Society, and the Failures of France in Algeria, Israel in*

Lebanon, and the United States in Vietnam (New York: Cambridge University Press, 2003), 74.

80. Scott Shane, "A Flood of Troubled Soldiers in the Offing, Experts Predict," *New York Times*, December 16, 2004.

81. Gregg Zoroya, "Psychologist: Navy Faces Crisis," *USA Today*, January 17, 2007.

82. Karen Seal, Daniel Berenthal, Christian Miner, Saunak Sen, and Charles Marmar, "Bringing the War Back Home," *Archives of Internal Medicine* 167: 479.

83. Robert Lewis and Kate McCarthy, "War Vets Fighting Addiction," *Military.com*, November 26, 2007, http://www.military.com/features/0,15240,156956,00.html?ESRC+dod-b.nl.

84. Ibid.

85. Yet fears about the potential abuse of drug among Canadian forces serving in Afghanistan have not materialized. A 2003 Canadian Military Police report stated that the presence of cheap and available narcotics in Afghanistan may risk higher incidence of drug abuse. (See Stephanie Rubec, "Drug Use Nightmare for Cdn Forces," *Toronto Sun*, November 14, 2004.) While Canadian participation has gradually intensified over the years, drug abuse has not risen. This could be because Canadian participation has not been the same as American and British contributions in Iraq and Afghanistan. Canadians are not using as many reservists, and tours of duty for their professional, full-time troops have not been as long. These two elements may mitigate much of the atmosphere that stimulates a widespread desire to turn to drugs. Conversely, the intensity of fighting has recently increased for Canadian forces in southern Afghanistan, and if recent history proves instructive, the effects of this may yet to be felt by the Canadian military establishment when veterans return and seek treatment for any mental health issues.

86. United States Pacific Command, "Combating Terrorism in the Phillipines," http://www.pacom.mil/piupdates/abusayyafhist.shtml (accessed July 16, 2006).

87. Martin Van Creveld, *The Transformation of War: The Most Radical Reinterpretation of Armed Conflict Since Clausewitz* (New York: Free Press, 1991), 204.

88. Sebastian Rotella, "The World; Jihad's Unlikely Alliance; Muslim extremists who attacked Madrid funded the plot by selling drugs, investigators say," *Los Angeles Times*, May 23, 2004, A1.

CHAPTER 4: NARCOTICS AND NATION-BUILDING

1. However, disrupting the market for illegally traded licit goods has proven exceptionally difficult as well; international monitoring and certificate schemes have made small impacts in the cases of diamonds, oil, and timber. Certification programs have even spawned other illicit cottage industries to manufacture false documents and have in-

creased the number of transshipment points as an effort to fool monitoring. Certification regimes for illegal narcotics are not practical and, as the history of the prohibition of drugs has demonstrated, neither are efforts to trace and track their transportation.

2. Le Billon, "Fuelling War," 57.

3. Michael Ross, "Oil, Drugs and Diamonds: The Varying Roles of Natural Resources in Civil War," in *The Political Economy of Armed Conflict: Beyond Greed and Grievance*, eds. Karen Ballentine and Jake Sherman (Boulder, CO: Lynne Reinner Publishers, 2003), 54.

4. Kimberley Thachuk, "Transnational Threats: Falling Through the Cracks?" *Low Intensity Conflict and Law Enforcement* (2001): 51.

5. Gretchen Peters, "Taliban Drug Trade: Echoes of Colombia," *Christian Science Monitor*, November 21, 2006, 4.

6. Le Billon, "Fuelling War," 46.

7. Mancur Olson, "Dictatorship, Democracy and Development," *American Political Science Review* (September 1993): 568.

8. Ralf Mutshcke, "The Threat Posed by the Convergence of Organized Crime, Drugs Trafficking, and Terrorism," testimony to the Subcommittee on Crime of the Judiciary Committee, U.S. House of Representatives, December 13, 2000.

9. Sarita Kendall, "Colombia Measures the Cost of Violence," *Financial Times*, November 11, 1996.

10. It should come as no surprise that political causes of rebel groups can be upended by the drug trade. After all, if agents of the government are susceptible to corruption by drug trafficking, armed groups that have no accountability and operate beyond the law are no less immune.

11. David Keen, "War and Peace: What's the Difference?" in *Managing Armed Conflict in the Twenty-First Century*, eds. Adekeye Adebajo and Chandra Lekha Siriam (London: Frank Cass, 2001), 2.

12. To connote the commercial nature of the dispute, the British preferred to call what is commonly known as the first Opium War, the War for Free Trade.

13. In fact, the Treaty of Nanking, which ended the first Opium War, does not mention opium anywhere in the text. See W. Travis Hanes III and Frank Sanello, *The Opium Wars* (Naperville, IL: Source Books, 2002), 163.

14. Jonathan Goodhand, "Afghanistan in Central Asia," in *War Economies in a Regional Context: Challenges of Transformation* (Boulder, CO: Lynne Reinner Publishers, 2004), 59.

15. Paul Stares, *Global Health* (Washington, DC: Brookings Institution, 1996), 95.

16. Ivelaw Griffith, "From Cold War Geopolitics to Post-Cold War Geonarcotics," *International Journal* (Winter 1993–1994): 25.

17. Parliament of Canada, "Sub-Saharan Africa Facing the Problems of Drugs," April 2001, http://www.parl.gc.ca/37/1/parlbus/commbus/senate/com-e/ille-e/presentation-e/labrousse1-e.htm.

18. Tara Kartha, "Controlling the Black and Gray Markets in Small Arms in South Asia," in *Light Weapons and Civil Conflict*, eds. Jeffrey Boutwell and Michael T. Klare (Latham, MD: Rowman and Littlefield, 1999), 53.

19. Larry Goodson, *Afghanistan's Endless War: State Failure, Regional Politics, and the Rise of the Taliban* (Seattle: University of Washington Press, 2001), 95–96.

20. Philip Dine, "Picking a Different Target," *St. Louis Post-Dispatch*, September 24, 2006.

21. Peters, "Taliban Drug Trade," 4.

22. Additionally, even if interdiction efforts are successful outside a country's borders, smuggling routes within a country can still be put to use for other illicit trade such as cigarettes, oil, bogus consumer goods, and people.

23. Pugh and Cooper, "Bosnia and Herzegovina in Southeastern Europe," in Pugh and Cooper, *War Economies*, 154.

24. Ibid.

25. Andreas, "The Clandestine Political Economy of War and Peace in Bosnia," *International Studies Quarterly* (June 2004): 46.

26. Rich Smyth (political advisor to the commander, Combined Joint Task Force–76, Baghram, Afghanistan, 2005–2006), interview, U.S. Army War College Carlisle Barracks, PA, December 3, 2006.

27. David Rohnde, "Afghan Symbol for Change Becomes a Symbol of Failure," *New York Times*, September 5, 2006, 14.

28. Sharon Behn, "Al Sadr Militia Pumping Up with Drugs," *Washington Times*, October 5, 2004, 5.

29. "A Small Success for the UN," *The Economist*, August 4, 2007.

30. Andreas, "The Clandestine," 44.

31. Marie-Joelle Zahar, "Proteges, Clients and Cannon Fodder: Civil-Militia Relations in Internal Conflicts," in *Civilians in War*, ed. Simon Chesterman (Boulder, CO: Lynne Rienner Publishers, 2001), 50–52.

32. Segell, 47.

33. Jeremy Weinstein, *Inside Rebellion: The Politics of Insurgent Violence* (New York: Cambridge University Press, 2007), 255. Interestingly, other warring groups that use illegal narcotics make it clear in their manuals that commanders should prohibit excessive drinking among their fighters. See Weinstein, *Inside Rebellion*, 371.

34. Parliament of Canada, "Sub-Saharan Africa Facing the Problems of Drugs."

35. Weinstein, *Inside Rebellion*, 124.

36. Judith Gentleman, *Implementing Plan Colombia* (Carlisle Barracks, PA: Strategic Studies Institute, 2001), 9.

37. Martin Smith, *Burma: Insurgency and the Politics of Ethnicity* (New York: Zed Books, 1991), 398.

38. Paul Battersby, "Border Politics and the Broader Politics of Thailand's International Relations in the 1990s," *Pacific Affairs* 71 (1998).

39. Richard Gibson and John Haseman, "Controlling Narcotics Production and Trafficking in Myanmar," *Contemporary Southeast Asia* (April 2003): 5.

40. United States Department of State, "Source Countries and Drug Transit Zones," *International Narcotics Control Strategy Report 2004*, http://www.whitehouse drugpolicy.gov/international/senegal.html.

41. Sharon Behn, "Coalition Troops Seize $30 Million in Heroin," *Washington Times*, October 11, 2004, 1.

42. Sharon Behn, "Al Sadr Militia Pumping Up with Drugs," 5.

43. Bill Berkeley, *The Graves Are Not Yet Full: Race, Tribe, and Power in the Heart of Africa* (New York: Basic Books, 2001), 207.

44. Martin Booth, *Opium: A History* (New York: St. Martin's Griffin, 1996), 342.

45. "Men of War," *Far Eastern Economic Review*, February 27, 1992.

46. Bernard Castelli, "Colombia: Here Today, Gone Tomorrow," *Sources* (April 1999): 8.

47. "Drive on Afghan Poppy Crop Due," *Los Angeles Times*, March 28, 2005.

48. "PAKISTAN: Drug injecting refugees vulnerable to HIV infection," *IRINnews.org*, February 5, 2007, http://www.irinnews.org/report.asp?ReportID=55613&SelectRegion=Asia&SelectCountry=PAKISTAN.

49. Parliament of Canada, "Sub-Saharan Africa Facing the Problems of Drugs."

50. Mona Mahmoud and Melanie Eversley, "Hospitals Wage a Different War: Against Addiction," *USA Today*, June 23, 2005. For the health conditions in Iraq, see Salman Rawaf, "The Health Crisis in Iraq," *Critical Public Health* 15, no.2 (June 2005): 12.

51. "Drug Crisis Grips Baghdad," *BBC News*, October 4, 2003, http://news.bbc.co.uk/2/hi/middle_east/3156048.stm.

52. Martin Boas and Anne Hatloy, "Alcohol and Drug Consumption in Post War Sierra Leone—An Exploration," Oslo, Norway: Institute for Applied International Studies, 7.

53. Bard O'Neill, *Insurgency and Terrorism: From Revolution to Apocalypse* (Washington, DC: Brassey's Inc., 1990), 143.

54. Thachuk, "Transnational Threats," 57.

55. Rachel Morarjee, "Taliban Goes for Cash Over Ideology," *London Financial Times*, July 26, 2006.

56. Barry McCaffrey, *Visit to Afghanistan and Pakistan February 16–23, 2007 After Action Report*.

57. Ahmed Rashid, "Letter from Afghanistan: Are the Taliban Winning?" *Current History* (January 2007): 18.

58. Steven Dudley, "Drug Mafia's Infiltration of Military Grows Clearer," *Miami Herald*, July 5, 2006.

59. There has been little study of the effects of anhedonia as discussed in chapter 3 on the recurrence of violence. Combatant leaders and their followers may be suffering from anhedonia where violence becomes associated with the feelings caused by the drug. Returning to violence may not only allow continued accessibility to the desired drug, but actually remind the fighter of the positive effects of that drug.

60. Kim Gamel, "UN: Liberia Peacekeeping Mission on Track," *Associated Press*, December 14, 2004.

61. "DR Of Congo Violence Provides Work For UN Peacekeepers," *Europaworld*, January 28, 2005, http://www.europaworld.org/week209/drofcongo28105.htm.

62. Ross, "Oil, Drugs and Diamonds," 58.

63. Weinstein, *Inside Rebellion*, 156.

64. Ibid., 157.

65. Stephen John Stedman, "International Implementation of Peace Agreements in Civil Wars," in *Turbulent Peace: The Challenges of Managing International Conflict*, eds. Chester Crocker, Fen Osler Hampson, and Pamela Aall (Washington, DC: United States Institute of Peace, 2001), 741.

66. Rashid, "Letter from Afghanistan," 17.

67. Robert Burns, "US Officials say Taliban Attacks Surge," *The Guardian*, January 16, 2007, http://www.guardian.co.uk/worldlatest/story/0,,-6348568,00.html.

68. Stedman, "International Implementation," 741.

69. Parliament of Canada, "Conflicts, Drugs and Mafia Activities," *Contribution to the Preparatory Work for the Hague Peace Conference May 11–16, 1999*, March 1999, http://www.parl.gc.ca/37/1/parlbus/commbus/senate/com-e/ille-e/presentation-e/labrousse2-e.htm.

70. "A Double Spring Offensive," *The Economist*, February 24, 2007.

71. Gentleman, *Implementing Plan Colombia*, 11, emphasis added.

72. Dine, "Picking a Different Target."

73. Judy Dempsey, "General Calls Drugs Biggest Test for Afghans," *International Herald Tribune*, May 20, 2006.

74. Dine, "Picking a Different Target."

75. Svante E. Cornell, "Narcotics, Radicalism, and Armed Conflict in Central Asia: The Islamic Movement of Uzbekistan," *Terrorism and Political Violence* (Winter 2005): 634.

76. "US Sees Setbacks in Coca Eradication in Southern Colombia," *ACAN-EFE*, May 16, 2006. The increase in coca growth in the Narino region may explain why the street price of cocaine in the United States has not changed as a result of successes in Putumayo.

77. In 1998, the 20th Brigade of the Colombian Army, together with right-wing militias, committed such flagrant abuses of human rights in its territory that the United States demanded its eventual dissolution.

78. Thorin Martin Wright, "Warlord Choices: An Inquiry into the Instititutional Choices in Post-Conflict State Building," paper presented at the Southern Political Science Association Annual Conference, January 4, 2007.

79. Justin Huggler, "Afghan Anti-Corruption Chief is Drug Dealer," *The Independent*, March 10, 2007; Scott Baldauf and Faye Bowers, "Afghanistan Riddled with Drug Ties," *Christian Science Monitor*, May 13, 2005.

80. Manuel Pastor and Michael Conroy, "Distributional Implications for Macroeconomic Policy: Theory and Applications to El Salvador," in *Economic Policy for Building Peace: The Lessons of El Salvador*, ed. James Boyce (Boulder, CO: Lynne Rienner Publishers, 1996), 159.

81. John Walton and David Seddon, *Free Markets and Food Riots: The Politics of Global Adjustment* (Cambridge, MA: Blackwell, 1994).

82. World Bank, *Sub-Saharan Africa: From Crisis to Sustainable Growth* (Washington, DC: World Bank, 1989).

83. "Bullet Points," *The Economist*, January 20–26, 2007, 48, 50.

84. Roland Paris, *At War's End: Building Peace after Civil Conflict* (Cambridge: Cambridge University Press, 2004), 5.

85. Ibid., 5.

86. Thachuk, "Transnational Threats," 62.

87. Booth, *Opium*, 269.

88. Khatharya Um, "Cambodia in 1993: Year Zero Plus One," *Asian Survey* (January 1994): 80.

89. Booth, *Opium*, 303.

90. Svante E. Cornell, "Narcotics and Armed Conflict: Interaction and Implications," *Studies in Conflict and Terrorism* (February 2007): 217.

91. Cornell, "Narcotics, Radicalism, and Armed Conflict in Central Asia," 623–624.

92. United Nations Information Service, "Iraq Emerging as a Transit Country for Drugs, INCB Presidents Says," May 12, 2005.

93. Sharon Behn, "Coalition Troops Seize $30 Million in Heroin."

CHAPTER 5: SOBER LESSONS FOR THE FUTURE

1. John Fishell, Max Manwaring, and Edwin Corr, *Uncomfortable Wars Revisited* (Norman, OK: University of Oklahoma Press, 2006).

2. Parliament of Canada, "Conflicts, Drugs and Mafia Activities," *Contribution to the Preparatory Work for the Hague Peace Conference May 11–16, 1999*, March 1999,

http://www.parl.gc.ca/37/1/parlbus/commbus/senate/com-e/ille-e/presentation-e/
labrousse2-e.htm.

3. Josh Meyer, "Burdened U.S. Military Cuts Role in Drug War," *Los Angeles Times*, January 22, 2007.

4. R. Pear and P. Shenen, "Customs Switches Priority from Drugs to Terrorism," *New York Times*, October 10, 2001.

5. James O'Gara, "The Wrong Plan for Afghanistan," *Washington Post*, January 24, 2007 (emphasis added).

6. Russell Crandall, "Clinton, Bush and Plan Colombia," *Survival* 44, no. 1 (Spring 2002): 165.

7. "Profile of Ly Wen-huan, Last of the Kuomintang Warlords," *Associated Press*, August 1, 1984.

8. Ahmed Rashid, "From Deobandism to Batken: Adventures of an Islamic Heritage," Central Asia-Caucasus Institute, *Forum Transcripts*, April 13, 2000.

9. Svante E. Cornell, "Narcotics, Radicalism, and Armed Conflict in Central Asia: The Islamic Movement of Uzbekistan," *Terrorism and Political Violence* (Winter 2005): 624.

10. Chris Harmon, *Terrorism Today*, 2nd ed. (New York: Routledge, 2008), 77 (emphasis added).

11. Paul Collier, "Doing Well Out of War," in *Greed and Grievance: Economic Agendas in Civil Wars*, eds. Mat Berdal and David Malone (Boulder, CO: Lynne Rienner Publishers, 2002), 103.

12. "U.S. Drug Ring Tied to Aid for Hezbollah," *New York Times*, September 3, 2002.

13. "IRA Accused Over Colombia Bombings," *The Telegraph*, August 11, 2002.

14. Bill Berkeley, *The Graves Are Not Yet Full: Race, Tribe, and Power in the Heart of Africa* (New York: Basic Books, 2001), 261.

15. Timothy Brook and Bob Tdashi Wakabayashi, "Opium's History in China," in *Opium Regimes: China, Britain, and Japan, 1839–1952*, eds. Timothy Brook and Bob Tdashi Wakabayashi (Los Angeles: University of California Press, 2000), 16–17.

16. "Drug Running: West Africa," *Africa Research Bulletin*, August 2007.

17. Shona Morrison, "The Dynamics of Illicit Drugs Production: Future Sources and Threats," *Crime, Law, and Social Change* (March 1997): 134.

18. Svante E. Cornell, "Narcotics and Armed Conflict: Interaction and Implications," *Studies in Conflict and Terrorism* (February 2007): 214.

19. Ahmed Rashid, "Letter from Afghanistan: Are the Taliban Winning?" *Current History* (January 2007): 17.

20. Donna Leinnwand, "Hyde Asks Rumsfeld to Bolster Fight Against Afghan Heroin," *USA Today*, October 24, 2006.

21. "The senior Republican on the House Foreign Affairs Committee, Representative Ileana

Ros-Lehtinen of Florida, released a statement criticizing the speech. Ms. Ros-Lehtinen and several other Republicans have been pressing the Bush administration to do more to crack down on Afghanistan's opium trade; she said the new strategy lacked 'practical initiatives to target major drug kingpins and warlords whose trade in opium finances the Taliban's campaign.'" Sheryl Gay Stolberg, "Pressing Allies, President Warns of Afghan Battle," *New York Times*, February 16, 2007.

22. "Tories Raise Afghan Heroin Alarm," *BBC online*, August 1, 2004, http://news.bbc.co.uk/2/hi/uk_news/politics/3526498.stm.

23. Chloe Fox, "The Rise and Rise of Drugs in Africa," *Sources* no. 111 (April 1999): 9.

24. Michael Shifter, "Latin America's Drug Problem," *Current History* (February 2007): 62.

25. Peter Andreas, "Criminalizing Consequences of Sanctions: Embargo Busting and Its Legacy," *International Studies Quarterly* (May 2005).

26. Moisés Naím, *Illicit: How Smugglers, Traffickers, and Copycats Are Hijacking the Global Economy* (New York: Doubleday, 2005), 19.

27. Bernard Fall, "The Theory and Practice of Insurgency and Counterinsurgency," *Naval War College Review* (Winter 1998): 2, 8.

28. Anthony James Joes, *Resisting Rebellion: The History and Politics of Counterinsurgency* (Louisville: University of Kentucky Press, 2004), 9.

29. Crandall, "Clinton, Bush and Plan Colombia," 167.

30. Paul Rexton Kan, "What Should We Bomb? Axiological Targeting and the Abiding Limits of Airpower," *Air and Space Power Journal* (2004): 28–29.

31. Arlene Tickner, "Colombia and the United States: From Counternarcotics to Counterterrorism," *Current History* (February 2003): 79, note 3.

32. Patrick L. Clawson and Rensaller W. Lee III, *The Andean Cocaine Industry* (New York: St. Martin's Press, 1998), 150.

33. Booth, 295.

34. Ali Jalali, former Counternarcotics Minister of Afghanistan, presentation to the Non-State Armed Groups Symposium, Kent Island, MD, July 10, 2007.

35. Martin Booth, *Opium: A History* (New York: St. Martin's Griffin, 1996), 342.

36. Hubert Bagley, "Afghanistan: Opium Cultivation and Its Impact on Reconstruction," U.S. Army War College Strategy Research Project, Carlisle, PA, March 19, 2004, 8–9.

37. Roland Paris, *At War's End: Building Peace after Civil Conflict* (Cambridge: Cambridge University Press, 2004), 3.

38. Ibid., ix.

39. Michael Scheurer, "Clueless into Kabul," *The American Interest* (September–October 2006): 115.

40. Michael Shifter, "Latin America's Drug Problem," *Current History* (February 2007): 59.

41. Keith Gottschalk, "Vigilantism vs. the State: The Rise and Fall of PGAD, 1996–2000," *International Studies Institute Paper*, no. 99 (February 2005).

42. The impact of the curtailing of charity funding for al Qaeda may force it into greater narcotics activities. See Audrey Kurth Cronin, "How Al Qaeda Ends," *International Security* (Summer 2006).

43. Mark Duffield, "Post-modern Conflict: Warlords, Post-adjustment States and Private Protection," *Civil Wars* (Spring 1998): 97.

44. Hedley Bull, *The Anarchical Society* (New York: Columbia University Press, 1977), 255.

45. John Arquilla and David Ronfeldt, "A New Epoch—and Spectrum—of Conflict," in *In Athena's Camp*, eds. Arquilla and Ronfeldt (Santa Monica, CA: RAND, 1997), 5.

46. Glen Segell, "Warlordism and Drug Trafficking: From Southeast Asia to Sub-Saharn Africa," in *Warlords in International Relations*, ed. Paul Rich (New York: St. Martin's Press, 1999), 39–40.

CHAPTER 6: SHAKY PATHS FORWARD

1. Arthur Lykke, "Toward an Understanding of Military Strategy," *Military Strategy: Theory and Application* (Carlisle Barracks, PA: U.S. Army War College, 1989), 6–7.

2. Harry Yarger, "Toward a Theory of Strategy," in *U.S. Army War College Guide to National Security Policy and Strategy*, 2nd rev. ed., ed. J. Boone Bartholomees, (Carlisle Barracks, PA: U.S. Army War College, 2006), 111.

3. These approaches are reminiscent of those described by Charles William Maynes for the direction of American foreign policy. See Charles William Maynes, "Contending Schools," *National Interest* (Spring 2001).

4. Charles Maynes, "Contending Schools," *National Interest* (Spring 2001): 4.

5. Joseph Murphy, "A White Paper on Economic Measures to Support the Counternarcotics Campaign in Afghanistan," Brussels, October 20–24, 2006.

6. Ibid., 5–6.

7. Barnett Rubin and Omar Zakhilwal, "A War on Drugs, Or A War on Farmers?" *Wall Street Journal*, January 11, 2005.

8. Karen Ballentine, "Beyond Greed and Grievance: Reconsidering the Economic Dynamics of Armed Conflict," in *The Political Economy of Armed Conflict: Beyond Greed and Grievance*, eds. Karen Ballentine and Jake Sherman (Boulder, CO: Lynne Reinner Publishers, 2003), 279.

9. Ibid.

10. Nancy Reagan, "We Must Not Tolerate Drug Abuse," *USA Today*, August 8, 1986.

11. Douglas Davids. *Narco-Terrorism: A Unified Strategy to Fight a Growing Terrorist Menace* (New York: Transnational Publishers, 2002), 69.

12. Kimberley Thachuk, "Transnational Threats: Falling Through the Cracks?" *Low Intensity Conflict and Law Enforcement* (2001): 59.

13. Thomas Fowler, "Winning the War on Drugs: Can We Get There from Here?," *Journal of Social, Political, and Economic Studies* (Winter 1990): 405.

14. *Foreign Assets Control Regulations for the Financial Community*, U.S. Department of the Treasury, July 3, 2002.

15. Vanda Felbab-Brown, "Opium Wars," *Wall Street Journal*, February 20, 2007.

16. Carolyn Nordstrom, "Out of the Shadows," in *Authority and Intervention in Africa*, eds. Thomas Callaghy, Ronald Kassimir, and Robert Latham (Cambridge: Cambridge University Press, 2001), 14, fn 40.

17. Duffield, *Global Governance and the New Wars: The Merging of Development and Security*, 143.

18. Roy Godson and Phil Williams, "Strengthening Cooperation Against Transnational Crime," *Survival* (Autumn 1998): 80.

19. Ibid.

20. Michael Shifter, "Latin America's Drug Problem," *Current History* (February 2007): 63.

21. "Anti-Money Laundering: New Rules, New Challenges, New Solutions," Price Waterhouse Coopers (Menlo Park, CA: Price Waterhouse Coopers Global Technology Center, 2002), 8.

22. Ibid.

23. Peter Van Ham and Jorrit Kamminga, "Poppies for Peace: Reforming Afghanistan's Opium Industry," *Washington Quarterly* (Winter 2006–2007): 70.

24. Roland Paris, *At War's End: Building Peace after Civil Conflict* (Cambridge: Cambridge University Press, 2004), 7.

25. Malcolm Waters, *Globalization: The Reader* (New York: Routledge, 1995), 66.

26. Michael Pugh and Neil Cooper, eds. *War Economies in a Regional Context: Challenges of Transformation* (Boulder, CO: Lynne Reinner Publishers, 2004), 196.

27. Timothy Luke and Gearoid O'Tuathail, "On Videocameralists: The Geopolitics of Failed States, the CNN International, and (UN) Governmentality," *Review of International Political Economy* 4, no. 4 (1997): 709.

28. Kimberly Martin, "Warlordism in Comparative Perspective," *International Security* (Winter 2006–2007): 41.

29. For a deeper discussion of offshore balancing, see John Mearshimer, *The Tragedy of Great Power Politics* (New York: WW Norton, 2001); Robert Art, *A Grand Strategy for America* (New York: Cornell University Press, 2003); and Christopher Layne, "From Preponderance to Offshore Balancing," *International Security* (Summer 1997): 86–124.

30. This has occurred in Afghanistan where Colombian officials have met their Afghan counterparts to share and compare strategies to overcome drug-fueled conflicts. See for example, Chris Kraul, "Calling in the Drug Calvary," *Los Angeles Times*, September

6, 2006; and Andy Webb-Vidal, "Bogota Set To Assist in Kabul's Drug Battle," *Financial Times*, August 8, 2006.

31. See for example, Bernard Fall, "The Theory and Practice of Insurgency and Counterinsurgency," *Naval War College Review* (Winter 1998); David Galula, *Counterinsurgency Warfare: Theory and Practice* (New York: Praeger, 1964).

32. Zhou Yongming, *Anti-Drug Crusades in Twentieth-Century China: Nationalism, History, and State-Building* (New York: Rowman and Littlefield, 1999), 171.

33. Joseph Nunez, "Challenges and Opportunities in the Americas: A Liberal Regime for Security and Defense Cooperation," (Ph. D. diss., University of Virginia, May 2006), 120.

34. "The Perils of Parapolitics," *The Economist*, March 24, 2007, 42.

35. Ivelaw Griffith, "From Cold War Geopolitics to Post-Cold War Geonarcotics," *International Journal* (Winter 1993–1994): 20.

36. John R. Mills, "All the Elements of National Power: Reorganizing the Interagency Structure and Process for Victory in the Long War," *Strategic Insights* (July 2006): 1.

37. Martin Booth, *Opium: A History* (New York: St. Martin's Griffin, 1996), 339.

38. Michael Pollan, *The Botany of Desire* (New York: Random House, 2001), 139.

39. Rensselaer Lee, *White Labyrinth: Cocaine and Political Power* (Somerset, NJ: Transaction Publishers, 1989), 224.

40. Monica Serrano, "Globalization, Economic Reform, and Organized Crime," in *Transnational Organized Crime and International Security*, eds. Mats Berdal and Monica Serrano (Boulder, CO: Lynne Rienner Publishers, 2002), 30.

41. Eva Bertram, et al., *Drug War Politics: The Price of Denial* (Los Angeles: University of California Press, 1996), 3.

42. In some ways, the worldwide spread of cigarette smoking offers a preview of such a dilemma. When the United States adopted more regulation of the cigarette industry, companies shifted their focus to overseas markets. Countries seeking to protect their own domestic cigarette industry and to limit cigarette smoking due to public health concerns were subjected to powerful lobbying in the WTO to allow overseas competition from American cigarette companies. See Allan Brandt, *The Cigarette Century: The Rise, Fall, and Deadly Persistence of the Product That Defined America* (New York: Basic Books, 2007), 449–465.

43. Michael Klare, "Redefining Security: The New Global Schisms," *Current History* (November 1996): 354.

44. Mark Duffield, "Post-modern Conflict: Warlords, Post-adjustment States and Private Protection," *Civil Wars* (Spring 1998): 69–70.

45. Booth, *Opium*, 290–291.

46. Philippe Le Billon, "Fuelling War: Natural Resources and Armed Conflict," *Adelphi Paper 373* (London: Routledge, 2005), 70.

47. "Face Value: Shining a Light," *The Economist*, March 10, 2007.

48. Moisés Naím, *Illicit: How Smugglers, Traffickers, and Copycats Are Hijacking the Global Economy* (New York: Doubleday, 2005), 280.

49. Roy Godson and Phil Williams, "Strengthening Cooperation Against Transnational Crime," *Survival* (Autumn 1998): 75.

50. Daniel Anderson (associate special agent in charge, Drug Enforcement Administration New York Field Division), briefing to the U.S. Army War College, September 29, 2005.

51. Ian Daly, "White-Collar America's New Wonder Drug," *Details* (December 2005): 102–106.

52. Schwartz, 51.

53. Michael Kenney, *From Pablo to Osama: Trafficking and Terrorist Networks, Government Bureaucracies, and Competitive Adaptation* (University Park: Pennsylvania State University, 2007), 6.

54. Naím, *Illicit*, 239.

55. Steve Metz, "Rethinking Insurgency," (Carlisle Barracks, PA: Strategic Studies Institute, 2007), 45.

56. Paul Rexton Kan, "The Blurring Distinction Between War and Crime in the 21st Century," *Defense Intelligence Journal* 13, no. 1 & 2 (2005): 42.

57. Stephen Stedman, "International Implementation of Peace Agreements in Civil Wars," in *Turbulent Peace: The Challenges of Managing International Conflict*, eds. Chester Crocker, Fen Osler Hampson, and Pamela Aall (Washington, DC: United States Institute of Peace, 2001), 742.

58. James F. Dobbins, "America's Role In Nation-Building," *Survival* (Winter 2003–2004): 103–110.

59. Ali Jalali, "Afghanistan: Regaining Momentum," *Parameters* (Winter 2007–2008): 12.

60. Metz, "Rethinking Insurgency," 56.

61. Ibid.

62. Peter Andreas and Ethan Nadelman, *Policing the Globe: Criminalization and Crime Control in International Relations* (New York: Oxford University Press, 2006), 246.

63. Tamara Marenko, "Crime, Terror and the Central Asian Drug Trade," *Asia Quarterly* (Summer 2002): 26.

64. Weinstein, 341.

65. H. B. Morse, *Trade and Administration of the Chinese Empire* (Shanghai: Kelly and Walsh, 1908), 323.

BIBLIOGRAPHY

Adebajo, Adekeye, and Chandra Lekha Siriam, eds. *Managing Armed Conflict in the Twenty-First Century*. London: Frank Cass, 2001.

Aisin-Gioro, Pu Yi. *From Emperor to Citizen: The Autobiography of Aisin-Gioro Pu Yi*. Translated by W. J. F. Jenner. Oxford: Oxford University Press, 1987.

Aksakova, E. "Tajik Border Guards Seize at least Two Tons of Drugs." U.S. Embassy, Dushanbe, December 7, 2006.

Amnesty International. *Child Soldiers: A Global Issue*. http://web.amnesty.org/pages/childsoldiers-background-eng.

———. "War Children Tell Their Story." *Amnesty Magazine* (November–December 2000): 3.

Andreas, Peter. "The Clandestine Political Economy of War and Peace in Bosnia." *International Studies Quarterly* (June 2004).

———, and Ethan Nadelman. *Policing the Globe: Criminalization and Crime Control in International Relations*. (New York: Oxford University Press, 2006.

Arquilla, John, and David Ronfeldt, eds. *Networks and Netwars: The Future of Terror, Crime, and Militancy*. Santa Monica: RAND Corporation, 2001.

Art, Robert. *A Grand Strategy for America*. New York: Cornell University Press, 2003.

Bagley, Hubert. "Afghanistan: Opium Cultivation and its Impact on Reconstruction." U.S. Army War College Strategy Research Project, Carlisle, PA, March 19, 2004, 8–9.

Ball, Nicole. "The Challenge of Rebuilding War-Torn Societies." In *Turbulent Peace: The Challenges of Managing International Conflict*, eds. Chester Crocker, Fen Osler Hampson, and Pamela Aall. Washington, DC: United States Institute of Peace, 2001.

Ballentine, Karen and Jake Sherman, eds. *The Political Economy of Armed Conflict: Beyond Greed and Grievance*, Boulder, CO: Lynne Rienner Publishers, 2003.

———. "Beyond Greed and Grievance: Reconsidering the Economic Dynamics of Armed

Conflict." In *The Political Economy of Armed Conflict: Beyond Greed and Grievance*, eds. Karen Ballentine and Jake Sherman, Boulder, CO: Lynne Rienner Publishers, 2003.

Bannon, Ian, and Paul Collier, eds. *Natural Resources and Violent Conflict: Options and Actions.* Washington, DC: The World Bank, 2003.

Bartholomees, J., ed. *U.S. Army War College Guide to National Security Policy and Strategy,* 2nd rev. ed. Carlisle Barracks, PA: U.S. Army War College, 2006.

Baum, Dan. *Smoke and Mirrors: The War on Drugs and the Politics of Failure.* New York: Little, Brown and Co., 1997.

Bechtol, Bruce. *Red Rogue: The Persistent Challenge of North Korea.* Washington, DC: Potomac Books, 2007.

Beeching, Jack. *The Chinese Opium Wars.* New York: Harcourt, Brace, Jovanovich, 1975.

Behn, Sharon. "Al Sadr Militia Pumping Up with Drugs." *Washington Times,* October 5, 2004.

————. "Coalition Troops Seize $30 Million in Heroin." *Washington Times,* October 11, 2004.

Bennett, Brian. "Stolen Away." *Time,* May 1, 2006.

Berdal, Mats, and David Malone, eds. *Greed and Grievance: Economic Agendas in Civil Wars.* Boulder, CO: Lynne Rienner Publishers, 2000.

Berkeley, Bill. *The Graves Are Not Yet Full: Race, Tribe, and Power in the Heart of Africa.* New York: Basic Books, 2001.

Bertam, Eva, Morris Blachman, Kenneth Sharpe, and Peter Andreas. *Drug War Politics: The Price of Denial.* Los Angeles: University of California Press, 1996.

Boas, Martin, and Anne Hatloy. "Alcohol and Drug Consumption in Post War Sierra Leone— An Exploration." Oslo, Norway: Institute for Applied International Studies.

Booth, Martin. *Opium: A History.* New York: St. Martin's Griffin, 1996.

Borovik, Artyom. *The Hidden War: A Russian Journalist's Account of the Soviet War in Afghanistan.* New York: Grove Press, 1990.

Bougarel, Xavier. *Bosnie: Anatomie d'un Conflit.* Paris: La Découverte, 1996.

Bounds, Andrew, and James Wilson. "Colombian Rebels Trade Drugs for Arms." *Financial Times,* May 16, 2002.

Boutwell, Jeffrey, and Michael T. Klare, eds. *Light Weapons and Civil Conflict.* Lanham, MD: Rowman and Littlefield, 1999.

Boyce, James, ed. *Economic Policy for Building Peace: The Lessons of El Salvador.* Boulder, CO: Lynne Rienner Publishers, 1996.

Brandt, Allan. *The Cigarette Century: The Rise, Fall, and Deadly Persistence of the Product That Defined America.* New York: Basic Books, 2007.

Brecher, Edward. *Licit and Illicit Drugs: The Consumers Union Report on Narcotics, Stimulants, Depressants, Inhalants, Hallucinogens, and Marijuana—Including Caffeine.* New York: Little, Brown & Co., 1972.

Brissard, Jean-Charles, and Damien Martinez. *Zarqawi: The New Face of Al-Qaeda*. New York: Other Press, 2005.

Brook, Timothy, and Bob Tadashi Wakabayashi. "Opium's History in China." In *Opium Regimes: China, Britain, and Japan, 1839–1952*, eds. Timothy Brook and Bob Tadashi Wakabayashi. Los Angeles: University of California Press, 2000.

Bull, Hedley. *The Anarchical Society*. New York: Columbia University Press, 1977.

Burns, Robert. "U.S. Officials Say Taliban Attacks Surge." *The Guardian*, January 16 2007, http://www.guardian.co.uk/worldlatest/story/0,,-6348568,00.html.

Butcher, John, and Howard Dick. *The Rise and Fall of Revenue Farming (Studies in the Economics of East & South-East Asia)*. New York: St. Martin's Press, 1993.

Cain, Kenneth, Heidi Postlewait, and Andrew Thomson. *Emergency Sex: And Other Desperate Measures*. New York: Miramax Books, 2004.

Callaghy, Thomas, Ronald Kassimir, and Robert Latham, eds. *Authority and Intervention in Africa: Global-Local Networks of Power*. Cambridge: Cambridge University Press, 2001.

Castelli, Bernard. "Colombia: Here Today, Gone Tomorrow," *Sources* (April 1999).

Charles, Robert. "The Afghan Dilemma." *Washington Times*, April 26, 2005.

Chesterman, Simon, ed. *Civilians in War*. Boulder, CO: Lynne Rienner Publishers, 2001.

Chouvy, Pierre-Arnaud, and Joel Meisonnier. *Yaa Baa: Production, Traffic, and Consumption of Methamphetamine in Mainland Southeast Asia*. Singapore: Singapore University Press, 2004.

Clawson, Patrick, and Rensaller W. Lee III. *The Andean Cocaine Industry*. New York: St. Martin's Press, 1998.

Cohn, Ilene, and Guy S. Goodwin-Gray. *Child Soldiers: The Role of Children in Armed Conflict*. New York: Oxford University Press, 1994.

Collier, Paul. "Development and Conflict." Presentation given at the Centre for the Study of African Economies, Department of Economics, Oxford University, October 1, 2004.

———, Anke Hoeffler, and Mans Soderbom. "On the Duration of Civil War." Policy Working Paper 2861, World Bank, 2001.

———. "Rebellion as Quasi-Criminal Activity." *Journal of Peace Research* (December 2000): 852.

Corchado, Alfredo, and Irene Barcenas. "Mexico: Desertion Rate Isn't a Concern." *Dallas Morning News*, January 6, 2006.

Cornell, Svante E. "Narcotics and Armed Conflict: Interaction and Implications." *Studies in Conflict and Terrorism* (February 2007).

———. "Narcotics, Radicalism and Armed Conflict in Central Asia: The Islamic Movement of Uzbekistan." *Terrorism and Political Violence* (Winter 2005).

———. "Stemming the Contagion: Regional Efforts to Curb Afghan Heroin's Impact." *Georgetown Journal of International Affairs* (Winter–Spring 2005).

Corum, James, and Wray Johnson. *Airpower in Small Wars: Fighting Insurgents and Terrorists.* Lawrence: University of Kansas Press, 2003.

Courtwright, David. *Forces of Habit: Drugs and the Making of World History.* Cambridge, MA: Harvard University Press, 2001.

Crandall, Russell. "Clinton, Bush and Plan Colombia." *Survival* 44, no. 1 (Spring 2002).

Crocker, Chester, Fen Osler Hampson, and Pamela Aall, eds. *Turbulent Peace: The Challenges of Managing International Conflict.* Washington, DC: United States Institute of Peace, 2001.

Daly, Ian. "White-Collar America's New Wonder Drug." *Details* (December 2005).

Daly, Sara, John Parachini, and William Rosenau. *Aum Shinrikyo, Al Qaeda, and the Kinshasa Nuclear Reactor: Implications of the Three Case Studies for Combating Nuclear Terrorism.* Santa Monica: RAND Corporation, 2005.

Davids, Douglas. *Narco-Terrorism: A Unified Strategy to Fight a Growing Terrorist Menace.* New York: Transnational Publishers, 2002.

Diehl, F. W. "Revenue Farming and Colonial Finances in the Netherlands East Indies." In *The Rise and Fall of Revenue Farming (Studies in the Economics of East & South-East Asia)*, eds. John Butcher and Howard Dick. New York: St. Martin's Press, 1993.

Dempsey, Judy. "General Calls Drugs Biggest Test for Afghans." *International Herald Tribune*, May 20, 2006.

de Soysa, Indra. "The Resource Curse: Are Civil Wars Driven by Rapacity or Paucity." In *Greed and Grievance: Economic Agendas in Civil Wars*, eds. Mats Berdal and David Malone. Boulder, CO: Lynne Rienner Publishers, 2000.

Deudney, Daniel. "Environment and Security: Muddled Thinking." *Bulletin of Atomic Scientists* (April 1991).

Dine, Philip. "Picking a Different Target." *St. Louis Post-Dispatch*, September 24, 2006.

Dubey, Prakash. "Maoist Rebels Sell Looted Petrol to Raise Funds." www.asianews.it/view.php?l=en&art=5570.

Douglass Jr., Joseph. *Red Cocaine: The Drugging of America and the West.* Atlanta, GA: Clarion House, 1990.

———, and Neil C. Livingston. *America the Vulnerable: The Threat of Chemical-Biological Warfare.* Washington, DC: Health and Company, 1987.

Dudley, Steven. "Drug Mafia's Infiltration of Military Grows Clearer." *Miami Herald*, July 5, 2006.

Duffield, Mark. *Global Governance and the New Wars: The Merging of Development and Security.* London: Zed Books, 2001.

———. "Globalization, Transborder Trade and War Economies." In *Greed and Grievance: Economic Agendas in Civil Wars,* eds. Mats Berdal and David Malone. Boulder, CO: Lynne Rienner Publishers, 2000.

————. "Post-modern Conflict: Warlords, Post-adjustment States and Private Protection." *Civil Wars* (Spring 1998).

Dunlap Jr., Charles. "Preliminary Observations: Asymmetric Warfare and the Western Mindset." In *Challenging the U.S. Symmetrically and Asymmetrically*. Carlisle Barracks, PA: U.S. Army War College Strategic Studies Institute, July 1998.

Eisner, Bruce. *Ecstasy: The MDMA Story*. Berkeley, CA: Ronin, 1994.

Ellis, Eric. "Afghanomics." *Fortune*, October 6, 2006.

Ellis, Stephen. *The Mask of Anarchy: The Destruction of Liberia and the Religious Dimension of an African Civil War*. New York: New York University Press, 2006.

————. "Liberia 1898–94: A Study of Ethnic and Spiritual Violence." *African Affairs* (Fall 1995).

Fall, Bernard. "The Theory and Practice of Insurgency and Counterinsurgency." *Naval War College Review* (Winter 1998).

Felbab-Brown, Vanda. "Opium Wars." *Wall Street Journal*, February 20, 2007.

Flynn, Stephen. "The Worldwide Drug Scourge: The Expanding Trade in Illicit Drugs." *The Brookings Review* (Winter 1993).

Fishell, John, Max Manwaring, and Edwin Corr. *Uncomfortable Wars Revisited*. Norman, OK: University of Oklahoma Press, 2006.

Foreign Policy Council. *Eurasia Security Watch* no. 86. Washington, DC: Foreign Policy Council, May 18, 2005.

Forero, Juan. "U.S. Indicts 50 Leaders of Colombian Rebels in Cocaine Trafficking." *New York Times*, March 23, 2006.

Fowler, Thomas. "Winning the War on Drugs: Can We Get There from Here?" *Journal of Social, Political, and Economic Studies* (Winter 1990).

Fox, Chloe. "The Rise and Rise of Drugs in Africa." *Sources* no.111 (April 1999).

Friman, H. Richard, and Peter Andreas, eds. *The Illicit Global Economy and State Power*. New York: Rowman and Littlefield, 1999.

Fuchs, Dale. "Spain Says Bombers Drank Water from Mecca and Sold Drugs." *New York Times*, April 15, 2004, national edition, section A.

Gahlinger, Paul. *Illegal Drugs: A Complete Guide to Their History, Chemistry, Use, and Abuse*. New York: Plume, 2001.

Galula, David. *Counterinsurgency Warfare: Theory and Practice*. New York: Praeger, 1964.

Gamel, Kim. "UN: Liberia Peacekeeping Mission on Track." *Associated Press*, December 14, 2004.

Garcia, Michelle. "Alleged Afghan Drug Kingpin Arrested by DEA in New York." *Washington Post*, April 26, 2005.

Gat, Azar, and Zeev Maoz. "Global Change and the Transformation of War." In *War in a Changing World*, eds. Azar Gat and Zeev Maoz. Ann Arbor: University of Michigan Press, 2001.

Gat, Azar, and Zeev Maoz, eds. *War in a Changing World*. Ann Arbor: University of Michigan Press, 2001.

Gentleman, Judith. *Implementing Plan Colombia*. Carlisle Barracks, PA: Strategic Studies Institute, 2001.

Gibson, Richard, and John Haseman. "Controlling Narcotics Production and Trafficking in Myanmar." *Contemporary Southeast Asia* (April 2003).

Godson, Roy, and Phil Williams. "Strengthening Cooperation Against Transnational Crime." *Survival* (Autumn 1998).

Goodson, Larry. *Afghanistan's Endless War: State Failure, Regional Politics, and the Rise of the Taliban*. Seattle: University of Washington Press, 2001.

Graham, Bob, and Michael Evans. "How War on Drugs May Have Helped Hezbollah." *London Times*, August 21, 2006.

Griffith, Ivelaw. "From Cold War Geopolitics to Post-Cold War Geonarcotics." *International Journal* (Winter 1993–1994).

Guaqueta, Alexandra. "The Colombian Conflict: Political and Economic Dimensions." In *The Political Economy of Armed Conflict*, eds. Karen Ballentine and Jake Sherman. Boulder, CO: Lynne Rienner Publishers, 2003.

Gugliotta, Guy, and Jeff Leen. *Kings of Cocaine: The Astonishing True Story of Murder, Money, and Corruption*. New York: Harper and Row, 1989.

Handleman, Stephen. *Comrade Criminal: Russia's New Mafiya*. New Haven: Yale University Press, 1995.

Hanes III, W. Travis, and Frank Sanello. *The Opium Wars: The Addiction of One Empire and the Corruption of Another*. Naperville, IL: Source Books, 2002.

Harmon, Chris. *Terrorism Today*, 2nd ed. New York: Routledge, 2008.

Healthcare Customwire. "Beslan School Attackers Were Drug Addicts." October 17, 2004.

Honwana, Alcinda. "Children of War: Understanding War and War Cleansing in Mozambique and Angola." In *Civilians in War*, ed. Simon Chesterman. Boulder, CO: Lynne Rienner Publishers, 2001.

Inciardi, James. *The War on Drugs III: The Continuing Saga of the Mysteries and Miseries of Intoxication, Addiction, Crime, and Public Policy*. Boston: Allyn and Bacon, 2002.

Institute of War and Peace Reporting (IWPR). "The Killing Fields of Afghanistan." *Afghan Recovery Report* no.16, June 26, 2002.

International Narcotics Control Board. "Iraq Emerging as a Transit Country for Drugs, INCB President Says." Press Release, Vienna, May 12, 2005.

Isralowitz, Richard, Mohammed Afifi, and Richard Rawson, eds. *Drug Problems: Cross-Cultural Policy and Program Development*. Westport, CT: Auburn House, 2002.

Jaffe, Greg. "Army's Recruiting Push Appears to Have Met Goals." *Wall Street Journal*, July 10, 2006.

Jane's Sentinel Security Assessment—West Africa, December 2005.

Joes, Anthony. *Resisting Rebellion: The History and Politics of Counterinsurgency*. Louisville: University of Kentucky Press, 2004.

Jordan, David. *Drug Politics: Dirty Money and Democracies*. Norman: University of Oklahoma, 1999.

Jordan, Mary. "British Soldiers Allegedly Traded Guns for Cocaine." *Washington Post*, September 25, 2005.

Joxe, Alain. "Narco-stratégie: de l'île de la Tortue à l'espace Mondial." In *La Planéte des Drogues, Organisations Criminelles, Guerres et Blanchiment*, eds. A. Labrousse and A. Wallon. Paris: Édition du Seuil, 1993.

Kan, Paul. "The Blurring Distinction Between War and Crime in the 21st Century." *Defense Intelligence Journal* 13, no. 1 & 2 (2005).

———. "Drugging Babylon: The Illegal Narcotics Trade and Nation-Building in Iraq." *Small Wars and Insurgencies* (forthcoming).

———. "What Should We Bomb? Axiological Targeting and the Abiding Limits of Airpower." *Air and Space Power Journal* (2004).

Kartha, Tara. "Controlling the Black and Gray Markets in Small Arms in South Asia." In *Light Weapons and Civil Conflict*, eds. Jeffrey Boutwell and Michael T. Klare. Lanham, MD: Rowman and Littlefield, 1999.

Keen, David. "The Economic Function of Violence in Civil Wars." *Adelphi Paper 320*. Oxford: Oxford University Press, 1998.

———. "Incentives and Disincentives for Violence." In *Greed and Grievance: Economic Agendas in Civil Wars*, eds. Mats Berdal and David Malone. Boulder, CO: Lynne Rienner Publishers, 2000.

———. "War and Peace: What's the Difference?" In *Managing Armed Conflict in the Twenty-First Century*, eds. Adekeye Adebajo and Chandra Lekha Siriam. London: Frank Cass, 2001.

Kendall, Sarita. "Colombia Measures the Cost of Violence." *Financial Times*, November 11, 1996.

Klare, Michael. "Redefining Security: The New Global Schisms." *Current History* (November 1996).

Kleiman, Mark. "Illicit Drugs and the Terrorist Threat." Congressional Research Service, April 20, 2004.

Kolodziej, Edward. "Renaissance in Security Studies? Caveat Lector!" *International Studies Quarterly* (December 1992).

Kraul, Chris. "Calling in the Drug Calvary." *Los Angeles Times*, September 6, 2006.

Labrousse, Alain, and Michel Koutouzis. *Géopolitique et Géostratégie des Drogues*. Paris: Economica, 1996.

————, and A. Wallon, eds. *La Planéte des Drogues, Organisations Criminelles, Guerres, et Blanchiment*. Paris: Édition du Seuil, 1993.

Layne, Christopher. "From Preponderance to Offshore Balancing." *International Security* (Summer 1997).

Le Billon, Philippe. "Fuelling War: Natural Resources and Armed Conflict," *Adelphi Paper 373*. London: Routledge, 2005.

————. "The Political Ecology of War: Natural Resources and Armed Conflict." *Political Geography* (June 2001).

Lee, Rensselaer. *White Labyrinth: Cocaine and Political Power*. Somerset, NJ: Transaction Publishers, 1989.

Leinnwand, Donna. "Hyde Asks Rumsfeld to Bolster Fight Against Afghan Heroin." *USA Today*, October 24, 2006.

Leppard, David. "Soldiers in 'Guns for Coke' Scandal." *The Sunday Times*, September 24, 2006.

Lintner, Bertil, and Shawn W. Crispin. "For U.S., New North Korea Problem." *Wall Street Journal*, November 18, 2003.

Luke, Timothy, and Gearoid O'Tuathail. "On Videocameralists: The Geopolitics of Failed States, the CNN International, and (UN) Governmentality." *Review of International Political Economy* 4, no.4 (1997).

Lykke, Arthur. "Toward an Understanding of Military Strategy." *Military Strategy: Theory and Application*. Carlisle Barracks, PA: U.S. Army War College, 1989.

MacCoun, Robert, and Peter Reuter. *Drug War Heresies: Learning from Other Vices, Times, and Places*. New York: Cambridge University Press, 2001.

MacDonald, Scott, and Bruce Zagaris. "Introduction: Controlling the International Drug Problem." In *International Handbook on Drug Control*, eds. Scott MacDonald and Bruce Zagaris. Westport, CT: Greenwood, 1992.

MacKinnon, Mark. "Russian Forces Jittery Even on Army Base." *Toronto Globe and Mail*, November 30, 2002.

Mahmoud, Mona, and Melanie Eversley. "Hospitals Wage a Different War: Against Addiction." *USA Today*, June 23, 2005..

Manwaring, Max. "Non-State Actors in Colombia: Threats to the State and to the Hemisphere." In *Non-State Threats and Future Wars*, ed. Robert Bunker. Portland, OR: Frank Cass, 2003.

Marenko, Tamara. "Crime, Terror and the Central Asian Drug Trade." *Asia Quarterly* (Summer 2002).

Martin, Kimberly. "Warlordism in Comparative Perspective." *International Security* (Winter 2006/2007).

Mathers, Chris. *Crime School: Money Laundering*. Buffalo, NY: Firefly Books, 2004.

Maynes, Charles. "Contending Schools." *National Interest* (Spring 2001).

McCaffrey, Barry. "Visit to Afghanistan and Pakistan After Action Report," February 16–23, 2007.

McCoy, Alfred. *The Politics of Heroin in Southeast Asia: CIA Complicity in the Global Drug Trade*. New York: Harper and Row, 1972.

McAllister, William. *Drug Diplomacy in the Twentieth Century: An International History*. New York: Routledge, 2000.

Mearshimer, John. *The Tragedy of Great Power Politics*. New York: W. W. Norton, 2001.

Mehlum, Lars. "Alcohol and Stress in Norwegian United Nations Peacekeepers." *Military Medicine* (October 1999).

Merom, Gil. *How Democracies Lose Small Wars: State, Society, and the Failures of France in Algeria, Israel in Lebanon, and the United States in Vietnam*. New York: Cambridge University Press, 2003.

Meyer, Josh. "Burdened U.S. Military Cuts Role in Drug War." *Los Angeles Times*, January 22, 2007.

Meyer, Kathryn, and Terry Parssinien. *Webs of Smoke: Smugglers, Warlords, Spies, and the History of the International Drug Trade*. New York: Rowman and Littlefield, 1998.

Meyers, Stephen. "Top Chechen Rebel Dies in Russian Raid." *International Herald Tribune*, June 18, 2006, http://www.iht.com/articles/2006/06/18/news/chechnya.php.

Midgley, Mary. *Beast and Man: The Roots of Human Nature*. Ithaca, NY: Cornell University Press, 1978.

Milligan, Susan. "Drug Use Seen on the Rise in Iraq." *Boston Globe*, August 28. 2003.

Mills, John. "All the Elements of National Power: Reorganizing the Interagency Structure and Process for Victory in the Long War." *Strategic Insights* (July 2006).

Montblatt, Steven. "Terrorism and Drugs in the Americas: The OAS Response." *Americas Forum* (February–March 2004), http://www.oas.org/ezine/ezine24/Monblatt.htm.

Morarjee, Rachel. "Taliban Goes for Cash Over Ideology." *London Financial Times*, July 26, 2006.

———. "Drug Lords Reap Human Rewards of Poor Afghan Opium Harvests." *Financial Times*, May 10, 2006.

Morse, H. B. *Trade and Administration of the Chinese Empire*. Shanghai: Kelly and Walsh, 1908.

Mueller, John. *Remnants of War*. Ithaca, NY: Cornell University Press, 2004.

Murphy, Joseph. "A White Paper on Economic Measures to Support the Counternarcotics Campaign in Afghanistan." Brussels, October 20–24, 2006.

Mutshcke, Ralf. "The Threat Posed by the Convergence of Organized Crime, Drugs Trafficking and Terrorism." Testimony to the Subcommittee on Crime of the Judiciary Committee, U.S. House of Representatives, December 13, 2000.

Naím, Moisés. *Illicit: How Smugglers, Traffickers, and Copycats Are Hijacking the Global Economy*. New York: Doubleday, 2005.

Nair, Roshila. "'The Courage to Be Myself': The Life and Times of an Ex-Gangster Turned Peacemaker." *Track Two* (December 1999), http://ccrweb.ccr.uct.ac.za/archive/two/8_3/p28_be_myself.html.

Nankoe, Hakiem, Jean-Claude Gerlus, and Martin J. Murray. "The Origins of the Opium Trade and Opium Regimes in Colonial Indochina." In *The Rise and Fall of Revenue Farming*, eds. John Butcher and Howard Dick. New York: St. Martin's Press, 1993.

Narconon. "History of Methamphetamine." 2004. http://www.friendsofnarconon.org/drug_education/drug_information.

Napoleoni, Loretta. *Modern Jihad: Tracing the Dollars Behind the Terror Networks*. London: Pluto Press, 2003.

Nordstrom, Carolyn. "Out of the Shadows." In *Authority and Intervention in Africa*, eds. Thomas Callaghy, Ronald Kassimir, and Robert Latham. Cambridge: Cambridge University Press, 2001.

Nunez, Joseph. "Challenges and Opportunities in the Americas: A Liberal Regime for Security and Defense Cooperation." Ph. D. diss., University of Virginia, May 2006.

O'Gara, James. "The Wrong Plan for Afghanistan." *Washington Post*, January 24, 2007.

Olson, Mancur. "Dictatorship, Democracy and Development." *American Political Science Review* (September 1993).

O'Neill, Bard. *Insurgency and Terrorism: From Revolution to Apocalypse*. Washington, DC: Brassey's, Inc., 1990.

Osterling, Jorge. *Democracy in Colombia: Clientelistic Politics and Guerrilla Warfare*. New Brunswick, NJ: Transaction Press, 1989.

Paris, Roland. *At War's End: Building Peace after Civil Conflict*. Cambridge: Cambridge University Press, 2004.

Parliament of Canada. "Conflict, Drugs and Mafia Activities." *Contribution to the Preparatory Work for the Hague Peace Conference May 11–16 1999*, March 1999, http://www.parl.gc.ca/37/1/parlbus/commbus/senate/com-e/ille-e/presentation-e/labrousse2-e.htm.

Parliament of Canada. "Sub-Saharan Africa Facing the Problems of Drugs." April 2001. http://www.parl.gc.ca/37/1/parlbus/commbus/senate/com-e/ille-e/presentation-e/labrousse1-e.htm.

Pastor, Manuel, and Michael Conroy. "Distributional Implications for Macroeconomic Policy: Theory and Applications to El Salvador." In *Economic Policy for Building Peace: The Lessons of El Salvador*, ed. James Boyce. Boulder, CO: Lynne Rienner Publishers, 1996.

Pear, R., and P. Shenen. "Customs Switches Priority from Drugs to Terrorism." *New York Times*, October 10, 2001, national edition, section B.

Perry, Tony. "Fallouja Insurgents Fought Under Influence of Drugs, Marines Say." *Los Angeles Times*, January 13, 2005.

Peters, Gretchen. "Taliban Drug Trade: Echoes of Colombia." *Christian Science Monitor*, November 21, 2006.

Pettifer, James. "Asylum Seekers: Time for a New Approach." Conflict Studies Research Center—United Kingdom Ministry of Defence (September 2004).

Pollan, Michael. *The Botany of Desire*. New York: Random House, 2001.

Porter, Bruce. *Blow: How a Small-Town Boy Made $100 Million with the Medellin Cocaine Cartel and Lost It All*. New York: St. Martin's Press, 1993.

Pugh, Michael, and Neil Cooper, eds. *War Economies in a Regional Context: Challenges of Transformation*. Boulder, CO: Lynne Rienner Publishers, 2004.

Ramsbotham, Oliver, and Tom Woodhouse. *Humanitarian Intervention in Contemporary Conflict: A Reconceptualization*. Cambridge, MA: Polity Press, 1996.

Rawaf, Salman. "The Health Crisis in Iraq." *Critical Public Health* 15, no.2 (June 2005).

Rashid, Ahmed. "From Deobandism to Batken: Adventures of an Islamic Heritage." Central Asia-Caucasus Institute, *Forum Transcripts*, April 13, 2000.

———. "Letter from Afghanistan: Are the Taliban Winning?" *Current History* (January 2007).

Renner, Michael. "The Anatomy of Resource Wars." *World Watch Paper* 162. Washington, DC: World Watch Institute, 2002.

Restrepo, German. Interview, U.S. Army War College, Carlisle Barracks, PA, March 24, 2006.

Reuter, Peter, and Edwin Truman. *Chasing Dirty Money*. Washington, DC: Institute for International Economics, 2004.

Rich, Paul, ed. *Warlords in International Relations*. New York: St. Martin's Press, 1999.

Robinson, Jeffrey. *The Merger: The Conglomeration of International Organized Crime*. New York: Overlook Press, 2000.

Robinson, Linda. "Terror Close to Home: In Oil-Rich Venezuela, A Volatile Leader Befriends Bad Actors from the Mideast, Colombia and Cuba." *U.S. News and World Report*, October 6, 2003, http://www.usnews.com/usnews/issue/031006/usnews/6venezuela.htm (accessed on October 9, 2003).

Rogers, Rick. "Some Troops Headed Back to Iraq are Mentally Ill." *San Diego Union Tribune*, March 19, 2006.

Rohnde, David. "Afghan Symbol for Change Becomes a Symbol of Failure." *New York Times*, September 5, 2006.

Ross, Michael. "Oil, Drugs and Diamonds: The Varying Roles of Natural Resources in Civil War." In *The Political Economy of Armed Conflict: Beyond Greed and Grievance*, eds. Karen Ballentine and Jake Sherman. Boulder, CO: Lynne Rienner Publishers, 2003.

Rotberg, Robert, and Gregg Mills, eds. *War and Peace in Southern Africa: Crime, Drugs,*

Armies, and Trade. Washington, DC: Brookings Institution Press, 1998.

Rubin, Barnett, and Omar Zakhilwal. "A War on Drugs, Or A War on Farmers?" *Wall Street Journal*, January 11, 2005.

Sanderson, Thomas. "Transnational Terrorism and Organized Crime: Blurring the Lines." *SAIS Review* (Winter–Spring 2004).

Scheurer, Michael. "Clueless into Kabul." *The American Interest* (September–October 2006).

Seal, Karen, Daniel Berenthal, Christian Miner, Saunak Sen, and Charles Marmar. "Bringing the War Back Home." *Archives of Internal Medicine* 167: 479.

Segell, Glen. "Warlordism and Drug Trafficking: From Southeast Asia to Sub-Saharn Africa." In *Warlords in International Relations*, ed. Paul Rich. New York: St. Martin's Press, 1999.

Seper, Jerry. "DEA Says Afghanistan's Heroin Begets Violence." *Washington Times*, June 29, 2006.

———. "Mexican Military Incursions Reported." *Washington Times*, January 17, 2006.

Seybolt, Taylor. "Major Armed Conflicts." *SIPRI Yearbook 2005*. Oxford: Oxford University Press, 2006.

Shane, Scott. "A Flood of Troubled Soldiers in the Offing, Experts Predict." *New York Times*, December 16, 2004.

Shelley, Louise. "Transnational Organized Crime: The New Authoritarianism." In *The Illicit Global Economy and State Power*, eds. H. Richard Friman and Peter Andreas. New York: Rowman and Littlefield, 1999.

Shifter, Michael. "Latin America's Drug Problem." *Current History* (February 2007).

Siegel, Ronald. *Intoxication: The Universal Drive for Mind Altering Substances.* Rochester, NY: Park Street Press, 2005.

Singer, P. W. "Caution: Children at War." *Parameters* (Winter 2001–2002).

———. *Corporate Warriors: The Rise of the Privatized Military Industry.* Ithaca, NY: Cornell University Press, 2003.

Smith, Martin. *Burma: Insurgency and the Politics of Ethnicity.* New York: Zed Books, 1991.

Spiegel, Peter. "Fear of Fighting and Economic Ruin Hold Back Bid to Stamp Out Opium." *London Financial Times*, January 4, 2005.

Stares, Paul. *Global Health*. Washington, DC: Brookings Institution, 1996.

Stedman, Stephen. "International Implementation of Peace Agreements in Civil Wars." In *Turbulent Peace: The Challenges of Managing International Conflict*, eds. Chester A. Crocker, Fen Osler Hampson, and Pamela Aall. Washington, DC: United States Institute of Peace, 2001.

———. "The Spoiler Problem in Peace Processes." *International Security* (Fall 1997).

Stolberg, Sheryl. "Pressing Allies, President Warns of Afghan Battle." *New York Times*, February 16, 2007.

Streatfeild, Dominic. *Cocaine: An Unauthorized Biography*. New York: Picador, 2001.

Swartz, Peter. "The War on Drugs." *Foreign Policy* (September–October 2005).

Szasz, Thomas. *Ceremonial Chemistry: The Ritual Persecution of Drugs, Addicts, and Pushers*. New York: Anchor Press, 1974.

Thachuk, Kimberley. "Transnational Threats: Falling Through the Cracks?" *Low Intensity Conflict and Law Enforcement* (2001).

Tickner, Arlene. "Colombia and the United States: From Counternarcotics to Counterterrorism." *Current History* (February 2003).

Troki, Carl. *Opium, Empire, and the Global Political Economy: A Study of the Asian Opium Trade*. New York: Routledge, 1999.

Tuan, Shi-wen. *Weekend Telegraph*, March 10, 1967.

United Nations. "Afghanistan's Opium Survey 2006." United Nations Office on Drugs and Crime.

———. United Nations Department for Disarmament Affairs, "Small Arms and Light Weapons." http://disarmament.un.org/cab/salw.html (posted April 24, 2006).

———. UN General Assembly Special Session on the World Drug Problem, June 8–10, 1998, *Money Laundering*. New York: United Nations, 1998.

———. United Nations Information Service. "Iraq Emerging as a Transit Country for Drugs, INCB Presidents Says." May 12, 2005.

———. United Nations Office on Drugs and Crime. *Addressing Organized Crime and Drug Trafficking in Iraq: Report of the UNODC Fact Finding Mission*, 2005.

———. United Nations Office on Drugs and Crime, *Annual World Drug Report 2006*. New York: United Nations, 2006.

———. United Nations Office on Drugs and Crime. *Ecstasy and Amphetamines Global Report 2003*. New York: United Nations, September 2003.

———. United Nations Office on Drugs and Crime. *Trafficking in Persons Global Report*. (April 2006).

———. United Nations Office on Drugs and Crime, *World Drug Report 2007*. New York: United Nations, 2007.

———. *Report of the United Nations Conference on the Illicit Trade in Small Arms and Light Weapons in All Its Aspects*. New York, July 9–20, 2001.

United States Department of State. Source Countries and Drug Transit Zones. *International Narcotics Control Strategy Report 2004*, http://www.whitehousedrugpolicy.gov/international/mexico.html.

United States Department of the Treasury. *Foreign Assets Control Regulations for the Financial Community*. July 3, 2002.

United States Marine Corps. *Child Soldiers: Implications for U.S. Forces Seminar Report*. Quantico, VA: Center for Emerging Threats and Opportunities, September 23, 2002, http://www.ceto.quantico.usmc.mil.

United States Office of National Drug Control Policy. *Marijuana Fact Sheet 2004.* http://www.ondcp.gov/publications/factsht/marijuana/index.html.

United States Pacific Command. "Combating Terrorism in the Phillipines." http://www.pacom.mil/piupdates/abusayyafhist.shtml (accessed on July 16, 2006).

Van Creveld, Martin. *The Transformation of War: The Most Radical Reinterpretation of Armed Conflict Since Clausewitz.* New York: Free Press, 1991.

Van Ham, Peter, and Jorrit Kamminga. "Poppies for Peace: Reforming Afghanistan's Opium Industry." *Washington Quarterly* (Winter 2006–2007).

Von Zeilbauer, Paul. "For U.S. Troops at War, Liquor Is Spur to Crime." *New York Times,* March 13, 2007.

Walt, Stephen. "The Renaissance of Security Studies." *International Studies Quarterly* (June 1991).

Walton, John, and David Seddon. *Free Markets and Food Riots: The Politics of Global Adjustment.* Cambridge, MA: Blackwell, 1994.

Webb-Vidal, Andy. "Bogota Set to Assist in Kabul's Drug Battle." *Financial Times,* August 8, 2006.

Weinstein, Jeremy. *Inside Rebellion: The Politics of Insurgent Violence.* New York: Cambridge University Press, 2007.

Williams, Ian. *Rum: A Social and Sociable History.* New York: Nation Books, 2006.

Williams, Phil. "The Nature of Drug Trafficking Networks." *Current History* (April 1998).

———. "Transnational Criminal Networks." In *Networks and Netwars: The Future of Terror, Crime, and Militancy,* eds. John Arquilla and David Ronfeldt. Santa Monica: RAND Corporation, 2001.

Williams, Sue. "The Globalization of the Drug Trade." *Sources,* no. 111 (April 1999).

Winer, Jonathan, and Trifin Roule. "Follow the Money." In *Natural Resources and Violent Conflict: Options and Actions,* eds. Ian Bannon and Paul Collier. Washington, DC: The World Bank, 2003.

World Bank. *Sub-Saharan Africa: From Crisis to Sustainable Growth.* Washington, DC: The World Bank, 1989.

Wright, Thorin. "Warlord Choices: An Inquiry into the Institutional Choices in Post-Conflict State Building." Paper presented at the Southern Political Science Association Annual Conference, January 4, 2007.

Yarger, Harry. "Toward a Theory of Strategy." In *U.S. Army War College Guide to National Security Policy and Strategy,* 2nd rev. ed., ed. J. Boone Bartholomees. Carlisle Barracks, PA: U.S. Army War College, 2006.

Yongming, Zhou. *Anti-Drug Crusades in Twentieth-Century China: Nationalism, History, and State-Building.* New York: Rowman and Littlefield, 1999.

Zahar, Marie-Joelle. "Proteges, Clients and Cannon Fodder: Civil-Militia Relations in

Internal Conflicts." In *Civilians in War*, ed. Simon Chesterman. Boulder, CO: Lynne Rienner Publishers, 2001.

Zoroya, Gregg. "Psychologist: Navy Faces Crisis." *USA Today*, January 17, 2007.

INDEX

ABOUT THE AUTHOR

PAUL REXTON KAN is an associate professor of national security studies at the U.S. Army War College. He has presented on this topic at the Southern Political Science Association and has published articles in such journals as *Small Wars and Insurgencies*, *Defense Intelligence Journal*, and *Air and Space Power Journal*. He lives in Carlisle, Pennsylvania.